MAKING THE CORPS

Thomas E. Ricks

SCRIBNER

SCRIBNER
1230 Avenue of the Americas
New York, NY 10020

Copyright © 1997 by Thomas E. Ricks
All rights reserved, including the right of reproduction
in whole or in part in any form.

SCRIBNER and design are trademarks
of Simon & Schuster Inc.

Designed by Colin Joh
Set in Garamond

Manufactured in the United States of America

1 3 5 7 9 10 8 6 4 2

Library of Congress Cataloging-in-Publication Data

Ricks, Thomas E.
Making the Corps/Thomas E. Ricks.
p.   cm.
Includes index.
1. United States. Marine Corps—Military life. I. Title.
VE23.R5   1997   97–25174
359.9'6'0973—dc21   CIP

ISBN 0-684-83109-0

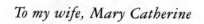

To my wife, Mary Catherine

A NOTE ON SOURCES

This is a true book. No names have been changed. Much of what is reported here was witnessed firsthand. Some of it was related later, usually by several participants and observers, but always by at least one person present. A few events were video-taped. I also have relied on the log of Platoon 3086 and other documentation, such as "Recruit Incident Reports" filed after unusual occurrences, and each recruit's continuously updated "Recruit Evaluation Card."

CONTENTS

CHAIN OF COMMAND

Platoon 3086, Kilo Company, Third Battalion, Recruit Training Regiment, Marine Corps Recruit Training Depot, Parris Island, S.C., as of March 1995:

Drill Instructors for 3086:
Senior Drill Instructor: Staff Sgt. Ronny Rowland
Heavy Hat: Sgt. Darren Carey
Third Hat: Sgt. Leo Zwayer

Series Commander (for Platoons 3084, 3085, and 3086):
Lt. David Richards
Series Senior Sergeant: Gunnery Sgt. David Camacho

Kilo Company Commander: Capt. Jeffrey Chessani
Kilo Company Senior Sergeant: 1st Sgt. Charles Tucker

Third Battalion Commander: Lt. Col. Michael Becker

Recruit Training Regiment Commander:
Col. Humberto Rodriguez (Succeeded soon after 3086's graduation by Col. Douglas Hendricks)

Depot Commander: Brig. Gen. Jack Klimp

Depot Senior Sergeant: Depot Sgt. Maj. Harold Moore

We few, we happy few, we band of brothers;
For he today that sheds his blood with me
Shall be my brother. Be he ne'er so vile,
This day shall gentle his condition;
And gentlemen in England now abed
Shall think themselves accursed they were not here.
                    —Shakespeare, *Henry V,* IV, iii

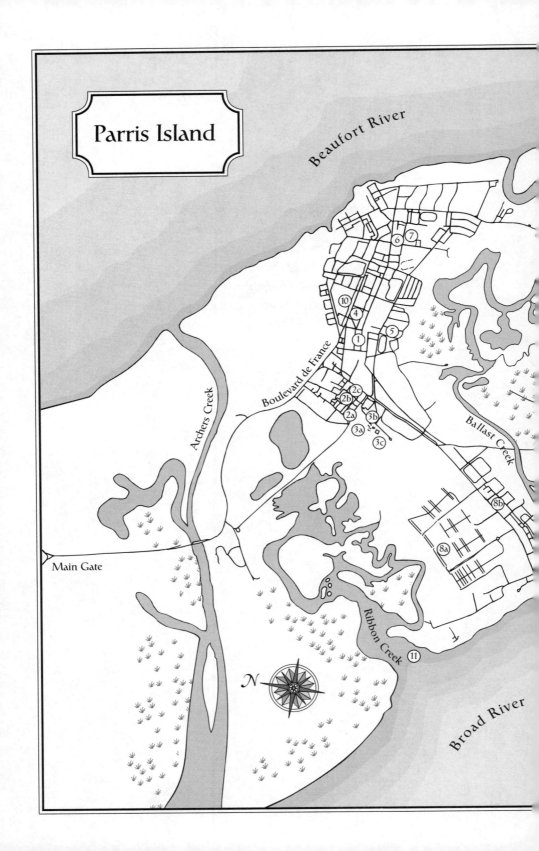

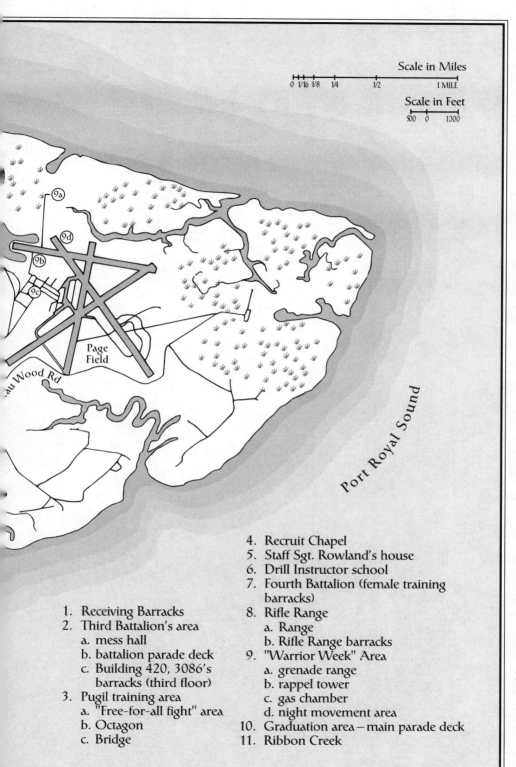

Scale in Miles

0 1/16 1/8   1/4   1/2   1 MILE

Scale in Feet

500   0   1000

(9a)

(9d)

(9b)

(9c)

Page
Field

...au Wood Rd

Port Royal Sound

1. Receiving Barracks
2. Third Battalion's area
   a. mess hall
   b. battalion parade deck
   c. Building 420, 3086's
      barracks (third floor)
3. Pugil training area
   a. "Free-for-all fight" area
   b. Octagon
   c. Bridge

4. Recruit Chapel
5. Staff Sgt. Rowland's house
6. Drill Instructor school
7. Fourth Battalion (female training
   barracks)
8. Rifle Range
   a. Range
   b. Rifle Range barracks
9. "Warrior Week" Area
   a. grenade range
   b. rappel tower
   c. gas chamber
   d. night movement area
10. Graduation area – main parade deck
11. Ribbon Creek

MOGADISHU, DECEMBER 1992

This book is mainly about Marine boot camp at Parris Island, South Carolina, but it has its origins on the other side of the world. For me, the story begins on a dark night in Somalia in December 1992, just a few days after U.S. troops landed.

It was my first deployment as a Pentagon reporter. I flew nonstop from California to Somalia in a huge Air Force cargo plane that refueled twice in midair. I didn't know what I was doing, but I realized soon after I stepped into the humid dawn at the ruined airport that I was in a miserable situation. By the end of my first day in Mogadishu I was worried, scared, tired, and a bit disoriented. I hadn't known enough to pack sunglasses and a hat, but I did bring the most essential tool, a big two-quart canteen, which I soon learned to drain at least three times a day.

It was a confusing and difficult time for the U.S. military: Americans had been brought to this dusty but sweaty equatorial nation to help with the logistics of famine relief, and there now was shooting going on. This was the first U.S. brush with "peacemaking"—a new form of post-Cold War, low-intensity chaos that is neither war nor peace, but produces enough exhaustion, anxiety, boredom, and confusion to feel much like combat.

I went out on night patrol in the sand hills just west of Mogadishu with a squad from Alpha Company of the 1st Battalion of the 7th Marines. The city below was dead silent. There were no electric lights illuminating the night, no cars moving, no dogs barking at the patrol, no chickens clucking. The only sound in the night was the occasional death-rattle cough of sick infants. As we walked in single file, with red and green tracer fire arcing across the black sky over the city, I realized that I had placed my life in the hands of the young corporal leading the patrol, a twenty-two-year-old Marine. In my office back in Washington, we wouldn't let a twenty-two-year-old run the copying machine without adult supervision. Here, after just two days on the ground in Africa, the corporal was leading his squad into unknown territory, with a confidence that was contagious.

The next morning I walked to the Mogadishu airport along a hot road ankle deep in fine dust with another returning patrol from Alpha Company, led by Cpl. Armando Cordova, a precise-seeming man with a small mustache and wire-rimmed glasses. A native of Puerto Rico who was raised in the Bronx, he once left the Marines and then, after ten months back in New York City, reenlisted. "You don't make friends in the world like you do here," he explained, his M-16 slung horizontally across his chest. "We are like family. We eat together, sleep together, patrol together."

The last thing I wrote in my notebook as I flew out of Somalia was that "in an era when many people of their age seem aimless, these Marines know what they are about: taking care of each other." Of course, that ethos isn't always honored. Some Marines rob and beat one another, or lie to Congress, or rape Okinawan girls. But over the last four years in Somalia, in a sniper's nest in Haiti, aboard amphibious assault ships in the Atlantic and the Adriatic, and at Marine installations in the U.S., I consistently have been impressed by the sense of self that young Marines possess.

The U.S. military is extremely good today—arguably the best it has ever been, and probably for the first time in its history, the best in the world. It also has addressed in effective ways racial issues and drug abuse, problems that have stymied the rest of American society. At a time when America seems distrustful of its young males, when young black men especially are figures of fear for many Americans, the military is a different world. As the sociologist Charles Moskos has observed, it is routine in the military, unlike in the rest of the nation, to see blacks boss around whites.

But the Marines are distinct even within the separate world of the U.S. military. Theirs is a culture apart. The Air Force has its planes, the Navy its ships, the Army its obsessively written and obeyed "doctrine" that dictates how to act. Culture—that is, the values and assumptions that shape its members—is all the Marines have. It is what holds them together. They are the smallest of the U.S. military services, and in many ways the most interesting. Theirs is the richest culture: formalistic, insular, elitist, with a deep anchor in their own history and mythology. Much more than the other branches, they place pride and responsibility at the lowest levels of the organization. The Marines have one officer for every 8.8 enlistees. That is a wider ratio than in any other service—the Air Force, at the other end of the spectrum, has one officer for every 4.2 enlistees.

Alone among the U.S. military services, the Marines have bestowed their name on their enlisted ranks. The Army has Army officers and soldiers, the Navy has naval officers and sailors, the Air Force has Air Force officers and airmen—but the Marines have officers and Marines. "Every Marine a rifleman," states one key Corps motto. It means that the essence of the organization resides with the lowest of the low, the peon in the trenches. That's especially significant because 49 percent of Marines are in the service's three lowest ranks (that is, E-3 and below). That's roughly twice the percentage in the other three services. "The Marine is the Corps and the Corps is the Marine," wrote Lt.

Gen. Victor Krulak, father of the current commandant of the Corps.

I like the Marine culture. It intrigues me. In a society that seems to have trouble transmitting values, the Marines stand out as successful and healthy institution that unabashedly teaches values to the Beavises and Buttheads of America. It does an especially good job in dealing with the bottom half of American society, the side that isn't surfing into the twenty-first century on the breaking wave of Microsoft products. The Corps takes kids with weak high school educations and nurtures them so that many can assume positions of honor and respect.

The Marine Corps "works" as a culture, and is adept at addressing its own faults. It strikes me as the most well-adjusted of the U.S. military services today, at ease with its post-Cold War situation. Indeed, it is the only service that isn't on the verge of an identity or cultural crisis, as the Navy steams in the circles of its post-Tailhook malaise, the Army tries to figure out what it is supposed to do for the next fifteen years and gnashes its teeth over gender integration, and the Air Force has quiet nightmares about unmanned aircraft dominating the skies of the twenty-first century. I suspect the Marine Corps also is one of the few parts of the federal government that retains the deep trust of most of the American people.

Because of their culture, the Marines tend to be an enjoyable service for a reporter to cover. Because they are so proud of their story, and because the Marines' existence has always been threatened, they are happy to have a journalist write about them—even if in their political conservatism they don't particularly like the media. They are more open than the Army tends to be; the average Marine lance corporal speaks with more self-confidence to a reporter than does the average Army captain. I frequently hear responses from Army officers along the lines of, "I don't want to say anything I shouldn't say." I have never heard anything like that from Marines. They know that if a reporter has been permitted within their lines, they can talk about who they are and what they are doing. (The Army tends to blame Vietnam for its bad relations with the media, but that alibi is losing credibility as the last Vietnam-era veterans retire. But I do think the Army is getting better at dealing with reporters as it realizes that for the first time in its history, it too must begin to justify its existence to the American people, whose economic, cultural, and political elites in the post-Cold War era generally know little and care less about the military.) The average Marine is far livelier to interview than is the average Navy sailor, who tends to be less informed about the mission, and less interested in the world. And the Marine infantryman lacks the know-it-allness I've encountered in many Navy and Air Force pilots, who watch a few minutes of CNN and then hold forth on world politics. A day on the ground somewhere will teach you more than a year of flying over it.

The Marines tend to display a kind of funky joie de vivre, especially in the field. In their own parlance, they know how to "pack their trash," something the Army is learning slowly and painfully as it too becomes "expeditionary" in hellholes like Somalia and Haiti. A naval officer told me once that as disembarkation day approached, he had his sailors hide the galley's little bottles of Louisiana hot sauce to keep the Marines from stealing them when they left the ship. In Somalia, I saw why. After one grueling patrol across the outskirts of Mogadishu, Corporal Cordova's squad pulled out a camping stove and cooked up a mess of what they called "Somali Stew": mix in a big pot one package of ham slice rations, one of chicken stew, one of tuna with noodles, one packet of cheese sauce, several tiny bottles of Tabasco sauce, and liberal shakes of onion and garlic powder. As they cooked, the squad played Little Richard's greatest hits on a Walkman connected to miniature speakers. They knew how to live— a sharp contrast to the infantry squad from the Army's 10th Mountain Division that I saw in Haiti sitting bored in a tent, reading dirty magazines, and grousing about its cold rations.

At the same time, I am worried by some aspects of today's Marines, especially their remoteness from American society. This is a matter of degree. There has always been an element of aloofness from society in the Marines' stance, as with any elite military organization. But over the last thirty years, as American culture has grown more fragmented, individualistic, and consumerist, the Marines have become more withdrawn; they feel they simply can't afford to reflect the broader society. Today's Marines give off a strong sense of disdain for the very society they protect. They view it, in much the same way the Japanese do, as decadent.

There is a history to the Corps' alienation. During the 1970s the Marines hit bottom. They were riven by the Vietnam War, in which the Corps suffered more casualties than it did in World War II. Race relations were lousy; in 1970, for example, the Corps logged 1,096 violent racial incidents. Drug abuse was rampant: 37 percent of all Marines in 1980 were estimated to be using illegal drugs at least occasionally. The Marines haven't taken draftees since 1970, but with the end of the draft in 1973, the Corps discovered that many of its "volunteers" in fact had joined to avoid the Army; in the mid-seventies, the quality of volunteers for the Marines plummeted. For a time, fewer than half of Marine recruits were high school graduates. "Many ill-adjusted, antisocial young men ended up in our ranks," then-Brig. Gen. Bernard Trainor observed in the *Marine Corps Gazette* in 1978.

Then the Marines, along with the rest of the U.S. military, rebounded. Today they are on the road American society didn't travel. Over the last twenty years, the Corps improved the quality of its recruits. It confronted its drug problems in effective ways. While it hasn't done as well as the Army has in finding and promoting black officers, it has defused racial tensions. Among senior sergeants, race simply doesn't appear to be an issue; as career Marines, they have far more in common with one another than they do with members of their races outside the military. And throughout the military, it is clear that a whiff of racism—at least of whites toward blacks—will end a career.

Over the last twenty years, as they rebounded, the Marines

moved from thinking of themselves as a better version of American society to a kind of dissenting critique of it. But theirs isn't an empty alienation. The Marines are rebels with a cause, articulately rejecting the vague nihilism that pervades American popular culture. With their incessant emphasis on honor, courage, and commitment, they offer an alternative to the loneliness and distrust that today seem so widespread, especially among American youth.

But the gap between the military and society can't be attributed entirely to improvements in the military. While American military officers always have tended toward conservatism, over the last twenty years they have become more politically involved, and effectively "Republicanized." But far more than civilian Republicans, they seem to look down on American society in a way that the pre-World War II military didn't. The U.S. military's new contempt for American society is especially troubling because it comes at a time when the end of the Cold War has cut adrift the U.S. military from its traditional roles. With the demise of the Soviet threat, many in the Marines, from commandant to drill instructor, seem to define the enemy as "chaos." That is worrisome because it can blur the line between foreign and domestic missions. Take this view to extremes—and some Marines do—and you wind up believing that the next war the U.S. military fights could be here at home.

The gap between the military and society is exacerbated by the public's new ignorance of military affairs. For two centuries, the military has played an important role in shaping the United States. We are, in the phrase of one historian, "a country made by war." But today the military's role in the nation (and its uses abroad) is troubled, uncertain, and shifting. For the first time in our history, we are—if the Cold War is indeed considered a kind of war—maintaining a large military establishment during peacetime. What's more, it is all-volunteer, and has been for two decades. It is no longer broadly representative of society, especially the elites. Even during the Vietnam War, two-thirds of the members of Congress had some military experience. Today about two-thirds have none. A dwindling number of people on the Armed Services Committees are able to reach back to their time as mud soldiers to skeptically quiz the military brass. We are, argues Harvard political scientist Michael Desch, moving toward having a semiautonomous military.

The coming years will be interesting as the U.S. military sorts out its role, at home and abroad, in the post-Cold War world. The best way to see where the U.S. military is going is to look at the Marines today. The Army, Navy, and Air Force are becoming more like the Marines as they become smaller, isolated, and expeditionary. Indeed, I've noticed lately that some of the Army's cutting-edge units, such as its "Southern European Task Force," a paratrooper brigade that was one of the first U.S. units sent to Bosnia, and has been in and out of Africa in recent years, are remaking themselves in the Marines' image. For decades, the U.S. Army sat in Europe waiting to slug it out with the tanks of the Red Army. But these paratroopers are a contingency force able to move in quickly in small numbers, do the job, whether it be evacuating an embassy or protecting Rwandan refugees, and get out just as quickly. That may sound simple, but it is a radical departure from the Army's traditional approach of going in big and heavy and slow, with tanks and hordes of troops and huge logistical bases, as it did even in the Gulf War.

With the end of the Cold War, and the rash of small, messy interventions in Somalia, Rwanda, and Haiti, the Marines have moved back to center stage in U.S. military operations. These tend to be conflicts that spotlight the kind of small-unit action in which Marines shine, partly because they are able to reach back to their pre-World War II role as the nation's "small war" force. In these operations, the kid whom we wouldn't trust to run the copier is the squad or platoon leader addressing questions that could alter national policy: Do I shoot at this threatening mob in Mogadishu? Do I fire first when a Haitian police officer levels his automatic weapon in my direction? If I am in a limited peacekeeping role, do I stop a rape when it occurs fifty yards in front of my position? And he is doing it under the glare of real-time global television broadcasts.

Ever since I went on night patrol in Mogadishu, I have wanted to discover how these young Americans acquired that sense of Marine self-confidence that enables them to make those decisions. Ultimately I decided to look at boot camp, where American youths make the transition from civilian society to the military, bridging the growing gap. I wanted to see how an organization could take fifty or so American kids—a group steeped in a culture of individualism and consumerism, many of them users of recreational drugs, few of them with much education or hope of prospering in the American economy—and turn them into Marines who saw themselves as a band of brothers, overcoming deep differences of race and class. I wanted to see who would "make" it into the Corps, who wouldn't, and why. I also wanted to see how drill instructors would make them into Marines. (Almost all writing about Marine boot camp is in the form of memoirs, meaning that we usually see the place through the eyes of an adolescent.) Finally, I wanted to explore how the Marine Corps rebounded from its post-Vietnam low point and remade itself in the late 1970s and 1980s, and contrast its recovery with the increasing fragmentation of American society.

To do that I had to begin on Parris Island. That is how I came to stand outside the receiving building in the fifty-six degree fog at 1:50 in the morning waiting for a bus from Charleston, South Carolina, to arrive. Aboard were thirty-six young men, the bulk of a new recruit platoon, Platoon 3086.

CHAPTER ONE

DISORIENTATION

It begins just like in the movies: A busload of recruits traverses a causeway across the tidal swamps of Archer Creek and arrives at the Marine Corps boot camp on Parris Island. It is 1:50 a.m., the middle of a chilly late-winter night on the coast of South Carolina, when the bus' air brakes sigh and the bus rolls to a halt outside the red-brick receiving station. Most of the thirty-six recruits on the bus already have been awake twenty hours or more, since they reported to military processing stations at dawn Wednesday. They won't sleep for another eighteen, until sunset Thursday. A haze of cigarette smoke hangs in the air of the silent bus. It is the last tobacco they will smell for eleven weeks.

Staff Sgt. Gregory Biehl, his face half-hidden by his big flat campaign hat—drill instructors hate it when tourists call it a Smokey the Bear hat—charges up the metal footsteps of the bus and faces the thirty-six faces, all male, most adolescent, many strained with fear.

"Now!" begins Staff Sergeant Biehl. It is the first word they hear on Parris Island, and it is entirely appropriate. For the next eleven weeks, every order they hear will carry a tacit insistence that it be executed immediately. That first word locks them into the present, and that is where they will remain. For nearly three months, no one in a position to know will tell them anything about their schedule. All they really have to go on are the movies they've seen on television, such as *Sands of Iwo Jima* and *Full Metal Jacket,* plus a few tall tales from older brothers and neighborhood kids who have come home wearing Marine uniforms. In their new lives here on the island, they simply will be ordered to march, and will find out what they are going to do next when ordered to stop marching.

At Parris Island, officers think about the weeks ahead, drill instructors think about the days ahead, and recruits think about the task at hand. The recruits don't know it and won't be told, but the Marines' theorists of boot camp indoctrination break the eleven-week process into five distinct phases. First is the initial receiving of recruits, which lasts about four disorienting days. Next is a period of similar length, the "Forming" of platoons, when the recruits are turned over to the drill instructors who will take them through the rest of boot camp. Then comes the main body of boot camp, "Training," which begins with basic drilling and rudimentary fighting, proceeds to riflery, and then puts it all together with basic combat training. Then, because Marine boot camp is three weeks longer than the other services', comes an odd ten-day period called "Advanced Training" in which nothing much appears to happen, but is significant because it puts on the recruits the final touches of indoctrination, polishing the best and sometimes reaching the recalcitrant. Finally comes the series of ceremonies and rituals that constitute graduation into the Marine Corps.

Many of the bewildered young men staring at Staff Sergeant Biehl will never make it that far. Some will be gone within a few days. But even for those who will make it the whole way, graduation at this moment is an unimaginably remote goal. Simply getting through each next moment of boot camp will consume all their mental and physical energies. And for most of the rest of their careers in the Marines, their officers will strive to keep them just as tightly focused: Not on whether they might eventually die, not on whether the mission will succeed, not on where their wife or girlfriend is and what she might be doing, but on the here and now.

"Now!" the sergeant repeats. "Sit up straight. Get your eyes on me. If you have anything in your mouth, get it out now." They stare at the sergeant, not knowing he is a passing figure in their lives, one who will move them along for exactly an hour and then never be seen again. The actual moment of shock will come three days later, at the "Forming," when they will meet the three drill instructors who will dominate every waking moment of their lives, and even some of their dreams, for the next eleven weeks. But right now, the Corps wants only to disorient the arriving recruits, not shatter them. The job now is to strip them of their old civilian identities before building new Marines.

"Now, get off my bus," shouts Staff Sergeant Biehl. They hadn't known it was his bus—but they soon will realize that they are on *his* island, in *his* Corps, and playing by *his* rules. Every drill instructor they meet will talk to them the same way. Nothing here is theirs, not even the right to be called "Marine." They are simply "recruits." They will have to earn the title "Marine"—and that is why most of them joined the Corps. Staff Sergeant Biehl pauses a moment, sufficient time for any attentive Marine to get going, and then raises the volume: "Let's go. Now. Move. Move! *Move!*"

They charge off the bus onto rows of yellow footprints painted on the asphalt: in their first moment on the ground of Parris Island, they also have stepped into the Marine Corps' powerful and distinctive culture. The footprints, four to a row, eighteen rows, are so closely packed that the newcomers can't been seen as individuals. Standing nearly heel to toe in the dark night their faces are hardly visible, and their bodies become one mass. The effect is intentional: Marine Corps culture is the culture of the group, made up of members who are anonymous. Later, Lt. Col. Michael Becker, commander of the Third Battalion, of which these men will soon become a part, will make the point by gesturing to the framed reprint on his office wall of perhaps the most famous photograph from World War II, that of the Marines raising the American flag at Iwo Jima. "Who are they? Just five Marines and a corpsmen. It isn't Patton. It isn't Eisenhower. It's five Marines and a corpsmen—you can't even see their faces." Indeed, two have their backs turned to the camera, two have their sides turned, and the fifth is hidden except for his arms and hands supporting the flag.

Who are these thirty-six recruits standing on the yellow footprints? Where are they from? How did they get here? Among them are an accountant fired by Ernst & Young because he flunked his CPA exam; a self-professed gang member from Washington, D.C.; the son of a Merrill Lynch bond trader; a Dutch-American who considers himself a pacifist; a former white-supremacist skinhead from Mobile, Alabama; a dozen former employees of Taco Bell and other fast food joints; and a handful of one-time workers at small, off-the-books construction firms.

They are mainly eighteen and nineteen years old, with a smattering of men in their twenties. The youngest is seventeen, the oldest twenty-seven. They come to Parris Island without strong prospects in the civilian economy. With a few exceptions, they are drawn from the 39 percent of young American males who don't attend college, and so live on the wrong side of the widening gap between the earnings of high school graduates and college graduates. To a surprising degree, they have been living part-time lives—working part time, going to community college part time (and getting failing grades), staying dazed on drugs and alcohol part time. They are, with a few exceptions, denizens of the bottom half of the American economy, or on the way there—poor kids with lousy educations, and a few wealthier ones sliding off the professional tracks their parents had taken. Consciously or not, they don't see much of a place open to them in postindustrial America. Most of them knew they were heading for mediocre jobs at wages that will always seem to lag behind inflation. They have come here from Shubuta, Mississippi, from Bayonne, New Jersey, from Destin, Florida, from Pittsburgh, Pennsylvania, and from forty other small towns and crumbling eastern cities to pursue one of the few rites of passage left in America. Here they can try to attain excellence.

In truth, society sees many of these kids more as threats than as contributing members. They are off the map—literally, in some cases. "You go into any high school in April, you'll see a map of the United States up on the wall showing where kids are going to college," says Staff Sgt. Michael Marti, a Marine recruiter in Boston who helped enlist Andrew Lee and Charles Lees III, two members of the group getting off this bus. "But that's only seventy-five percent or so. The other kids, the ones that are going the nontraditional route, they don't put them on the map at all. A kid who joins the military isn't honored, but the kid who goes to college is."

Spending their days in high schools, pool halls, and gyms, trolling for prospects, recruiters see a lot of adolescent America, probably more so than most parents of teenagers. Their reports are chilling. "I don't believe any of the statistics I see," says Sgt. Arthur Banester, who works the suburbs south of Boston. "I haven't seen one kid who hasn't used marijuana.

"It's rich down there," he continues. "It's midway between Providence and Boston, and there's a lot of nothing to do. So we get drugs, assault and batteries, breaking and entering. Alcohol's really bad."

Yes, echoes Staff Sergeant Marti, the chief of the recruiting station: "Alcohol's worse than anybody's nightmare."

The new recruits are propelled from home by fear of failure and drawn here by their desire to be Marines. That is very different from what attracts American youth to the other military services. One current recruiting pamphlet for the Navy carries the headline "What's in it for you." For years, the Army has advertised under the self-actualizing motto, "Be all you can be." The Marines, by contrast, take an ascetic, even forbidding approach: "Maybe you can be one of us," one of "a few good men," "the few, the proud."

For high-strung Andrew Lee, rippling with muscles and tension, there was never a question about where he wanted to be. He grew up just across the street from the Vietnam Veterans Memorial in South Boston. The first such monument in the country, it displays the names of twenty-five dead. Some fifteen of those names are followed by the letters "USMC." He grew up with the brothers and cousins of those names.

Suffering from dyslexia, Lee never liked school much. But he loved the summers. As a teenager he began working as a lifeguard at South Boston's Farragut Beach. "I met this guy Herb Cavellas there," Lee will later recall. "He's the reason I joined the Marines. He was a quiet guy. He wore a 'Semper Fi' hat. He talked to me about Vietnam, where he was a scout/sniper. He talked to me about the Marines being a true brotherhood. Despite everything they went through—I wasn't there, but, you know, government lies, hypocrisy—they still hold true to the Marines."

One day late in 1994, Lee went downtown and signed up with the Marines on a delayed entry program. Then he caught a bus back to South Boston and told his parents. His mother, a social worker in a Boston school, was distraught. For months she tried to talk him out of it. "My mother, there's a real generation gap between she and I," Lee will later explain. "She's a good women, an excellent mother, but she comes out of the Vietnam thing."

"She wouldn't hang up on me," recalled Sgt. Rodney Emery, Lee's recruiter, who would check up on Lee two or three times a month. "But every once in a while she'd voice her opinion." Lee's father, the principal of South Boston's middle school, wasn't much pleased either.

On the morning he was to "ship" to Parris Island, his mother got up early and made him a big breakfast. She cried the whole time.

Traveling with Lee from Boston is Charles Lees III, a big two hundred seventy-five-pound Samoan with a Band-Aid on his forehead. The wound on his head was sustained while trying to qualify for boot camp; just getting to this point has been a struggle for Lees. A graduate of Holy Cross, Lees was looking for something more in life than computer sales. He came into the recruiting office heavily overweight. The recruiters determined that he would need to drop forty-seven pounds simply to qualify to begin boot camp. They had him visit once a day, then twice, to exercise him into shape.

He reported as ordered the night before he was to ship, in mid-February. But he was still six pounds over the limit. The sergeants at the processing station dressed him in a heavy sweat suit and kept him running all night. To keep the weight off, he wasn't allowed to eat. When thirsty, he was given an ice cube to lick. Toward morning, he later recalls, "everything went yellow." He woke up on the floor, looking up at the master sergeant. In fainting he somehow cut his forehead. He was sent home to recuperate for two weeks.

So, by chance, Lee and Lees ship out the same day. The two Bostonians with similar names will become the heart of their platoon at Parris Island. Assigned by the alphabet to share a bunk bed, they become a team: Andrew Lee, the small, wiry, inarticulate leader by example, and Charles Lees, the hulking, reflective recruit who has the intelligence to teach his slower comrades, the maturity to know how to do it, and the physical strength to ensure that they listen.

Also part of the Boston shipment is Paul Bourassa, a graduate of the University of Massachusetts who enlisted after being fired by Ernst & Young. He broke the news to his parents over dinner at an Applebee's restaurant in Methuen, up near the New Hampshire border. "She began crying, made a scene. She said I was gonna die. My dad said I was crazy."

Parents' resistance to their sons' joining the Marines is common among this group. "My mother and uncles tried to talk to me. They didn't want me to go anywhere dangerous," James Andersen, one of five recruits shipped here today from Pittsburgh, says later. "I said, 'It's my choice, and I need it.' " The nineteen-year-old had been a shift manager at a Taco Bell in the Pittsburgh suburb of Bethel Park, "partying" every night; he "didn't give a shit about anything."

In eastern Pennsylvania, just outside Philadelphia, Nathan Weber, who had been sliding from one dead-end job to another, enlisted and then went to a friend's house for dinner. When his friend's father heard the news over the meal, he gave him a disgusted look and said, "Kids these days want to be so tough." Several other friends, and his parents, are puzzled by his decision.

Failing to persuade her son to renege on enlisting, the mother of another Pittsburgh recruit, Joshua Parise, decided to wrest from the recruiting sergeant a promise that her son would be safe at boot camp. Then at dawn she was shocked when a different sergeant appeared at the front door to collect her boy. She stood in her bathrobe hugging her son—and refused to let go. This went on for several minutes, until he finally lifted her arms and extracted himself. "She kind of wigged out," Parise later says.

If some parents try to bar the door, others actively open it. Craig Hoover's dad, a retired government cartographer, suggested that his son try something new in life. Hoover had just dropped out of Montgomery College, in the prosperous Maryland suburbs of Washington, D.C., and he'd quit his job as a waiter because he didn't like some of the other staff at the diner. "I needed a break, a change of scene," he says later.

At dawn on March 1, 1995, this wave of recruits reported to military processing stations across the eastern United States. Their recruiters already had given them physicals and vetted their names with local police for criminal records. Each was checked for open wounds and fresh scars. Then a recruiting sergeant interrogated them one last time. "Did you get in any trouble? Did you smoke some dope? We know you have going-away parties, drink a few beers, have some trouble." After a final paperwork check, each was driven to a local airport in a government minivan, usually with three or four other recruits. At Boston, the recruits left for Logan Airport at 12:30. On arrival at Charleston, South Carolina, they were met by a Marine and taken to a special room. They were told to sit with their hands flat on their knees, facing forward, and to remain silent. They waited for hours, stock still.

Finally, just after midnight, thirty-six recruits had accumulated. They were told to file onto a bus illuminated by the other-worldly orange lights of the airport parking lot. They immediately felt the humidity and relative warmth of the Deep South. The bus cut south and surprisingly soon left behind motels and automobile dealers on the outskirts of town. Route 17 narrowed to two lanes and plunged into the pitch darkness of the South Carolina sea marshes, a land of rice, cotton, alligators, and mud, one of the most remote areas east of the Mississippi. The recruits were permitted to talk, but no one did. They stared out the window trying to see something in the piney woods and marshes along the Edisto River basin. The blackwater stream itself was invisible in the night, just a negative strip of emptiness. They caught glimpses of Spanish moss hanging in great masses from the branches of live oaks. Some smoked. Charles Lees asked himself, *What have I done?*

Nearly ninety minutes later, the lights of the Parris Island guardpost looming out of the dark signal the beginning of the answer to that question. Symbolically, boot camp begins here as the bus slows, but doesn't stop at the gate at the mainland end of a causeway that leads out to the island. The Marine guard waves the bus through, and it takes the recruits across the border from the America they know into Marine territory, where they will remain until they graduate months from now, or until they are washed out and sent home.

The bus is again in darkness as it traverses the 2.3-mile-long causeway. *Good-bye, world,* Lees thinks, sensing the psychological remoteness of the place. This isolated atmosphere is somewhat artificial. In reality, the bright lights and yacht-set bistros of antebellum Beaufort, South Carolina, are just a few miles from the Marine camp. But to the recruits, the 7,000 flat, wet acres of sand that make up Parris Island might as well be a thousand miles out in the Atlantic Ocean.

The Devil's Island atmosphere of the place is no accident. In the late nineteenth century, after a naval station and dry dock were established on the island, the Navy used the installation as a "disciplinary barracks"—that is, a military jail. The Marines first began training recruits on the island in 1915, for service in World War I. Since then, the Marines are fond of saying, more than a million recruits have trained on the island, with about 20,000 coming through annually nowadays. At any given point, there are about 4,300 recruits training on Parris Island—fewer in mid-winter, more during the late summer and early fall, as the high school graduation bulge passes through. They are governed by just under 600 drill instructors.

This being the history-minded Marine Corps, the roads on Parris Island are named after the Corps' great battles and campaigns. The bus leaves the causeway and enters Boulevard de France, evoking World War I, the conflict that did more than any other to elevate the Corps from a naval police force into a legitimate fighting force that could stand as an alternative to the U. S. Army. The Marine base on the island is a haphazard, charmless collection of two- and three-story brick buildings with live oaks and pines growing in the grassy areas between them, but grass fights a losing battle in the salty, sandy soil; walk five minutes away from the main buildings, and the green thins and gives way to the sand that is the natural ground cover here. Beyond the sand ripples the deceptive waters of Atlantic Ocean inlets. As the tide recedes, it becomes clear that the water is just a few inches deep. The water peels back to reveal slick black mudflats, aromatic ooze that almost seems to have a pulse, and wafts hints of shrimp and crab toward shore. The locals call this rich tidal mud "pluff," for the sighing sound it makes when a foot plunges into it.

The bus heads toward the billboard-size sign that spans the boulevard, supported by four steel legs, proclaiming PARRIS ISLAND: WHERE THE DIFFERENCE BEGINS. Then it turns right toward the receiving building and disgorges the recruits onto those yellow footprints.

The thirty-six recruits stand dazed as Staff Sergeant Biehl initiates them by reading two articles of the Uniform Code of Military Justice: First, they may not strike a Marine. Second, if they run away, they are subject to military law. It is similar to a police officer's reading the Miranda rights to a suspect—except that here the rights are those of the institution, not the individual.

The sergeant ushers them into the processing station and sits them in a kind of classroom, a brick room filled with rows of stainless steel one-piece desk-chairs. The walls are decorated with photographs of boot camp training. Waiting in the chairs are eleven other recruits who had arrived earlier from points south, kids from northern Florida and the Carolinas who simply were driven to Parris Island from Marine recruiting stations. After the dark of the cloudy night outside, the fluorescent overhead lights blaze like spotlights on the shiny steel desktops.

"Now," says Staff Sergeant Biehl, "I'm going to 'splain something to you. You are not at home. You are not back on the block. Everything you do will be done quickly and loudly." This emphasis on behavior and language, not military training, will form the core of their boot camp experience. It may not be what the recruits expected, but it is central to the process of transformation they are about to experience. Marine Corps basic training is more a matter of cultural indoctrination than of teaching soldiering, which comes later, at combat training or, for the real grunts, at infantry school. Before they can learn to fight, they must learn to be Marines. "We're getting them from a society that is in many ways disintegrating," the commandant of the

Marine Corps, Gen. Charles Krulak, says in his speeches. "Unless there is a change in this nation, this problem is going to manifest itself in larger proportion as we go along." That view is widely shared in the Marines. Sergeant Biehl, in a private moment, sums up the mission of Parris Island this way: "The Marine Corps is like a family, and we teach family values."

As if to underscore that they have entered a new world, Staff Sergeant Biehl begins to teach them a new language. Its peculiarly nautical tone grows out of the Marines' origins as a sea service. "We don't call it a floor, we call it a deck," he lectures, striding purposefully back and forth at the front of the desks. "We don't call it a door, we call it a hatch." For no apparent reason relating to the sea, writing pens are now to be called inksticks and sneakers are go-fasters.

Then he introduces them to another aspect of language on Parris Island: Orders generally are issued in the future imperative, the drill instructor's favorite verb tense. "You are going to write this number," Staff Sergeant Biehl says, perfectly confident that they will. "Three-zero-eight-six." They use Magic Markers to write the four numbers on their left hands. "This is now your platoon number," he says. "You are now part of Platoon Thirty Eighty-six." That number is now more important than their own names.

With a unit assigned, the recruits now have an address, which means they can mail a letter home and tell their families how to contact them. Then they are given the letter to mail: It is from Col. Humberto "Rod" Rodriguez, commanding officer of the Recruit Training Regiment. "Your Marine recruit has arrived safely at Parris Island," the letter states. "We have instructed him to write to you regularly."

Recruits alert enough to scan the letter get a hint of the pace that awaits them. "Please do not be alarmed if his first letters to you report that he has not received any mail yet," it continues. "Due to the rigorous training, recruits lose track of days."

The colonel's letter then gets to the point of Parris Island: "Our responsibility in the Recruit Training Regiment is to transform your young man and thousands like him from a civilian into a basically trained Marine, capable of accepting full responsibility for his present and future roles in our Corps. . . . In the process, he must prove to himself, his comrades, and his officers and drill instructors that he is worthy of the respect and confidence which are part of our title and uniform."

Next, as if they were entering prison, the recruits inventory the civilian clothes they are about to place in a brown bag. (Lacking civilian clothes makes it much harder for recruits to flee the island.) "We don't call them pants, we call them trousers," the sergeant helpfully reminds the newcomers. Moving back to the future imperative, the sergeant says, "Right now, all jewelry will come off your body."

Johnny Thomas Jr., a skinny black recruit from Delray Beach, Florida, not destined to make it through Parris Island, finds this order somehow humorous or embarrassing, and looks up at the sergeant with a slight smile. Unfortunately, he has a gold tooth in the middle of the smile that catches the sergeant's eye. "On your feet," Sergeant Biehl shouts, charging at him and waving a finger a few inches in front of his mouth. "I guarantee you that in the next couple of hours I'll wipe that smile off your face."

It is a very credible threat. Recruit Thomas's smile is gone in seconds. The sergeant resumes the in-processing. "Now, this is your last chance to cough up anything that shouldn't be on your body." Without explanation, he orders them to turn over any weapons, knives, cigarettes, matches, lighters, candy, food, gum, soda, drugs of any kind, liquids of any kind, dice, playing cards, subversive material, "pornographic material, naked pictures of your girlfriend or mother, rubbers, prophylactics, or any of that trash, put them in that orange crate right now, 'cause you ain't got any need of that now."

At 2:50 A.M., precisely one hour after meeting the bus, he ushers them into the next room and turns them over to Sgt. Ansil Lewis, a fine-boned infantry scout from the Virgin Islands who will run Platoon 3086 for the next three days.

Sergeant Lewis begins with the next big step in the disorientation process: He withdraws from the recruits the right to use the first person. Their first names also are banished. "From now on, you are no longer he, she, it, or whatever you was," he says in a clear, quiet voice. "You are now 'Recruit-and-your-last-name,' understand?" Coming from a society that elevates the individual, they are now in a world where the group is supreme. Using "I" raises suspicions: Why would you care more about your self than about your unit? You are 3086.

Sergeant Lewis's second move is to emphasize that no matter what they are doing, they are not doing it fast enough. He moves them in a single file toward the barber's stand in the back of the receiving station. "Let's go. Hurry up. Hurry. Tighter."

Buzz cuts begin at 3:30 A.M. and take twenty-five seconds per recruit. For some, six months' growth of hair flutters to the floor with each stroke of the barber's shaver. The barber is a broken-down looking civilian wearing a black T-shirt inscribed, in red letters, with the words PAIN FEAR IRONY DESPAIR DEATH. It is an unusual job, shaving the heads of terrified young men in the middle of the night. He doesn't speak as he does it. The recruits emerge from the barber's cubbyhole in the back of the receiving station and are made to line up in unnatural proximity, each recruit's toes almost touching the heel of the one before them, crotches within a foot of the buttocks of the recruit in front. This is far closer than the "comfort zone" of most Americans, especially adolescent males. But they already know enough to remain absolutely silent. As the last of the platoon is being shorn, Sergeant Lewis, in keeping with the drill instructor's ethic of using every available moment, begins teaching the shaveheads. "Whenever a drill instructor says 'Ears,' you say, 'Open.' Whenever a drill instructor says 'Eyeballs,' you say, 'Snap.' "

He plucks out two recruits to sweep the hair. He hurries them along, as DIs always do, by irritatedly saying, "Any day."

Then they are marched through a supply room and issued all the clothes they will wear and everything else they will need for eleven weeks, including such unique items as "rifle towels," which carry printed outlines showing where to place each piece of the M-16 as it is cleaned. The issuing clerk, an old man in casual civilian clothes, says the Marines used to do this in a roughshod way, having a sergeant distribute the gear and screaming at the recruits as they ran through, but found that caused so much trouble with confusion over equipment that they civilianized the task.

They carry their gear upstairs to the receiving barracks, a big unsympathetic chamber where identities evaporate. With its empty white cinderblock walls and bare floor, furnished only with sheetless mattresses on bunk beds, it may be the world's most anonymous room. The regular barracks on Parris Island at least display Marine Corps signs and instructive material on their walls; this lacks even the graffiti of a drunk tank. It offers absolutely no clues. It is 4:00 A.M., an empty hour. A recruit chancing on a mirror might not even recognize his own pasty-white hairless head.

The beds are inviting. But Platoon 3086 has long to go before it will sleep. Instead, at 4:50 A.M., Sergeant Lewis begins teaching it to toe the line. Literally. He assembles them along the two white lines painted the length of the spartan barracks. "Right in front of you is a little line," he says. "I want you to put your toe on it."

The sergeant then teaches them a few basic elements of how to walk in formation—"Left foot strikes the deck"—and marches them to the 3rd Battalion's mess hall. "When we go to the chow hall, nobody's going to run their mouth, understand?" he orders. The platoon moves through the windswept trees, a flashlight in each of their forty-seven hands, with forty-seven beams of light swinging and catching spooky glimpses of Spanish moss hanging from live oaks. Steam swirls around the platoon from the island's overground heating pipes. A fat raccoon squats and watches the group move by, its eyes flashing red in the swinging beams. It is an exotic and unsettling environment to the recruits from the cities and farms of the north, where palm trees and sea breezes signify vacation luxury, not boot camp.

The scene outside the mess hall in the predawn darkness is bewildering to outsiders. Young men appear in formation and move quickly amid great shouting, ranks of four peeling off at a time, but it isn't apparent how this high-energy system works, or why it requires continual yelling and stomping. Amidst this inexplicable whirl, 3086 stands in ragged formation on the veranda of the mess hall, a small rock in a rushing rapid. No one explains anything to it. "The disorientation is part" of the receiving process, says Master Sgt. Wilbert Altman, a receiving sergeant. "They never know what's going to happen next."

Some members of 3086 bite their lips. On the chins of others, baby fat quivers. Of the fifty-nine people who soon will make up the platoon, fourteen will be classified as overweight. They look like a mess, but they are typical of the platoons created at this time of year. There is an old Parris Island saying, "Summer from the school halls, winter from the pool halls." Most of this crew has more in common with Minnesota Fats than with Rambo. "Most of the kids got out of school last summer and then sat around playing Nintendo, eating potato chips, maybe working part time at McDonald's, or doing some construction work for a friend," says 1st Sgt. Charles Tucker, an eighteen-year-veteran of the Corps who is the senior sergeant for 3086's Kilo Company. "You sit around idle for eight or nine months, you can lose a lot psychologically."

Opposite 3086 on the cement veranda stands a seasoned platoon a day away from graduation. It is lean, cocky, and rock-band loud as it stands at crisp attention, chanting: "Three-zero-five-six/ We don't need no stinkin' chicks!" It stomps into the mess hall, driving its boot heels into the cement and shaking the floor.

At 5:20 in the morning the platoon sits down to a good breakfast—French toast, cereals, two apples, and orange juice. They remain stock still until Sergeant Lewis, standing over them, shouts an order: "Drink some water!" The drill instructors don't eat with the platoon, or even in front of them: It would make them appear human. The platoon's first meal on the island is over in eleven minutes, which is easy, because recruits in this battalion are forbidden to speak at meals, except to address their superiors. Swirling around them, more experienced recruits shout, "Morning, gentlemen," at a civilian standing with a drill instructor. The Third Battalion, of which they are a part, even though they don't yet know it, is known on Parris Island as the "Heavy D" unit, for its emphasis on discipline, a priority that seems to have been quietly decided by its drill instructors. "They're kind of strict in the Third Battalion," Sergeant Lewis later explains. The 2nd Battalion, by contrast, located across Boulevard de France, is known for its emphasis on weapons training: "All kill, no drill."

They march back outside, where dawn brings light but no more warmth. The pale sun rises on a group shorn of its past. "Everything is taken away—hair, clothes, food, and friends," says Navy Lt. James Osendorf, a Catholic priest for the 3rd Battalion. "It's a total cutoff from previous life. That's why you get so much loneliness, and so many suicidal tendencies." Religion will become important to many for the first time, he says, because it will be the only window they have back into their old lives.

"The sign on the road as you come into Parris Island says, WHERE THE DIFFERENCE BEGINS," adds Father Osendorf. "But to me it's more than that, it's where the transformation begins."

Over the next eleven weeks, the recruits will receive a value system transfusion, as they learn the Marine Corps way of walking, talking, and thinking. They will endure a pace of as many as fifteen orders per minute, every one a reminder that they have left a culture of self-gratification and entered a culture of self-discipline. Here, pleasure is suspect, and pain and sacrifice are good. The recruits will be denied all the basic diversions of the typical American youth—television, cigarettes, cars, cards, candy, soft drinks, video games, music, alcohol, drugs, and sex. Unlike in the other military services, they won't train alongside women. Here on Parris Island, women train separately, over in the 4th Battalion, in a citadel-like two-story barracks that shelters its own drill deck, gymnasium, mess hall, and beauty shop. "We don't have to go out of our own little world," says Lt. Mary Cogdill, the 4th Battalion's operations officer. But the atmosphere within the female battalion is very much that of Parris Island. A sign posted flat on the ceiling of one of its squad bays reads: PAIN IS GOOD, EXTREME PAIN IS EXTREMELY GOOD. It is located on the ceiling so recruits can contemplate it while doing punishment sit-ups. The only times the recruits of 3086 will encounter these female recruits will be on Sundays, at recruit chapel. Even then the females sit in their own assigned section of pews at the far side of the building.

Filling the vacuum in the recruits' lives will be their drill instructors. Many of these recruits have come here seeking a new identity. It is striking how little influence parents and family have had on most of the recruits. They don't define themselves through their families or work, as do many American adults. Asked about their pasts, many of these recruits talk about their leisure activities—"Drinking the forty ounce on the corner," as one Pittsburgh recruit puts it. They have come to boot camp to try the straightforward and simple definition of manhood offered by the Marines. To many, their drill instructors will become among the most important people they will ever meet, and these eleven weeks will become the central experience in their entire lives. Any Marine veteran can reach back thirty or forty years and summon the names of his drill instructors. Flying in a Marine jet over Parris Island, Brig. Gen. Randy West looks down on the swampy land and simply says, "I was born there."

The next step in the separation is "Recruitment Liaison," a process informally known as "the moment of truth." Mandatory one-on-one meetings with receiving sergeants, which take up the entire morning, give recruits a last chance to confess to previously undisclosed drug use or criminal convictions. This is also a way for the Corps to screen out unqualified or ineligible recruits that hard-pressed recruiters, trying to meet their quotas, might have tried to sneak by the authorities. Platoon 3086 and its companion platoon, 3085, move through together. The interviews reveal a cross section of the minor trouble that American youth can make. "I got into an argument with my mother, and this small-town cop, he didn't like me, and he took me out on a back road and beat me up," says a member of 3085 from Perry, New York, explaining a charge of assaulting an officer. One of his comrades has a record of burglary, aggravated assault, and breaking into cars in Fort Lauderdale, Florida, in 1992. But he told the recruiter about that, and he insists that nothing else will show up on his record when the Marines check.

For many members of 3086, marijuana use has been routine. Some tell Gunnery Sgt. Timothy Gulledge that they have dabbled in cocaine, LSD, and PCP. After each confession, Sergeant Gulledge asks, "Do you know the Marine Corps position on illegal drugs?" Each recruit is required to state that he understands the Corps doesn't tolerate drug use.

"You've used marijuana twenty-five times?" Sergeant Gulledge says to one recruit.

"Yes, sir," the uneasy recruit says. Both he and his interrogator know the number is probably far higher. But the point of the exchange is to underscore that, whatever the actual figure, it won't increase.

"You got a waiver for that. You understand you get no more chances?"

"Yes, sir." In fact, nearly half of all Marine Corps recruits enlist under some sort of "waiver" for crimes, drug use, and medical and psychological problems.

After a hurried lunch, Sergeant Lewis begins to teach them to march as a unit, beginning with how to stand erect like a Marine, how to lift a foot, how to stand in line. He repeats each step with a quiet, crisp tolerance.

By 5:30 that afternoon, the platoon, still without sleep since arriving the previous night, is dragging. But it already is looking more like a group of recruits, and less like a frazzled crowd of civilians. As the platoon enters its temporary barracks in the receiving building, most of its members remove their "utility hats"—the enlisted Marines' everyday headgear. Several say, "Good afternoon, sir," to a passing civilian. They also are learning to work as a group, rather than as individuals. They march to the mess hall for an early dinner, then back to the barracks, where Sergeant Lewis gives them twenty seconds to remove and hang up all their gear—hats, canteens, canteen web belts. The more astute members realize that the only way to do it within that limit is to aid one another. When Daniel Armstrong, a gangling, storklike road construction worker from Florida, gets tangled trying to remove his canteen belt, Christopher Anderson, a smart, short black recruit who plans to study criminology at the University of Maryland, leans over and helps him. Sergeant Lewis watches in silent approval: They are getting the message.

But that is a moment of clarity in a world of chaos. For the most part, the platoon learns by error. They live in a blur of anonymous drill instructors sweeping by them and yelling at them for committing sins they didn't know existed. One recruit gazes for a moment at a sergeant watching the platoon. "Get your eyeballs off me, recruit," the sergeant snarls. The platoon doesn't know it, but in a few weeks that small man will take on a godlike status for them. He is Staff Sgt. Ronny Rowland, who will become their senior drill instructor. He has come to quietly observe the material he will be inheriting from the receiving station.

By the approach of evening at the end of their first full day on Parris Island, the recruits' identities have been hollowed out. They know very little about anything, except toeing the line, which they are getting good at doing. The entire platoon can now be on line in just three seconds, down from twenty last night, and five this morning. Their heads are shaved. They are wearing anonymous military camouflage uniforms that don't yet have their names stenciled on them. The recruits around them are still strangers. They live in the disorienting, empty world of the receiving barracks. The sole clue to their identity is the black ink on their left hands: "3086."

They only want one thing: to lie down and go to sleep as soon as possible. They haven't slept for thirty-six hours, since they hugged their mothers and reported to the processing stations. But first they must learn how to make a bed in proper Marine style, with the sheets tucked at each corner with a forty-five-degree fold.

And they must do this through a haze of fatigue and dislocation, asking questions and making requests in the new language they are learning. Jonathan Prish, the self-declared former skinhead from Mobile, Alabama, is so tired that it takes him seven agonizing attempts before he is able to correctly formulate a simple question in proper Marine style.

"I need to . . ."

"No."

"Sir, I need to . . ."

"No."

"Sir, can I go to . . ."

"No."

Finally, after four more tries, he puts it all together, dropping the first person and including a "sir": "Recruit Prish requests permission to make a head call, sir."

The platoon never will be left alone at night on Parris Island, but on their first night here they are watched with special attention. Many members of 3086 are so disoriented that they seem incapable of considering where they are, and why. Sergeant Lewis keeps a close eye on them. "After a full day of this, everyone yelling at them, tired, scared, that's when they knock on my hatch and say, 'I don't want to stay here.' " Usually, he says, two or three do so on the first night.

Sure enough, at 7:00 P.M., the first recruit cracks—and hard. Recruit Campbell's tone is almost conversational, an eerie contrast to the hoarse shouts of most recruits' utterances, as he seeks to control himself. He quietly approaches Sergeant Lewis. "Is it possible I could go to the doctor tonight, if you don't mind?" he asks in a voice that strains to be casual, but clearly isn't.

Sergeant Lewis goes on full mental alert. This one won't be just a matter of sitting him down with a senior sergeant for a fatherly talk. This one could go sour fast. At the drill instructors' school on Parris Island, every drill instructor has pounded into him the fact that abuse of recruits has given the Marines a black eye in the past. In the most notorious incident, the Ribbon Creek "death march" of April 1956, Staff Sgt. Matthew McKeon, a DI from the Third Battalion, decided, after drinking heavily one night, to march a platoon into the tidal stream behind the rifle range. Six recruits drowned in the deep "trout holes" in the swirling tide. Later, during the demoralized post-Vietnam days of the 1970s, when the Corps was at a low point, poorly trained drill instructors, frustrated by the low quality of the recruits of that era, fell into a pattern of harassment and even maltreatment. Two recruits died during training, one after being beaten into unconsciousness in pugil stick training. "In the seventies, the process (of abuse) became institutionalized," concluded a report by Marine Lt. Gen. Bernard Trainor. These days, when a recruit hints that he feels bad, the Marines listen. They don't want recruits killing themselves on Parris Island, and the congressional inquiries that would provoke.

Partly to ensure that he has a witness, Sergeant Lewis leads the recruit downstairs to where Sergeant Biehl is doing paperwork. Recruit Campbell explains himself to the two men: "Sir, I feel real bad about something I did, sir. I feel kind of depressed about it."

"Do you feel suicidal?" Sergeant Lewis asks. It is the key question. The answer will determine whether Recruit Campbell will be off the island tomorrow morning.

"A little bit, sir." That alone is probably enough to win him a bus ticket home. His subsequent confession that he wasn't com-

pletely candid in his enlistment, that there was information he
should have told the recruiter but didn't, ensures that his career
in the Marines will end before it begins. Because all the doctors
have left the island for the day, Sergeant Lewis assigns shifts of
two recruits each to stay up and watch Recruit Campbell as he
sleeps. "Two shadows will be put on him all night."

So ends 3086's first long day in the Marines. At 8:00 P.M. they
tumble into their bunks and sleep.

But not for long. Less than seven hours later, at 2:50 A.M. Friday, March 3rd, Sergeant Lewis strides into the receiving barracks, flips on the fluorescent overhead lights, and shouts, "Get
on line NOW! Get on line! Get! On! Line!" The forty-eight
recruits wake up, scared, sleepy, and bald. If they had a moment
to think, they might ask where they were. But there is no time to
ponder. They are being berated in the middle of the night by a
black man demanding immediate and unquestioning obedience.
It is a novel experience for most white Americans. The membership of the platoon will change as some recruits drop out and
others, who have overcome injuries or other problems, are
"picked up" from preceding platoons. But 3086's racial and ethnic composition will remain throughout about three quarters
white and one quarter black and Hispanic.

What's more, there is the matter Sergeant Lewis is yelling
about: drugs. Yesterday they were told the Corps won't tolerate
drug abuse. Now it is going to prove it is serious. The sergeant
has them get on line, count off one through forty-eight, and then
get dressed as a unit. First, everyone dons a T-shirt. Then socks
and trousers. Then right sneaker. But when one recruit goes
ahead and puts on his left sneaker as well, the sergeant has them
take off the right sneaker and start again. Then each member of
the platoon is told to open his canteen, chug the entire quart,
and then hold the empty container upside down over his head.
Recruit Armstrong, the storklike Floridian, nearly overwhelmed
by the barrage of orders, looks near tears. At 3:30 A.M., Sergeant

Lewis lines them up and marches them into the latrine to provide samples for urinalysis. Anyone testing positive for heroin, cocaine, or opium will be ejected from the Corps.

Morning chow is wolfed down in silence and finished by 5:00 A.M. Next are two long bureaucratic processes, as much a part of military life as taking orders and doing exercise. First, starting at 6:30 A.M., their rifles are issued, with serial numbers duly logged in duplicate. Their M-16s will be constant companions, carried on marches, hung on the ends of their bunk beds at night. But they will never be given bullets, except at the rifle range, when each round will be tracked with laserlike precision. The rest of the morning is taken up by the dental check. Several members of the platoon have cavities and abscesses. The naval dentists issue them military fillings and a few false teeth.

The overcast afternoon brings the "initial strength test." The Corps wants to know if the recruits are even in sufficiently mediocre condition to *begin* getting in shape. Recruits whose bodies—especially their feet and legs—aren't able to absorb the impact of physical training constitute the leading cause of dismissal from Parris Island. "The kids I trained in '78, '80 were distinctly different" from today's recruits, says Brig. Gen. Jack Klimp, the island's commanding general. "A lot of them back then were tough, hard kids—a lot more physically tough, less fragile than today's kids. A lot of today's kids are the Nintendo generation, spending their lives looking into computers. They're the highest quality recruits we've ever had [in terms of education], but we've had to change our physical training to adjust to them. They are more fragile than recruits were ten years ago. A lot of them have never hit someone, or been hit."

For the entire afternoon the platoon is put through rounds of pull-ups, sit-ups, and running on a big field near the receiving building. The drill instructors of the Third Battalion make the five-minute walk over to the receiving area to watch these recruits and assess the material with which they will work for the next eleven weeks. One DI looks at Dana Patrick, struggling along, and calls him "a bowl of jelly." Five of the forty-seven recruits fail the strength tests, including Recruit Patrick, who doesn't complete the run. Judged unready to begin training, three will be sent to the Physical Conditioning Platoon to get them into sufficient shape to begin. The "PCP"—which inevitably becomes known as the "Pork Chop Platoon"—is Parris Island's purgatory. On average it is peopled by ninety recruits, most of them Initial Strength failures who can't do two pull-ups or run a mile in ten minutes and thirty seconds. For about thirty days, the PCPers are put through a regime of exercise, diet, and drill. Most are then "picked up" by a new platoon. But about one in five never is able to get in shape, and washes out of boot camp before really beginning it.

Staff Sergeant Rowland exercises his discretion to keep two borderline test failures. One of them is Shane Logan, a big, thoughtful kid from Oneonta, New York, who wants to be a social worker. "The kid only did one pull-up—the minimum is three—but he had such huge desire to be a Marine," Rowland explains. (His assessment is correct: By the time Logan graduates from boot camp, he will be doing fifteen pull-ups.) The platoon averages nine and a half pull-ups, fifty-two sit-ups, and twenty-four minutes for the three-mile run. By graduation it will be doing twice as many pull-ups, half again as many sit-ups, and will have cut three minutes from the run. As a new platoon, "I'd say they're about average," Staff Sergeant Rowland concludes.

They also look to be typical mentally, adds Staff Sgt. Ivan Pabon, the acting gunnery sergeant for this "series," or group, of platoons. "The biggest problem we have with these kids is that everybody in America thinks they know everything, and their way is the right way," he says as he watches the platoons stream in from the three-mile run, the first of many they will perform in the coming weeks. Parris Island is the first place many of them ever encounter absolute and impersonal standards of right and wrong, of success and failure, says Sergeant Pabon, a native of Puerto Rico who learned to speak English in boot camp. "When they mess up at home, they don't get punished, they get 'explained.' The parents, the media, want to 'explain' everything. Here, you screw up, we stop you and penalize you immediately, before you forget it."

"The broken family kids are one of the bigger problems we have here," adds 1st Sgt. Charles Tucker, the senior NCO for 3086's Kilo Company. "A lot of them have never had anyone get on them. It's a big shock when they come down here and get told, 'No, you are doing it wrong.' A lot of them, if they came from a single-parent household, and their mother's working, they've pretty much had free rein."

For Platoon 3086, the shock of the absolute looms just over the horizon. Here, the absolute actually has a body, title, and name: Sgt. Darren Carey, USMC, the "heavy hat" drill instructor who will land on them tomorrow morning. But they don't know that as they march to Friday night chow. They move almost as a unit. They are beginning to look like recruits. A few may even think they have this place figured out. They will soon find out they are wrong. Friday is their last day in the "low-stress environment" of receiving. On Saturday morning they will move to the real world of Parris Island.

CHAPTER TWO

THE FORMING

I will NOT accept substandard performance from you," shouts
Sgt. Darren Carey in a roar that rings off the barracks' white
cinderblock walls. He is kicking 3086 into high gear.

After a bit more than two days on Parris Island, 3086 is
deemed ready to meet its drill instructors. On a bright, dew-thick
Saturday morning, their boots reflect the sun. Sergeant Lewis
marches the shuffling platoon across Wake Boulevard to its new
home: Third Deck, Building 420, to begin the "Pick-up," the first
part of the "Forming," the phase in which the members of the
platoon, having shed their individual civilian pasts, prepare to
commence training. The "Pick-up" is shock theater, Marine Corps
style. Its purpose is to intensify the training experience, and to
push the recruits to move beyond what they believe to be their
limits. They will have to, just to keep up.

Before the platoon arrives, the three drill instructors who will
assume control of it this morning meet in the "DI house," which
is really just a cell-like room at the end of the barracks floor. Offering barely enough room for three men, it is furnished only with the
essentials: a desk for Staff Sergeant Rowland, the senior drill
instructor, to do his daily paperwork, which tracks each recruit's
performance, test results, weight, and offenses. A chair for another
DI to sit in. A bed for the DI on duty to sleep in—the recruits are
never left to themselves overnight. A small bathroom. A closet,

containing a seminude pin-up. A wooden rack on the cinderblock wall to preserve the crease on the all-important DI hat.

Sergeants Rowland and Carey are joined by the junior drill instructor, Sgt. Leo Zwayer, a twelve-year veteran of the Corps from Ashville, Ohio. All three men are trim, with not a loose thread between them; they sport Marine "high and tight" hair-cuts—shaved on the sides, a brush cut on top. They check them-selves in the mirror and energize themselves with quick reminders and small talk as they prepare to confront their new charges. The two senior sergeants, Rowland and Carey, similar-looking men—small, bantamlike, flat-stomached, and wasp-waisted—have strik-ingly different personalities. Sergeant Rowland, an Arkansan, is outwardly cordial, but fundamentally taciturn, with the air of one who wants to keep his personality out of public view. Sergeant Carey, a Long Islander, appears at first to be reserved but becomes voluble once he is comfortable with his surroundings. The two men mesh well.

"I feel good, da-na-*na*-na-na-na-na." Staff Sergeant Rowland sings James Brown, pumping himself up to his full 5-foot, 6-inches. He dons the shiny black belt that is the emblem of the senior drill instructor, a subtle mark of prestige that sets him apart from the junior DIs with their green web belts. He is thirty-seven years old, ancient for a staff sergeant. This is because he has what the Marines call "broken time": he joined the Marines in 1977, left in 1980, went home and worked in a sink factory in Searcy, Arkansas, for seven years, and then rejoined the Corps in 1987.

Sergeant Lewis marches the platoon into the barracks, but the DIs stay hidden in their DI house. First the officers in 3086's chain of command greet the unit. These men are the opening acts, and they are low key, even soft spoken. But then, Parris Island isn't an officer's show. For the most part, they are more like producers and directors. The DIs are the main actors.

"The training here is tough," begins Capt. Jeffrey Chessani, commander of Kilo Company. "We will accept nothing less than the very best effort from you at all times."

Then comes Lt. Dave Richards, a young artillery officer who sometimes wonders whether he should break with a family tradition of serving as a Marine officer and instead pursue his love of writing and literature. "There is only one way on—or off—this island," he warns them. "That is by the causeway." The Marine Corps doesn't want unhappy recruits trying to swim away and being washed out to sea by the tides, or chewed up by sharks.

Then Staff Sergeant Rowland strides out of the DI house, executes a sharp left flank, and takes over. He ups the intensity level a few notches, but he isn't shouting. His role is that of the father figure for the platoon, the one who tracks the progress of individuals and counsels those who lag.

"Every recruit here, whether he is fat or skinny, tall or short, fast or slow, has the ability to become a United States Marine, if you can develop self-discipline and spirit," he says, standing between the two pillars at the end of the barracks. If it seems like theater, it is: He in fact is reciting the "Pick-up" speech for senior drill instructors prescribed in *Standard Operating Procedures for Recruit Training,* the bible of Parris Island.

Stenciled on the pillars flanking Staff Sergeant Rowland in black and red letters are the words CORE VALUES: HONOR. COURAGE. COMMITMENT. ("These are things," explains former Marine Commandant Al Gray, "that come before the self.") The barracks is still spartan by the standards of the outside world— there is no TV, radio, telephone, or any other connection to civilian life. It is lurid in comparison to the barren holding tank of the receiving barracks, where the platoon has stayed since getting off the bus eighty hours ago. There are signs posted in black and red throughout the barracks, listing information that all recruits must learn: the birthplace of the Marine Corps, the muzzle velocity of an M-16 rifle and, over a bathroom sink, the answer to the question, "What is the Proper Position of a Victim with a Sucking Chest Wound?"

"We will give every effort to train you, even after some of you have given up on yourselves," declares Staff Sergeant Rowland, emphasizing a phrase that soon will creep into the prayers of some recruits, as the distinction between God and the senior drill instructor erodes. In fact, the prayer penned by some recruits and used at their graduation eleven weeks later will quote that phrase exactly. "Starting now, you will treat me and all other Marines with the highest respect and you will obey all orders without question." Why?: "We have earned our place as Marines and will accept nothing less than that from you."

He next touches on a key aspect of Parris Island's history: recruit abuse. "I am not going to threaten you with physical harm, abuse you, or harass you. Nor will I tolerate such behavior from anyone else, Marine or recruit. If anyone should abuse or mistreat you, I will expect you to report such incidents to me. Further, if you believe that *I* have mistreated you, I expect you to report it to the series commander."

Then he turns to what they must do to survive the next eleven weeks and come out the other side as Marines. "You will obey all orders. You must give one hundred percent of yourself at all times. You must do everything you are told to do, quickly and willingly. You must be completely honest in everything you do." It is a rigid code, bristling with values alien to many of these recruits.

Then, the man appears who will enforce that code, Sergeant Carey. He marches alone from the DI house and stands between the pillars. He is the "heavy hat," the disciplinarian who will dominate the recruits' lives. He is bellowing about the "seven steps" of learning, and about paying attention, but the words are irrelevant. His point is that he is making the recruits shout back at him "Yes, sir," ten times a minute, until he is satisfied with their volume. As he works the platoon, two additional sergeants materialize. They aren't part of the usual DI team, but have been imported for the occasion to increase the shock effect. The five DIs swarm over the platoon, shouting at individuals because of their posture, their answers, their expressions.

They are everywhere. One is shouting, "Back up. *Back up!* BACK UP!" To a second recruit, another sneers, "Take your sweet time." A third rasps, "Oh, we'll wait for you."

In some ways this is the most important moment of 3086's eleven weeks on Parris Island. This is the point when the drill instructors cut all those ties to the past and irrevocably establish the fact that they are in charge, entirely on their own terms, for the duration. "The reason we do this the way we do is to create uncertainty," explains Lieutenant Colonel Becker, commander of the Third Battalion. "From the recruit's perspective, it appears to be chaos. War is chaos. And then they see this drill instructor—this magnificent creature who brings order to chaos. They learn that if they follow orders, their life will be calmer." Boot camp is indeed a kind of war, he says. "The recruits aren't the enemy—don't get me wrong. The enemy is their values—their un-Marinelike values. Self-indulgence, me first, 'I'm-going-to-do-what-I-want-to-do.' "

The five DIs appear maniacally angry. Shouting, pointing their fingers, raising a foot and slamming it to the ground, then whirling to scream at their next victim, they never stop moving— and never appear remotely pleased with the recruits' frantic execution of their buzz of orders. They manage to turn the inventory of the mundane gear the recruits have brought with them from receiving into an extraordinarily intense, even excruciating experience. Each recruit must produce exactly the right item—a left sneaker, a towel, socks—at exactly the right moment. And instead of facing the soft-spoken, patient Sergeant Lewis from receiving, they are up against five strange new drill instructors who cackle in a frenzy of military-issue sarcasm, issuing an order, waiting a beat, then snarling, "Any day."

It is a shocking experience, repeated for every new platoon on the island. It is one they will remember for the rest of their lives. "I've been in a lot of combat" since boot camp, observes retired Marine Maj. Gene Duncan, now an author and commentator on the military and society, "and I'm telling you the truth, I never been as frightened in combat as I was here on Parris Island."

Leading the charge at all times is Sergeant Carey. He brings a combatlike intensity to the job of recruit training. Described by his father, a career police officer in Long Island's Nassau County, just outside New York City, as a "Huck Finn–type," Sergeant Carey joined the Marines in 1984 after graduating from high school and spending some time painting houses. His body tells the story of the eleven years since then. A mako shark tattooed on his leg commemorates his time as a combat scuba diver and a parachutist in "Force Recon," the Marines' elite reconnaissance units. Three short, curling scars above his left ear mark the time in 1985 when a speedboat in the Mediterranean ran him down and broke his jaw, fractured his skull, and knocked out his front teeth. After spending months in hospitals in Europe, he rejected the Marines' offer to send him home to finish recuperating. He chose instead to return to his unit aboard a ship off Beirut. Despite his severe injuries, he is now in great shape, thin but muscled. At age thirty he still scores a perfect 300 on the boot camp physical fitness test—though he aches for a day or two afterward. (There are entire platoons at boot camp that fail to have one recruit capable of that feat even after 10 intense weeks of physical fitness training here.)

The Corps has long been ambivalent about "Force Recon" Marines such as Sergeant Carey, fearing they would become an elite within an already elite service. Force Recon is exactly that. The true stories about it are amazing. One Force Recon Marine celebrated the Marine Corps' all-important birthday by doing 500 pushups—and then 2000 sit-ups. A routine Force Recon exercise calls for the men to sneak undetected in teams across a section of southern California hills, and then meet at a rally point miles away—out in the Pacific Ocean. During the entire Vietnam War, 362 of the 2,300 men who served in the Third Reconnaissance Battalion were killed—and in that small unit, five men were awarded the Medal of Honor. "We're kind of like bastard children," Sergeant Carey explains. "Everyone either really appreciates us, or dislikes us because of our attitudes. A lot of animosity comes from the rest of the Marine Corps thinking that you're a yahoo or a cowboy." He rejects that view, arguing that being in Force Recon, "You're just more Marine. What I learned in basic training about the Marines, that's what being Force Recon is."

In his time with the Marines, Sergeant Carey has attended just about every special warfare school operated by the U.S. military. In 1990 he graduated No. 2 in an Army Ranger class—a standing he suspects was rigged to ensure that a Marine didn't take the top spot. He has swum through Scuba School, climbed through Mountain Warfare School, shivered through Winter Survival School, and learned things he won't talk about in the Fort Bragg course on Special Forces Target Acquisition and Exploitation. He has taken other courses on hostage extraction, high altitude parachuting, and "platform disabling." (This last was really a series of exercises in the Gulf of Mexico aimed at figuring out how to shut down Iranian oil platforms without causing widespread environmental damage.) "He's an awesome Marine," says Staff Sergeant Matthew Balenda, the Third Battalion's drillmaster. "He keeps them fired up—his veins pop, his head starts to glow, the spit is flying."

Despite all that, he is still only a buck sergeant after eleven years in the Corps. That's partly because promotions have been hard to come by in the post-Cold War downsizing of the U.S. military, but also because his aggressive streak hasn't always helped him. Even among Force Recon Marines, Sergeant Carey stands out. As a twenty one-year-old corporal, "he was the Deion Sanders of the Recon community," recalls a senior Marine intelligence officer. That is, "He talked a lot, shot off his mouth—but he was as good as he talked."

The Marine culture encourages candor, but Sergeant Carey pursues that virtue with a vigor that sometimes startles his superiors, who aren't accustomed to disagreement from their juniors. One weekend in 1991, while he was off duty at Camp Lejeune, he committed a common offense among Marines: he had a bit too much to drink. Among other things, he wound up cursing at "a guy in the dark." The "guy" turned out to be a senior sergeant. It was a borderline offense, but the sergeant chose to write it up. Four years later, Sergeant Carey reported to Parris Island, only to find that the same sergeant was now his sergeant major—the big boss. Typically, Sergeant Carey reopened the unhappy acquaintance by asking the sergeant major why he had been such a hard-ass back at Lejeune.

He is just the sort of person that militaries need in wartime, but don't know how to handle at other times. "He makes people uneasy," Captain Chessani later observes. "He's outspoken, and a lot of people aren't used to sergeants being outspoken."

Sergeant Carey walks down the center aisle of the barracks. James Andersen, the nineteen-year-old former Taco Bell shift manager, extends his arms to display his shower flip-flops, as ordered. His hands shake slightly as he does, but he is on track. The brass belt buckle display doesn't go so well. Chad Shelton, a light brown-skinned twenty-one-year-old from Manchester, Connecticut, who came here from working in a Sizzler steakhouse, blurts out, "I don't have one."

Sergeant Carey is stunned. He looks dumbfounded, as if Recruit Shelton had challenged him to a fight or cursed Mother Carey. The drill instructor's neck cords bulge. "I?" His scars turn red. "I?" His face just inches from the recruits, he screams, "I? I? I? 'I' is GONE!"

Recruit Shelton begins to try to explain himself. We can work this out, his half-smile seems to say. "SHUT YOUR MOUTH," shouts Sergeant Carey. "UNDERSTAND." It isn't a question.

Recruit Shelton says, "Aye, sir."

Sergeant Carey shouts, "UNDERSTAND." He repeats the exchange eight more times, his mouth inches from Recruit Shelton. His spittle flies across the recruit's handsome brown face. The recruit later confesses quietly that he was seconds away from slugging the sergeant—an act that probably, but not definitely, would have gotten him tossed out of the Corps, a chance for leniency coming from his newness on the island and his clean record. But Recruit Shelton, the son of a Marine, thinks of himself as a leader, someone who can help along the other recruits. He restrains himself, waits until Sergeant Carey's wrath moves on, and then discreetly wipes his face.

Another recruit stumbles into the first person. "I?" screams Sergeant Carey, stomping a foot and raising an accusing finger. "You got on the wrong bus, 'cause there ain't no me, my's or I's here. The only eyes are in your head"—in fact, just a few inches from the drill instructor's wagging finger. "I" will soon disappear from the recruits' vocabulary. According to Parris Island legend, a recruit intent on escaping from boot camp stole a bicycle one evening and, wearing his physical training T-shirt and shorts and a baseball cap he found somewhere, pedaled out the causeway to the main gate. The guard, assuming the kid was a civilian or a Marine dependent, casually asked, "Where are you going this late at night?" The recruit jumped off his bike, stood at attention, and shouted, "Sir, this recruit is. . . ." He was hauled back to his barracks.

Awed by Sergeant Carey's ability to maintain a burning intensity for hours, day upon day, the recruits will come to idolize him. "Everyone looked up to Staff Sergeant Rowland and Sergeant Zwayer," Recruit Patrick Bayton will say months later, "but Carey was a step above. He was like the perfect Marine."

What drives Sergeant Carey is a love for the Corps and a fear that inferior recruits will drag it back into the muck of a lazy, selfish society. He doesn't just take it personally, he takes it to the center of his being. When regulations force him to give lagging recruits another chance to pass physical capability tests, he clenches his teeth. "I'm not politically correct to say this, but they shouldn't be given another chance," he spits. "They should be out. They haven't met Marine Corps standards. It hurts the attitude of the platoon. And it almost degrades me."

He isn't sure about some of the recruits he sees now. Several more of them, knocked off balance by the bizarre tumult of angry grown men shouting insanely about underwear and flip-flops, acting as if each recruit's survival somehow depended on these mundane items, slip and revert to the banned first person. "Whose cover is this?" asks Sergeant Carey, using Marine jargon for a hat.

"Me, sir," says an unwary recruit. He is chewed out and spat back into his place. Other recruits, wised up, demonstrate that they at least remember the correct "this recruit" method of referring to themselves. But then they hit another hurdle: Sergeant Carey finds it distasteful to see them show off, almost reveling in the misfortune of a comrade. "Shut your mouth," snaps Sergeant Carey. "Did you ask permission to speak?"

By 10:45 in the morning they look sweaty and wrung out. They have been in the hands of Sergeant Carey for just 45 minutes. Sergeant Pabon, the acting gunnery sergeant on hand for this performance, surveys the poleaxed platoon. "Just think, some of these guys probably are used to waking up at 9 A.M., not working, not exercising." He chuckles. "Look at them now."

Sergeant Carey pumps them back up. He has them chant: "Honor. Courage. Commitment. Kill, kill. Marine Corps!" It is a boot camp haiku that eventually will be tattooed on their brains, shouted almost every time they sit down for a class or mail call. He gives them the inviolable terminology of their new home. The stairs are the ladder; there are two sets, but recruits may only use the rear set. The lane down the middle of the barracks between the bunkbeds is the "DI highway"; when he is on it, recruits stay off it. The windows are "ports" and the beds are "racks."

He assembles them for a bedmaking class. "I want to stress teamwork. Nobody gets anywhere by themselves."

When they begin to flag again, he steps on the gas. "I guess we want the wrath of God to come down on us this early in the game, right?" This is a bit of a surprise to the platoon—they thought that is exactly what happened this morning. It is a scary thought: What else does this crazy sergeant have up his sleeve? Just a warning, it turns out: "We don't stinkin' lollygag, understand?" says Sergeant Carey. "You better start snappin' and poppin'. When I say something, you better move like freakin' lightning, understand?" A good drill instructor doesn't waste a moment of his time with the platoon, not if he is going to turn Beavis and Butthead into Marines he'd want covering his flank in combat.

On the way to the Third Battalion mess hall for lunch, Sergeant Carey works on their primitive marching abilities. Under his tutelage, the movement across the battalion parade ground, normally a one-minute stroll, takes a quarter of an hour. In a sense they are infants, still learning to walk and stand as Marines. In doing so, they are learning how to move as a group. That unity is the basic building block of drill—and drill is the basic element of the professional military unit. Historian William McNeill theorizes that humanity's first step in moving beyond small groups was engaging in large-scale movement together, the tribal dance. Moving as a group enlarged the sense of self and gave pleasure. From this, he argues, grew the body politic. The beginning point of a military society, he adds, is close order drill—the military dance. It is no accident that the sergeants who run boot camp platoons are not called "military instructors" but "drill instructors." Drill—boring, repetitive, and replete with sixty-two basic movements, each containing several subsets of requirements for the location of the rifle, the placement of the hands on the rifle, and the angle of the arms—is the heart of boot camp.

Sergeant Carey moves the platoon across the asphalt at a crawl, correcting hand movements, straightening arms, aligning files, enforcing forty inches of separation between each rank. The platoon finally arrives at the mess hall. There Sergeant Carey uses the wait in line to initiate 3086 into another aspect of Marine boot camp's Zen-like fetish for minor details, in which not a single action is left to individual improvisation. The mess hall tray is to be held with arms flush at the side, bent ninety degrees at the elbow, he instructs. But there is more to it than that. "You will hold your tray this way: thumbs on the outside," he continues. (In fact, this instruction will become a minor controversy with some other Third Battalion DIs, who insist that Standard Operating Procedure calls for thumbs on the inside.)

Even meals offer no respite. The recruits sit silently as Sergeant Carey circles them and lectures, just as DIs from other platoons are doing with their own units. "Drink water," says one DI.

Sergeant Carey eyes one recruit's tray. "Them cakes is nasty," he admonishes. "That ain't warrior food." He tries to steer them toward fresh vegetables and carbohydrates.

After lunch, Staff Sergeant Rowland simply reappears from nowhere, as DIs do in their godlike way, and takes the drivers' wheel. In private, he and the other DIs refer to commanding the platoon as "driving the bus." It is an apt metaphor for the art of keeping more than fifty young men, many of them dog-tired and confused, moving at the same speed in the same direction. Staff Sergeant Rowland assembles them on the tarmac of the parade ground for an introductory talk. "Before we leave my island, we will be thinking and breathing exactly alike." It is classic DI prose: it is hugely possessive, it speaks to the group, and it is confidently cast in the future imperative. "Nobody's an individual, understand?" That is, anybody who somehow remains an individual is by definition a nobody: not a Marine.

On the end of the formation, Recruit Moore rolls his eyes in dismay and even seems to shake his head in disagreement. Sergeant Rowland, alert to the smallest variation from the prescribed movement, strolls to the recruit's side. "You bored, recruit?"

After a closer look at the disconsolate recruit he pulls him out of the formation for a chat. "What is the problem?" he asks quietly.

"I can't handle this Marine life," says Moore, an eighteen-year-old high-school dropout from the Deep South. "This ain't for me." Tears begin streaming down his cheeks. "It's just too much to remember, sir."

Sergeant Rowland leans his head near the recruit's and softly asks, "This is probably the worst day of your life, right?"

Moore nods. "Yes, sir," he says just as quietly.

"There's been ten thousand Marines who felt like that," the sergeant says. "And you know what? They walked across that parade ground and graduated."

Recruit Moore looks doubtful. But he stands a little straighter when he is put back in formation. For the next ten weeks he constantly will look as though he is about to crumble. Not many people could take this stress, he will confide. Several times, it won't be clear if he can. Sergeant Rowland later concedes that his soft-spoken, paternal approach had been a duty. "He was boo-hooing all over the place. I wanted to choke him." The platoon would never guess it, but this is Staff Sergeant Rowland's first cycle as a senior drill instructor, playing the "daddy" role. Just a few weeks earlier, with his previous platoon, he had been the martinet heavy hat— and, by all accounts, a good and fearsome one.

Sergeant Carey, taking it all in from behind the platoon, isn't worried by Recruit Moore's faltering performance. Tears are nothing new here: eventually, almost every member of the platoon will cry while on Parris Island. "They're in culture shock now," says Sergeant Carey, not at all unhappy with the fact. He grins. "They're thinking, '*What* did I do?' "

During more introductory drill practice, one drill instructor issues orders to the group while the other moves along the ranks to correct individuals. The smallest of the services, the Marines cultivate frugality as part of their culture. Only one thing is lavished on the recruits: The energetic attention of at least one, and usually two, drill instructors at all waking moments. The platoon marches back to the barracks for its first class, in a typically austere "classroom"—just the open bay at the end of the barracks, with two recruits' wooden green footlockers stacked up as the teachers' desk. The recruits sit on the floor, cement painted Marine maroon. It is time for what the Corps calls "knowledge"—the one-word title of the twenty-three-page booklet the drill instructors now give to the platoon. The recruits will carry these little white booklets until the white pages are brown with sweat and dust. Whenever they have an idle moment—and there are many in the movement of any military unit, even on Parris Island—they are supposed to pull it out and study it. They learn the order of the ten persons in their "Chain of Command," from "1st—Senior Drill Instructor" to "10th—President of the U.S.—The Honorable Mr. Clinton." They read and reread "Marine Corps History." ("History relates to the courage of the person who wears the title Marine," says former Commandant Gray. "History is the glue that holds this together. A lot of people have worn the title Marine, and you don't want to let them down.") They become steeped in the two crucial pages called "Customs and Courtesies": "The statement used when passing an officer from behind is? 'By your leave, sir.' "

That is all to come. First is the definition: "Knowledge is what?" bellows Sergeant Carey.

"Power, sir," responds the platoon, sitting cross-legged on the cement floor.

"Power is what?"

That puzzles 3086. Faces scrunch up in thought. Eventually, one recruit hazards a guess. "Money?"

Sergeant Carey is dumbfounded that such a civilian attitude persists in his platoon after nearly three full days on Parris Island. "No," he shouts. "Power is VICTORY!" He turns the class over to the junior drill instructor, Sergeant Zwayer, and says, in a whispered aside, "I swear, I'm dealing with aliens." (Unlike many in American society, Sergeant Carey and his fellow drill instructors aren't in it for the money. He works as long as seventeen hours a day, six and a half days a week. He is paid $1,775 a month—a figure that works out to about the minimum wage.)

Fresh from the Drill Instructors' School across the island, this is Sergeant Zwayer's first "rotation" as a DI—he previously was a mess sergeant here on the island. What he lacks in finesse he makes up in volume as he shouts the platoon through its first "knowledge" class. It is pure rote, evoking the Japanese style of education: Loud, simple, and repetitive, the academic equivalent of close order drill. In the coming weeks, almost all the platoon's classes on everything from the inner life of the M-16 rifle to how to throw a hand grenade to how to move through the woods at night will be conducted in a similar fashion. The major motivator is fear. One classic example of the Marine use of fear as an educational device is the story related by Gene Duncan, the Marine writer and commentator, about the old sergeant who begins a class on secure communications by handing a pistol to a student and ordering him to shoot his buddy. After a heated confrontation, he backs down and explains that giving precise location information over an unsecured radio is the same as putting a loaded gun to other Marines' heads.

Sergeant Zwayer makes no effort to make his audience comfortable; the platoon either will memorize these facts or suffer the consequences, which range from being chewed out and given extra "physical training," to being dropped from the platoon and "recycled" back into a newer unit. That last cataclysmic option—being shipped as a stranger into another platoon that already has bonded—will come to be many recruits' greatest fear. Some will hide minor injuries out of worry that they will be recycled out of 3086.

"A sergeant major is an E-9, understand?" says Sergeant Zwayer.

"Yes, sir," the platoon bellows.

"What is an E-9?" he then asks.

"Sir, E-9 in the Marine Corps is sergeant major," the platoon responds. And so on down the rank structure.

In the back of the platoon, someone farts. Adolescent titters ripple across the platoon, as if it were back in high school. Sergeant Zwayer's restrained response is an elegant summary of the Marines' essentially conservative view of man generally, and the adolescent

American male particularly, as an ignoble savage in desperate need of external civilizing. The drill instructors aren't out to cultivate any Quaker-like inner light; they aim to transform these kids into Marines. "That's just human nature," Sergeant Zwayer says in a calm voice. He's not accepting it, just pointing out what the Marines intend to alter. He doesn't want to embarrass the offending recruit; in the DI's view, the entire platoon is so civilianlike that it is continually offensive, one big walking degradation. "We're here to refine you," he says to these crude recruits. "By the time you leave here, you ain't going to do that trash no more."

There are no rest breaks allowed for the recruits to catch their breath and clear their heads. "Knowledge" is followed by more drill. Then, on the way to evening chow, Sergeant Carey again uses the march to teach the rhythm of unit movement.

At 6:20, as night descends, Staff Sergeant Rowland begins another session with the platoon. He wears his thirty-seven years in a fatherly way as he pulls up a footlocker and gathers the bedraggled platoon around him. "You mind if I sit down?" he asks with a grin. The social distance between him and the platoon is so great that asking their permission is richly absurd. They grin back.

"There's an old saying in the Marine Corps that 'stuff rolls downhill,' " he begins. He actually means "shit rolls downhill," but neither he nor the other DIs in this platoon will use much profanity with the recruits. "Guess who's at the bottom of the hill?"

Despite the harshness of his message, the platoon is warmed by his tone, or perhaps his honesty. "We are, sir!" they happily shout, as one.

"Everything we teach you has a purpose," he continues. For example, he notes, sitting cross-legged in classes, awkward though it may be, is good preparation for the sitting position they will use on the rifle range. The point is minor, but the gesture is pleasant. This is the first time anyone has deigned to explain anything to the recruits since they arrived on Parris Island.

Then he delivers his key message, echoing his noontime lecture. It goes to the heart of the boot camp ethic of teamwork and anonymity—the antithesis of celebrity-besotted American culture. "I challenge you to be the recruit that walks across the parade ground on graduation day, and the doggone drill instructor doesn't even know your name." They can do that, he says, simply by being good recruits. In fact, it is the group of quiet recruits in the middle of the platoon who will undergo the greatest changes at boot camp. The best, like Andrew Lee, who arrive both fit and disciplined, will be able to charge through boot camp without significantly altering their personalities. The worst won't be able to change their personalities sufficiently to make it through boot camp. But it will be those in the middle, young men who have come here looking to change themselves, to discard failed or unfulfilling adolescent lives, who will undergo a quiet transformation as they acquire new lives as Marines.

The talk helps him establish his paternal role. "A lot of these kids have no fathers, or have abusive fathers," he later says, when asked to explain his job. "The drill instructor is the first father figure they've ever had who treats them with respect, who cares what happens to them."

Turning to what he expects to be a simple administrative task, he asks the forty-seven recruits present about their religion. Recruit Shelton says he isn't a Protestant, he's a Christian. When that is sorted out, the count is twenty-one Protestants and twenty-five Catholics, a mix that reflects the pull the Marines still have on the rural South and the blue-collar ethnics of the urban northeast—Irish, Italian, Polish, and Hispanic. (The Marines send recruits from east of the Mississippi River to Parris Island; those from the West generally are sent to the boot camp in San Diego.)

That accounts for forty-six. The forty-seventh is Earnest Winston Jr., a black recruit from the violent inner-city streets of southeast Washington, D.C. He says that he is not a Protestant. And he isn't a Catholic. Staff Sergeant Rowland cocks a questioning eyebrow. "Neither, sir," insists Recruit Winston, who speaks softly below lidded eyes and a hooked nose that clearly has been broken at least once. Sergeant Rowland looks at him with some disbelief, and pushes the issue, albeit gently. Maybe there is a misunderstanding, like the one Recruit Shelton had. No, responds Recruit Winston: "This recruit follows no denomination, sir." In fact, Recruit Winston practices a religion that he won't disclose here tonight. It is a mix of self-preservation and the beliefs of Black Muslims, but he isn't about to say that to a white cracker drill instructor he just met.

It is Recruit Winston's first exchange with his drill instructors, and it doesn't bode well. In the coming days the drill instructors, and even more so the senior sergeants who supervise them, will come to distrust Recruit Winston and debate whether he should be discharged.

But Recruit Winston has nothing if not an instinct for survival. In private conversation weeks later, he claims—credibly—to have shot ten people before joining the Corps at age nineteen. He regrets none of what he has done, not even hitting bystanders in drive-by shootings. "That was payback," he reasons. "If it hits someone in their neighborhood, that's payback, too." He does admit to a bit of remorse about certain armed robberies that went sour. "End of last year, I robbed an old black lady, and the guy that was with me beat her."

He says he was a first-class crook, but enlisted in the military to get away because he was involved in a pistol smuggling outfit the D.C. police were rolling up, and so wanted to get out before he was killed. That had been the fate of his friends Anton, Taurus, Darlwin, Fish, Rick, and Tarzan—on his block of Anacostia Road alone. "I was at the peak of my life. I knew all about being a thug out on the streets. But if I died, where would that leave my mother?" Of all the services, he joined the Marines because he likes to excel, whether at crime or soldiering. "I always wanted to be the best." He shows little fear of the rigors of Parris Island. "Ain't nothing the Marine Corps could put in front of me that could scare me more than my neighborhood," he reflects. "I had a friend who got beat to death with a stick by his father. I had a friend, they put duct tape around his eyes and mouth and shot him eight times in the head. His mother had to bury him with white spots on his eyelids. When I was in fifth grade, a friend of mine got put in a closet by his father and then his father killed his mother with a butcher knife."

Staff Sergeant Rowland stares at Recruit Winston, lists him as a Protestant and moves on in his evening colloquy. "We'll pray every night," he tells the platoon. But the Corps also gets its due: After the prayer, he has them jump into bed at precisely 9:00 P.M. shouting, "Honor, courage, commitment!" Then they lie in bed at attention while they review some "knowledge": "Sir," they shout in unison, "the birthday of the Marine Corps is ten November seventeen seventy-five, sir."

They see a harsher side of their fatherly senior drill instructor nine hours later. Because it is Sunday, they are allowed to sleep one extra hour, until 6:00 A.M. But because it is Parris Island, they are rolled out of bed with screams. By 6:01, the recruits have yelled "Yes, sir!" eight times. But Staff Sergeant Rowland isn't at all pleased with the volume of their responses. "You think you doggone back on the block. You. Are. Not. You are in recruit training!"

He chants in the Parris Island way that sometimes verges on poetry, or at least military doggerel, "I don't know why you're moving like snails/ So get your heads out of your tails/ And begin moving at the speed of light."

By 6:15 they have swept the barracks with hand brushes, on their hands and knees. Then, reading from a sign at the end of the barracks, they chant, "D. I. S. C. I. P. L. I. N. E. Discipline, sir. Discipline is the instant willing obedience to all orders, respect for authority, self-reliance, and teamwork, sir. Stop, sir." For good measure, they are ordered to do it again. And again. And again. And again. They will shout it before every meal for the next eleven weeks—and again whenever Staff Sergeant Rowland feels them slacking off a bit.

While they chant about discipline, one recruit turns his head to look at Sergeant Carey. The heavy hat doesn't bite off his head, this being Sunday morning, but issues a clear warning: "The only place you should be looking is up to God, 'cause he's the only one whose gonna save you, besides the senior drill instructor."

The "fat trays" are designated before the platoon marches to breakfast. These are the recruits who are deemed at least fifteen pounds overweight, and so will be allowed to eat only certain foods. There are seven. Over the next several weeks, six will begin to shed the pounds; one of them, Charles Lees, the big smart kid from Boston, eventually will drop seventy-six pounds, all told. The seventh, Charles Maletesta, will be dropped from the platoon for other reasons. He will be followed by several other recruits who begin to crumble under the sustained pressure.

CHAPTER THREE

TRAINING

Staff Sergeant Rowland kicks off the official training cycle on Tuesday, March 7th. This being the Marine Corps, the first formal training day focuses on how to use weapons safely. The second day includes three hours on the history of the Marine Corps. On the third, the platoon drills from 7:00 a.m. to 9:00 a.m., studies Marine Corps history until noon chow, then is lectured on the Uniform Code of Military Justice, then exercises for two hours.

Days quickly begin to blur at Parris Island. Most are endless rounds of drill, chow, drill, run, chow, instruction, drill, exercise, drill, march, chow, drill, and sleep. The soundtrack is a nonstop stream of barked orders and sarcastic comments from drill instructors.

About 14 percent of male recruits wash out of Parris Island, many of them during the first three weeks. For 3086, as for most platoons, this is the most difficult part of basic training. They are cut off from their old lives, but don't yet feel like Marines. Take Recruit Bayless. On March 10th, he emerges from the barracks bathroom totally naked. He shouts and slaps the cinderblock wall. When Sergeant Carey comes out of the DI house to investigate, the nude recruit swings and swats off the DI's "Smokey the Bear" hat. Sergeant Carey tenses, worried about defending himself against the big, muscled recruit—but also remembering that hitting a recruit could end his career as a drill instructor. "Get back," Sergeant Carey evenly instructs the wild-eyed recruit. "Remember who you are." In a few minutes, Recruit Bayless calms—and is sent packing.

"He just lost it," says Staff Sergeant Rowland, shaking his head as he reviews the incident. Sergeant Carey later candidly admits that the attack frightened him. Oddly, one recruit takes encouragement from the incident: Nathan Weber, the quiet, smaller kid from near Philadelphia, had noticed Bayless on the bus to Parris Island. "I saw this big bodybuilder and I thought, 'Oh, no, I'm gonna get crushed down there.' And when I saw him wash out, I thought, 'I'm gonna make it.' " He will.

The next day is notable only for a one-hour class on snake, insect, and animal bites. When the talk turns to the three types of poisonous snakes on Parris Island, some recruits quickly look around the barracks floor.

At 6:15 on the morning of March 13th, Charles Maletesta, the "fat tray" from Westfield, Massachusetts, stands up from his breakfast and slips out of the mess hall. He goes back to the squad bay, where the firewatch tells him to go back to chow. Instead, Maletesta goes for a walk. At 6:20 the base military police retrieve the recruit. He is ejected from Parris Island for "failure to adapt to the Marine Corps way of life."

That afternoon, Sergeant Carey gives punishment exercise to Recruit Moore, the slow-moving Mississippian. After each sit-up, Moore hisses, "Fuck this." When he finishes, he looks at the drill instructor and says, "I want to go home. I want to quit." Sergeant Carey is disgusted but dutifully tells Staff Sergeant Rowland, who again counsels Moore.

Most weeks bring one or two events that stand out from the routine of drill, exercise, and dull classes. The drill instructors look forward to these diversions more than the recruits, who generally aren't aware of what is coming. The big event of the first week after the forming is "combat hitting skills," essentially a series of boxing matches staged inside a three-sided padded wooden ring not much larger than a telephone booth.

Staff Sergeant Rowland, in a blue Third Battalion sweatshirt and fatigue pants, crouches over the edge of the ring, fists clenched as he shouts encouragement. A close combat instructor in a yellow sweatshirt begins each fight: "On my whistle, you explode. First straight punch to the head wins. No roundhouses, no uppercuts, no punch to the top of the head. No hugging."

Robert Warren, who comes to Parris Island from working as a stocker in a grocery store in Murfreesboro, North Carolina, moves into the ring wearing a three-sided padded helmet and a padded external crotch protector. He ducks down his head and gets punched out the open side of the ring. Recruit Moore leans over at the waist in a Japanese bow and fights looking at the ground. "Get your head up, Moore," shouts Staff Sergeant Rowland. The senior drill instructor is more impressed by Daniel Keane, the son of the Merrill Lynch bond trader, who has gone almost completely unnoticed in boot camp until now. Keane jabs three times at his opponent. The first hit knocks the other recruit backward. The second knocks him sideways. The third, to the head, knocks him out of the booth. The drill instructors nod in approval.

Craig Hoover, the community college dropout from the Maryland suburbs of Washington, D.C., disappoints Staff Sergeant Rowland by essentially backing out of the ring. "I'm not a fighter," Hoover shrugs later. "I didn't know what I was doing. I've never been in a fight in my life." He adds, in a phrase characteristic of his approach to life, "I was like, 'I don't want to deal with this.'"

The youngest member of the platoon, Paul Buijs—his name rhymes with "house"—a thin, dark-haired, doe-eyed seventeen-year-old who came here from the Netherlands, does even worse. He looks terrified entering the ring, eyes wide in a paralyzed crouch. His opponent's first punch lands square on his eyes. His head jerks back to the side. After being hit he appears to get mad, in a bug-eyed Harpo Marx-like way, wide-nostrilled and snorting. Two seconds later he is on his rear end in the sawdust.

Buijs contends in private conversation that he is a pacifist. It isn't clear why he left the Netherlands to join the Marines, but there is a hint in his personal history. He was born in New Jersey to a free-spirited Dutch girl who came to America to find the hippie life and instead found a man who left her one month after Paul was born in 1977. She took her baby back to Holland, and Paul grew up happy there. Though essentially Dutch in outlook, he seems somehow driven to prove that he really is an American—perhaps as much an American as his vanished father.

Earnest Winston Jr., the gang member from inner-city Washington, is as American as apple pie and violence. Poker-faced, he looks his opponent straight in the eye, then on the instructor's whistle wades into him. He fights ferociously but methodically. He is accustomed to taking hits. But he keeps pounding even after the instructor blows the whistle near his ear to signal him to stop. In his world, you don't stop fighting until the other guy is down. His violation of an implied order worries Staff Sergeant Rowland. "That's lack of discipline," he says later as he reviews a videotape of the event.

Andrew Lee is next. While his opponent tries to throw round-house punches, Lee follows the instructions and pumps a quick series of straight jabs, hitting the other recruit square on the chin. "Look, he's on fire," says Staff Sergeant Rowland. But when the whistle blows, Recruit Lee instantly stops, wheels, and places his gloved hands on the side of the fighting pit. He has displayed the combination of intensity and discipline that makes a leader in a small military unit.

Platoon 3086 wins the event, and with it the right to carry the flag for its "series" of three platoons. Then Staff Sergeant Rowland calls, "Recruit Lee, front and center," and hands him the flag, designating him as the "guide" for 3086. He will hold that leadership position for the rest of the platoon's time on the island.

That night, Staff Sergeant Rowland sits at his desk in the "DI

house" at the end of the barracks and makes some initial nota-
tions on the big white "Recruit Evaluation Card" kept for each
member of the platoon. First, Andrew Lee. "Highly motivated,"
the senior drill instructor writes. "In great physical condition."

He is worried by Winston. "Shows a lack of discipline," he
notes. "Still eyeballs the area when he should be at the position
of attention"—that is, gazing straight into the distance with an
impenetrable thousand-yard stare.

Sergeant Zwayer, the junior DI, writes the initial evaluation of
Buijs. "Displayed a less than desirable effort toward training. Is
constantly being corrected for all positions during drill and
repeatedly required to sound off."

Sergeant Zwayer has his own problem. He is the odd man out
among the three-man team. Unlike the other two, who come
from the combat arms of the Marines, he has been a mess
sergeant for the Third Battalion, making him a bit suspect. Also,
unlike them, he has a Fred Flintstone body type—big, jowly, and
prone to a five o'clock shadow. And he is fresh out of Drill
Instructor School, making him "Nick the New Hat." When he is
tense, which is often in his first few weeks as a drill instructor, he
walks stiffly and talks with a half-clenched jaw.

He tries harder, but doesn't always succeed. Drilling the platoon during this first week, he calls for a left "oblique" turn—but
calls it as the platoon is on the right foot. In a few weeks, the platoon will know how to adjust to such an out of place order by taking an extra step and then executing. But now the recruits just
grind to a confused and talkative halt. They know that the other
two DIs wouldn't commit a rookie blunder like that. Sergeant
Zwayer stops and glares at the platoon, clearly angrier at himself
than he is with them. "Look, everybody makes mistakes," he
says, tight-jawed, but with disarming candor. "I'm trying to do
my best out here. That's all you can do. Anybody got anything to
say?" Of course, no one does.

Sergeant Zwayer later confesses that during these first few

weeks, he had felt as stressed as the recruits. He was the man in the middle, being measured by both the platoon and the other two drill instructors. The fact that one of the other two was Force Recon Carey hadn't helped. "I knew Carey from being in the battalion, and I wanted to live up to his standards."

Sergeant Zwayer's first major test as a DI will result from the suspicion of the platoon's six black recruits that they are being picked on by 3086's team of drill instructors, which, unusually, is all white. Chris Anderson, the bright, alienated recruit who says he plans to become a criminologist, especially feels this way. "Bone, Winston, Moore, and I had deep talks about being of African descent in America," he later will recollect.

The drill instructors, in turn, grow suspicious of Anderson. Sergeant Carey jots the first disapproving notation on the recruit's evaluation card: "Displayed an individual-type attitude."

The issue builds over several days, beginning with Week Two's first big event, the four-day introduction to "combat water survival"—that is, how to stay afloat in combat gear. It is generally a pleasant but routine series of classes, more symbolic than anything else: If the Marines are the full-immersion Baptists of the U.S. military, this is the literal initiation. It doesn't always go well. In 1991, a recruit drowned in this training. The supervising drill instructor was convicted of involuntary manslaughter, sentenced to a year in prison, and given a bad conduct discharge.

Platoon 3086 sits through hours of classes alongside the island's sixty-meter indoor pool. Then it dons backpacks, helmets, and flak jackets and marches single file through the shallow end, weapons tilted across their chests at port arms, like some hopelessly lost patrol. Next the recruits lay on their backs in the pool, still in combat gear, rifles slung across their fronts, backpacks so tightly wrapped they act as flotation devices, and "bicycle" forty meters across the pool. Then, still in combat gear, they jump from a diving tower and swim fifteen meters.

On the second day of combat swimming, Chris Anderson is

climbing from the pool when, slowed by a boot that perhaps laced too loosely had filled with water, he bangs his knee on the edge of the pool. The knee will begin to hurt him the next day, touching off a long-running dispute between him and his drill instructors: Is he really hurt, or is he using a little bit of pain to slack off? He is put on light duty for several days.

He is back for the platoon's first five-mile conditioning march carrying combat packs, full canteens, and M-16 rifles, but he lags throughout. Sergeant Zwayer keeps saying, "Catch up, Anderson." The DI is displeased by the pouty "Aye, sir," that he gets each time in response.

The next morning, Anderson tests Sergeant Zwayer. The DI begins the day, as he generally does, by "quarterdecking" a recruit—that is, calling him up to the end of the barracks near the DI house and ordering him to do about fifteen minutes of intense push-ups, jumping jacks, and sit-ups. Today his target is Anderson. Uninvited, three other black recruits come up to do the exercise with Anderson.

"What's going on?" asks Sergeant Zwayer, who is on duty alone.

Recruit Anderson speaks for the group. "We got to stick together, 'cause there's not many dark greens here," he says, using Marine terminology for blacks—which, ironically, emphasizes the commonality of being Marines over the color of their skins.

Zwayer sends the other three recruits back down the barracks and then speaks privately to Anderson, who accuses him of racism. "You're wrong, Anderson," he says calmly. "And you're on the quarterdeck because you're wrong—not because of the color of your skin. But if you think that's why—if you think I am acting in a racist manner—then you need to, *you must,* take that to the Senior Drill Instructor." Anderson backs off.

Sergeant Zwayer concludes that the incident helps the platoon. "It was good that it happened. It stopped it early." Nonetheless, Recruit Anderson will harbor his suspicions throughout boot camp, and take them into the Corps. The drill instructors know this. "When he got in trouble, it couldn't be because he was wrong, or slow, it had to be because he was black," Sergeant Zwayer will later say. Anderson will continue to complain about his knee, but medics at the infirmary say it is just mild tendinitis. Partly because he is determined not to be considered a quitter, he doesn't demand X rays, or refuse to run until the knee has been more closely examined.

"Displays an immature and childish attitude since being diagnosed with a medical problem," Sergeant Carey writes on Anderson's evaluation card. "Has tried to play on the feeling of the drill instructor by crying after sick call. When it comes down to it Rct. Anderson is nothing but a whining boy."

The other big training event of Week Two is the first round of pugil stick fighting. The day begins as the others do, with the ritual quarterdecking of one recruit who does fifteen minutes of intense exercise. Then the platoon heads outside for close order drill in the predawn darkness. A quarter moon still reflects in bright silver spots on the slick tidal mudflats ringing the island. After a silent breakfast, the platoon marches to an exercise field. This morning is the first warm day of spring, which for the first time brings out Parris Island's notorious sand fleas. The fleas are small enough to escape notice until they bite, and then they feel like horseflies. In a whiff of Parris Island's manifestly unfair system, where the group suffers for the faults of its individuals—just as a unit sometimes does in combat—Sergeant Zwayer tells Johnny Thomas, the gold-toothed kid, that the next time he scratches a flea bite without permission, Recruit Thomas's squad leader, Mark Beggs, will be doing punishment exercises on the quarterdeck. "And you'll be watching him," the drill instructor adds.

As the platoon marches, it is swarmed by the three DIs. "Pivot on your left foot," reminds Sergeant Carey. Platoon 3086's first close order drill inspection looms in just a few days, and in the eyes of these drill professionals, much work remains to be done.

"Lean back, little end, you're just as proud as the front," says Sgt. Rowland, whose small size makes him sympathetic with the shorter recruits bringing up the rear of the size-ordered platoon. The DIs take the platoon for a one-mile warm-up run.

Once at the pits, four recruits climb into pugil gear: large external padded jockstraps, flak jackets, padded horse collars, and football helmets with a lineman's web of a mask. The pugil sticks themselves are really double-headed clubs about four feet long, with heavy green pads at either end, like great malevolent Q-Tips. Sergeant Carey exhorts them. "Kill or be killed, understand? If you come out a loser, you might as well consider yourself dead, understand?"

Today's preliminary round of pugil stick fighting is staged on a wooden fifty-foot-long boardwalk elevated about two feet above a pit of sawdust. Here simple two-man contests are staged to loosen up the recruits as the DIs stand nearby and instruct them, like handlers just outside a boxing ring. Members of 3086 are sent up the ramp to the boardwalk to confront head-on recruits from 3084, a companion platoon. Years from now, those recruits will be bosom buddies, Marine comrades who went through boot camp at the same time. But now the adversaries from 3084 are "the other"—masked strangers who might as well be aliens from another planet for all the comradeship 3086 feels with them. The goal is to land two "killing" blows—hits to the head, thrusts to the chest—before the opponent does the same to you.

Jonathan Prish, the former skinhead, slashes an opponent to the ground, then thrusts his pugil stick into the other recruit's chest for a solid "kill." "Awesome, Prish," says Sergeant Rowland.

"Good violence," seconds a visiting DI.

Daniel Armstrong, the gangly road worker from Stuart, Florida, gets tangled up with the pugil stick and never even hits his antagonist. "He kind of weenied on me," grimaces Sergeant Rowland.

Each match lasts about thirty seconds. The results split evenly between the two platoons, which means that each unit has about twenty-five recruits wondering what hit them. The experience is stunning, and it primes them for instruction in hand-to-hand combat. Sergeant Carey "drives the bus" to "Leatherneck Square," a sawdust-covered training area under a huge camouflage netting. He sits them in the sawdust in his typical manner: "I said align your rifles, not your bodies," he shouts. "Failure to follow simple instructions is going to get somebody killed in the Fleet! Understand?"

"Yes, sir." He makes them say it five times more.

Sgt. Joel Collins, the close combat instructor, stands arms akimbo in front of the assembled platoons sitting in the sawdust. "Here are six techniques you can use to kill a man in three to five seconds, with your bare hands," he bellows. "Pretty awesome, huh?" The first is a response to being strangled. The instructor demonstrates how to break the bone in the adversary's forearm, kick him in the face, drive a heel into his Achilles tendon, and then, when he falls to the ground, finish him off with a boot heel to the skull.

The other five methods are variations on that theme: Essentially, ignore what your attacker is doing and instead inflict massive pain on him by breaking one of his bones, jabbing one of his eyeballs, or yanking one of his testicles. Then, when he is distracted, flip him to the ground. Then stomp his skull.

Presiding over this introduction to mayhem is Gunnery Sgt. Hans Marrero, a native of Colombia who is now one of the Corps' preeminent philosophers of close combat. He wears his high position lightly. "Once you understand how to snap necks, everything else is just fancy stuff," he shrugs.

But that sort of knowledge is only half the game, he continues. "Before I teach my instructors anything, I teach them the honor code—which is to do the right thing always," he says with a whisper of a Spanish accent. "A warrior has to be ruthless in combat, but have empathy. My master taught me that fifty percent of a warrior is the skills of how to take a man's life. The other fifty percent is the philosophies engraved on your heart and soul so that you compromise for no one."

Off to one side, away from the recruits, Gunny Marrero offers a demonstration to a visitor. He has an assistant try to strangle him—"C'mon, choke. CHOKE!"—and defeats the attempt by jabbing one finger into his attacker's chest, sending him reeling backward in genuine pain. He doesn't show this move to the recruits. Nor does he display his reported ability to pull two golf balls through the fabric of zipped blue jeans.

On March 16th, near the end of Week Two, after the platoon returns to its barracks from noon chow, Recruit Poynor is accused of taking crackers from the mess hall. He begins to cry, then drops to his knees and bangs his forehead with his rifle five times. That afternoon he is seen by the Navy doctors. He, too, is labeled "FTA"—that is, a "failure to adapt."

"A classic case, one I hadn't seen before—he just broke," concludes the senior drill instructor. "One of the most ignorant displays of self-destruction I've ever seen."

Jonathan Enos, a recruit "picked up" from the Physical Conditioning Platoon, brought to Parris Island a burning desire to be a Marine. He has been on the island nearly four months, longer than most recruits who become Marines. But he once again suffers leg stress fractures and is put on a bus back to Baltimore.

Several other recruits appear near washing out. Scott Glica, a troubled pizza parlor worker from outside Buffalo, New York, looks like he might not make it one day in Week Two when he flatly refuses an order to get on line. "You can't make me," he responds. Staff Sergeant Rowland takes him aside and counsels him. He appears to shape up.

Daniel Sabella Jr., a former towtruck driver from Bethlehem, Pennsylvania, tells Staff Sergeant Rowland that he wants to quit.

Then he gets a letter from his girlfriend: "If you don't come home a Marine, don't come home." He will make it—but his troubles will begin, not suprisingly, when he is back in her arms.

Then there is Prish, who has brought with him evidence of his white supremacist past in Mobile in the form of seven tattoos, including "White Pride" and one made of three crossed sevens which together resemble a swastika. He came to Parris Island from a troubled relationship with his father, a former Marine who was wounded in Vietnam and who went on to become an executive with the International Paper Company. Prish also left behind a marijuana bust at age sixteen, and memories of nights spent with "skaters, skins, punks, and junkies," indulging in escapades like "mailbox baseball"—driving out to the countryside and swinging a baseball bat at rural mailboxes. To add to his woes, Prish's attention span is "minimal," Sergeant Carey notes on his evaluation card. James Andersen, the Pittsburgh Taco Bell man, is astonished by the fact that after much effort, including studying sessions in the latrine after lights out, Prish still can't memorize and recite "general orders" and "reporting at post," the things that all recruits must learn, such as, "Sir, this recruit's first general order is to take charge of this post and all government property in view, sir."

Sergeant Zwayer decides to make a project of Prish. "Prish was Zwayer's pick," Staff Sergeant Rowland would say months later, reviewing the progress of 3086. "He was gonna make or break him. And he made it."

All told, the platoon drops some members, picks up eighteen "recycles," quickly loses some of them, and so churns through Week Two with a total of sixty-three members. Most of them are making it. They do everything a bit quicker, a touch more seriously. But even the best recruits appear to be operating frequently in a state of catatonic disbelief. The nonstop seventeen-hour days are an exhausting contrast to the sleepy pace that most knew in American high schools. Recruit John Hall, a truck dispatcher from

Bayonne, New Jersey, will later remember that "the first few weeks were like detox for me," coming from a life where "I'd been smoking a pack a day and drinking like a fish."

On the morning of March 17th, as Week Two draws to a close, Andrew Lee waits until the quarterdecking is finished, and then pipes up, "Sir, Recruit Lee requests permission to speak to the platoon, sir."

"What is it, Lee?" asks Sergeant Zwayer.

Lee grins. "Happy Saint Patrick's Day, platoon."

"Shut your freaking mouth, Lee," says Zwayer—turning away to grin himself.

Week Three is the culmination of the first phase of boot camp. It literally brings the first set of hurdles: a run through Parris Island's "confidence course," a set of wooden obstacles and rope-climbing challenges ending with a slide off a thirty-foot-high tower down a rope slanting down over a pool of swamp water. The platoon zips though it, shinnying upside-down along the forty-five-degree angled rope, but a Hispanic recruit from another platoon loses his grip on the rope and drops into the cool black water. He emerges, soaked, loudly singing, as required, "The Marine Corps Hymn" in a heavy accent: "From the hells of Mont-ee-zoooom-uh, to de shaws of Treep-o-leee."

Week Three also will bring the first objective measures of 3086's progress: the first written test, the first physical test since receiving, the first inspection for individual appearance and knowledge, and the first inspection of the platoon's ability to drill in close order.

The recruits are unaware of most of these looming tests, but their DIs are only too conscious of them. Drill practice grows more intense, especially because the platoon isn't doing it particularly well. On the morning of March 20th, Sergeant Carey appears more than usually driven. As he puts the platoon through drill, he sees Recruit Travis Gay swipe at a sand fly biting his chin, causing him to miss a movement in the presentation of his rifle. The heavy hat lunges at him. "You missed it because you care more about the bug on your face. You care more about yourself. You're selfish." Warming to his subject, the sergeant yells in Recruit Gay's face, "You're just going through the freaking motions, aren't you?!" Recruit Gay knows enough to stare passively straight ahead and remain silent. But the sergeant isn't finished. He leans back and bellows at the hot blue sky, as if informing God Himself: "LA-ZY! American youth is LA-ZEEEEEEE!"

Euphemisms such as "freaking" and "frigging" are about as profane as Sergeant Carey ever becomes. Once notoriously foul-mouthed, Parris Island's drill instructors today are forbidden to use obscenities. At the same time, their recruits arrive steeped in casual vulgarity from pop music, cable TV, and everyday conversation. So it is all the more unnerving to face a DI who appears, as Sergeant Carey does now, to be insanely angry—but who rarely swears. (Occasionally, a drill instructor, growing impatient with a recruit who waits a second or two to reply, will yell, "Yes, sir—no, sir—fuck you, sir. Something like that?" Charles Lees, the observant Holy Cross graduate who has become 3086's "scribe," or clerk, keeping track of the platoon's laundry numbers, sick call chits, and other mundane data, observes privately that "that third offer sometimes is really tempting.") The physical abuses of recruits in the 1970s have resulted in strict limits on corporal punishment that DIs can mete out. With the sadism of the past largely weeded out, Parris Island today is far more heavily focused on cultural indoctrination. "You can't physically stress them out, so you get to them mentally," says Staff Sgt. Marvin Frasier, senior drill instructor for Platoon 3085. He thinks sleep deprivation would be a useful tool, if he were only permitted to use it. "You get the esprit de corps inside them and then whatever you tell them, they'll believe."

The hot spring day sees the launch of new squadrons of sand flies. Recruit Gay isn't the only one suffering. By noon the bare forearms of the recruits average five small but angry red sand flea bites per square inch. Those who have scratched are developing patches of skin that look like pizza.

Drill orders and the DI's corrections also buzz in the air: "Pivot. PIVOT! . . . Align to the right, cover, forty inches—don't close it up! . . . Drive your heels. Lean back and drive! . . . Don't rush it!" The one order the DIs never utter is "At ease."

Recruit Marcus Stephenson, a "fat tray" who came here from working for a temp company in Rhode Island, and who already has shed eight pounds and a double chin, recites the proper way to come to a stop while holding a rifle: "Left, right, port. And guide it to the seams—pause—and *ease* the weapon to the deck."

As the drill practice grinds on for another half hour, Recruit Eric Didier, whose parents are computer company executives living in the posh Washington, D.C., suburb of Potomac, Maryland, tries to quietly correct a fellow recruit in the ranks in sliding the bolt of his M-16. To compound his sin of preempting the DI, his own correction is wrong (he fails to curl his fingers into his palm). Sergeant Carey is so disgusted with this nearly invisible flaw that he doesn't even yell, and instead mutters, "If there was any rank lower than recruit, Didier, you'd be it right now."

Staff Sergeant Rowland suspects the platoon of lacking sufficient intensity, so he has them sit in formation. Then he has them stand: "On your feet NOW!" Then sit: "Sit down NOW!" He repeats this seven times, as a kind of warning shot. He keeps them standing at attention. Recruit Parise whispers a correction to the recruit next to him. Staff Sergeant Rowland hears it. "You are wearing my nerves thin, Parise," he shouts. "You were probably some big jock in high school. Well, you ain't crap now."

Staff Sergeant Balenda, the battalion drillmaster, strolls over to observe 3086 as it prepares for its initial close order drill evaluation. The signs aren't good. When stationary, "they're kind of fidgeting around," says Sergeant Balenda, watching them with a professional's eye. "By Week Eleven, you could give them 'Platoon, halt,' and go away for a cup of coffee, and they'd freeze." And when marching, "they're bouncing up and down, like an ocean. They should only be moving from the waist down, just floating forward."

Drill, he says, builds unit cohesion and unit and individual discipline. And for mental as well as physical reasons, he comments, 3086 needs to bear down and drill more. "It's also a look in the face," he says. "Half of them still don't know where they are. They're in culture shock." This isn't a novel view on Parris Island, where it is gospel that today's youths are strangers to values and standards. "It's today's generation," says the twenty-eight-year-old Sergeant Balenda, a ten-year veteran of the Corps originally from Bay City, Michigan. "They're raised by baby-sitters. There's a lot of broken families, and they're doing their own thing, on their own. My last platoon as a senior drill instructor, half the recruits came from broken families.

"The recruits have never had an authority figure," he says, watching Sergeant Carey, 3086's very authoritative heavy hat, put them through their paces. "A lot of them have never been held accountable for anything in their lives. Here, they begin to understand, and begin to rely on each other, which is what the Marine Corps is all about. That's the heart and soul of the Corps, values. I still hold the values my drill instructor instilled in me in 1985. Here they become brothers of the ones who died in the Beirut blast, of all the Marines who went before."

By the time they leave Parris Island, he says, most will be members of the Marine Corps family, holding its values. Unlike the families they left behind, he argues, this big Marine family works. "That's the appeal to the recruits, becoming part of a family of 174,000 Marines, 'cause of the society and all that mess out there, broken families and all."

A few minutes later, Sergeant Carey notices that Recruit Shelton is out of step. The recruit thinks of himself as one of the platoon's leaders, but Sergeant Carey disagrees. "He can't do nothing right," the sergeant loudly complains.

Hearing this, Gunnery Sgt. David Camacho, the top sergeant for this "series," or group of platoons, pulls Recruit Shelton out of the ranks. "What's the matter, recruit?" Shelton stands mute. The gunny leans into him. "You got a hearing problem? Speech impediment? Why can't you do anything right?"

Recruit Shelton responds almost conversationally, as if the gunnery sergeant actually were seeking his views on the subject. "Sir, you asked me . . ." he begins.

Sergeant Camacho, a lanky, hawk-nosed Hispanic from Austin, Texas, cannot believe what he is hearing. He ostentatiously staggers backward. " 'You'? 'Me'? Three weeks you been on this island, and you say 'me'?"

Recruit Shelton isn't the only one getting the one-on-one treatment. Staff Sergeant Rowland notices a five o'clock shadow on the face of Fernando Mendez Jr., who used to be a shipping clerk in a chemical warehouse in central New Jersey. The senior DI scrapes his thumbnail across the recruit's upper lip and cheek. "Shave more often," he orders. "I don't want you looking like trash."

When Earnest Winston Jr. misses a movement in the drill and looks at Staff Sergeant Rowland without being ordered to do so, the senior drill instructor sarcastically says, "Oh, we're big buddies, right, Winston?" The recruit shifts his cold stare to the edge of the distant woods. He wants to be in the Corps, but he isn't sure he wants to be like this sarcastic little cracker he could take in a fair fight.

Sergeant Rowland's reprimands are certainly personal, but far more docile than the boot camp of old. In his autobiographical novel *Battle Cry*, for example, Leon Uris recounts a encounter similar to Sergeant Rowland's with Recruit Mendez. When two recruits fail to shave, the drill instructor orders them to stand before the platoon and use rusty razors to shave each other without lather or water.

It is an article of faith among DIs, and among many Marine veterans as well, that boot camp today isn't nearly as tough as it should be. They blame politically sensitive officers for permitting too much of soft American society to creep into training. In a typical letter to the *Marine Corps Gazette,* published in January 1993, Gunnery Sgt. Daniel E. Paulak complains that "a much softer, less stressful environment is now commonplace. The pendulum has swung too far away from the instant obedience and discipline that were the norm from the start."

There is no question that boot camp is less abusive than it frequently was in the past. In his memoir of his World War II service with the Marines, William Manchester, who enjoyed his time on Parris Island, reports that "it was quite common to see a DI bloody a man's nose, and some boots were gravely injured." In a disturbing memoir of his Vietnam-era training, R. Wayne Eisenhart, a veterans' counselor, recalled that,

> While in basic training we were issued M-14 rifles. The breech of the weapon is closed by a bolt which is continually pushed forward by a large spring with considerable force. One night three men who had been censured for ineffectiveness in their assigned tasks were called forward in front of the assembled platoon, ordered to insert their penises into the breeches of their weapons, close the bolt, and run the length of the squad bay singing "The Marine Corps Hymn." This violent ritual ended as the drill instructor left and the three men sank to the floor, penises still clamped into their weapons. We helped them remove the rifles and guided them to their beds. There was considerable bleeding as the men cupped their wounded penises with their hands, curled into balls, and cried.

The question is whether anything good comes of such abuse. The minority in this debate among Marine veterans maintains that sadism isn't training, and that boot camp needn't be harsh to turn out good Marines. Today, this side says, Parris Island does an arguably better job than it did when DIs ran wild. These days, for example, recruits learn not just to swim, but how to survive in water while wearing combat gear. The majority simply shakes its head: If you don't break them down, stir their souls, and maybe clobber the recalcitrant, you can't build them back up.

Where both sides agree is that the bottom 10 percent of those who graduate from boot camp probably shouldn't. Most of the members of 3086, which never experiences anything remotely like the sadism of the old days, also will come to believe this. The 14 percent attrition rate for males on Parris Island is almost double the Army's boot camp dropout rate of 7.2 percent. (Indeed, there is quiet talk in the Army that its newer soldiers are being incompletely indoctrinated in its easier-going basic training, and some enviously look on the Marines' higher dropout rate as something to be emulated.) But if Sergeant Carey had his way, the rate would be about 25 percent. The better recruits agree with that view. "I expected it to be tougher," says Edward Linsky, a twenty-three-year-old former carpetlayer from southern New Jersey who manages to shout "Yes, sir!" louder than anyone else in the platoon, sometimes so fiercely that the DIs occasionally do doubletakes, suspecting he might be mocking them. He isn't. "I feel like I'm growing up," he says one night during Week Three as he sits on his footlocker in a brown military T-shirt and jockey shorts and shines his boots. He is one of the handful of recruits in 3086 who will never cry during his time on the island.

Even Recruit Armstrong, who more than once has leaned on other recruits for help, complains that the thing that irks him most about boot camp is "the other recruits who can't carry their own weight."

Sergeant Carey finishes the last drill of the morning and marches them to the mess hall, delivering an impromptu lecture on the way. The theme is less elevated than Sergeant Balenda's, but the point is essentially the same. "We all must sacrifice to be number one. Ain't nothing going to mean nothing to you unless you work for it. That girl who gave it up first time you asked, was it what you expected? But the girl who made you chase three months, that was worth it." The recruits, in the midst of their own agonizing three-month chase, grin at the analogy. The DIs may not seem like humans, but at least they seem to be familiar with sex.

The platoon's wait in line for lunch offers Sergeant Carey time to reprise one of his favorite lectures. "Listen up," he admonishes. "We got hot dogs and cheeseburgers. That's trash. That ain't warrior food. I want you to load up on salad, understand? We ain't eating no cookies, understand?"

As he listens, Recruit James Pitts, a former construction worker from the part of the Florida panhandle sometimes called the Redneck Riviera, issues a fart that sounds like a paper bag popping. This is Week Three, and the DIs are growing less tolerant of such crudeness. Sergeant Carey, leaning forward like a pointer hound, shakes a finger in the recruit's face. "No manners, no morals, no integrity. I blame your stinkin' parents, cause you got no respect." The recruit is invited to hold a rifle out in front of him while doing deep knee bends.

If boot camp today seems an anachronistic island of formality in a world of gangsta rap, crotch-grabbing comedians, and foul-mouthed preadolescents, it is society, not boot camp, that has changed, argues 1st Sgt. Charles Tucker, the senior sergeant for Kilo Company, to which 3086 belongs. The Marines, he says, have simply preserved civilities abandoned by the rest of society. Its insistence that recruits be courteous to superiors and civilians "is nothing more than good manners, being polite and respecting your elders. But most kids in American society don't respect their elders."

As the graying sergeant speaks, a recruit walks behind him. "By your leave, sir," he says, adding "Good morning, gentlemen." Sergeant Tucker nods his campaign hat in approval.

Of all the U.S. military services, the Marines cultivate the most formal culture. They pass it on at Parris Island. Recruits must say, "Good day, sir," each time they pass a superior. This formality extends to the drill instructors, who observe it whenever they are under the eyes of the recruits. Sergeant Carey, for example, always addresses Staff Sergeant Rowland by either title or rank and name: "Senior drill instructor" or "Staff Sergeant Rowland." Sergeant Camacho is addressed as "Series Gunnery Sergeant." When Staff Sergeant Rowland is asked the first name of Sergeant Carey, with whom he has worked side-by-side for weeks, he actually doesn't know.

Lunch on March 20th is followed by another two hours of close order drill, then an hour of exercise, and a three-mile run of alternating sprints and jogs. Even the post-run cooling off is regimented: They are ordered to walk in a giant circle, with each recruit sipping from his canteen. Recruit Moore, who wept on the parade ground during the forming and then cursed as he did punishment exercise, is dragging again today. "He does the minimum," worries Staff Sergeant Rowland. The senior DI also is bothered by a picture Recruit Moore has drawn in his little white "knowledge" booklet of a drill instructor being shot through the head. The recruit also has written an odd note to himself stating that the DIs are racists. In private, Recruit Moore confides that "if I could go back to civilian life now, boy, I wouldn't hesitate. This place is no place to be if you are a mama's boy, which I am." Nevertheless, he adds, with some ambivalence, "It's a good change. I really don't miss my old attitude that caused me to quit school and get into fights."

At 5:00 P.M. the platoon has been drilling, exercising, and running almost nonstop for twelve hours. Sergeant Rowland isn't sympathetic. "You ain't done nothin' yet," he shouts at the perplexed circle of recruits. "You ain't experienced HURT yet. Little cheesy three-mile run."

"Ain't no one ever died of sweat," Sergeant Carey reassures them. "The more you sweat in peace, the less you bleed in war."

"You won't die from running, you'll pass out first," chimes in Staff Sergeant Rowland. They appear to be enjoying themselves as they recite these boot camp clichés—and catch their own breath.

Sergeant Carey marches them back to the barracks, has them strip, and runs them into the showers and back out. Then he dresses them as a unit. "Now, when I give the command, I want you to get on your trousers and boots." He pauses one beat. "Ready—NOW!"

Evening chow is followed by still more drill. Sergeant Carey wants to hear fifty-nine rifle bolts simultaneously slide, see fifty-nine rifles come to "port" together. But Recruit Armstrong's rifle sling is twisted. "Why?" Sergeant Carey asks the red-faced, flea-bitten, former road worker from Florida. By now the entire platoon knows there is only one permissible answer to that question: "No excuse, sir." Recruit Armstrong, though addled by the sun and hours of drill, croaks out exactly that.

At 6:48 P.M. they march back home to the Third Deck of Building 420. But because of some unexplained minor flaw in their marching, Sergeant Carey pulls them back downstairs, and makes them march back up, then back out again. From a sand flea's point of view, it is a perfect evening: warm and windless, with the humidity settling in on the island like an unwelcome heavy coat. The fleas climb into nostrils, ear canals, and even the corners of recruit's eyes.

Finally satisfying the heavy hat, the recruits are allowed to march back up and remain in their barracks. There they relax by cleaning their rifles. Recruit Anderson, the short, smart black recruit from Maryland, once again helps the gangling Recruit Armstrong, who seems flummoxed by the steps of disassembling his rifle.

"We take better care of our weapon than we take care of WHAT?!" Sergeant Carey yells across the barracks.

It is a familiar refrain. "Ourselves, sir," respond fifty-nine recruits.

At 7:45 the platoon assembles cross-legged on the floor of the open squad bay at the end of the barracks for mail call. "Honor, courage, commitment! Kill, kill! Marine Corps, sir!" they shout.

Letters are flipped to the recruits, but all packages must be opened for inspection in front of Staff Sergeant Rowland. Didier's mother is mailing her son aspirin, wrapped inside the *Washington Post* Sunday comics. Staff Sergeant Rowland seizes this contraband.

Tonight's mail also brings a letter for Randy Barrows, one of 3086's quiet men in the middle. This close-mouthed group—which also includes Daniel Keane, Jason Picciuto, and Nathaniel Behrendt—meets Staff Sergeant Rowland's ideal of boot camp anonymity. They do what they are supposed to do without attracting notice. "Progressing at an average rate," Staff Sergeant Rowland first writes on Behrendt's recruit evaluation card. A month later, Sergeant Zwayer adds, "Completing tasks at an average rate." When Behrendt graduates, the senior will write, "An average recruit."

Only one thing distinguishes Recruit Barrows, who was a farmhand in central Alabama before enlisting. He has a brother who is a Marine lance corporal at Camp Lejeune, and who believes that boot camp should be harsher than it is. So this brother faithfully sends letters—sometimes simply empty envelopes—with insults to the drill instructors scrawled on the outside. Each one is guaranteed to set Barrows up for extra doses of physical training. Tonight's letter says, "Tell me about that cute DI of yours." A later one will say, "Make sure you send those saved rounds"—that is, mail me your bullets issued but not fired, which would be a major sin at boot camp. Most provocative of all is one that invokes the Army motto: "Be all that you can be." Each time, the drill instructor handing out the mail says, "Barrows—get up there and pay me," and Barrows obediently begins doing push-ups.

Talking about the importance of obeying orders, Sergeant Rowland suddenly says, "Pick your nose." Simultaneously, fifty-nine index fingers shoot into nostrils. Then the platoon sweeps the barracks with hand brushes. At 8:48 they stand at attention next to their footlockers and perform the final "count off" of the day. One fatigued recruit stumbles on his number, unable in his exhaustion to remember what comes after twenty-three. Recruit Thomas laughs, flashing his gold tooth like a lighthouse. Just as he does, Captain Chessani, Kilo Company's commander, strides into the barracks. After he leaves, Sergeant Carey furiously turns on the recruit. "Thomas, you are an awesome spectacle—laughing right in front on my company commander. You are crazy."

At 8:55 they again perform the "discipline" chant: "Sir, discipline is. . . ." At 9:00 P.M. the lights are switched off. The recruits lie in bed at attention for the "Protestant prayer" ("Lord God, help us to become United States Marines. . . .") and a nearly identical "Catholic prayer" ("Lord God, help us to work better together, as a team, to learn discipline. . . ."). Eventually, Christopher Cooke, the platoon's Catholic lay reader, will come to end his prayer every night with the phrase, "Platoon 3086: No place I'd rather be."

Some nights after lights out, Gregory Tenhet, a twenty-year-old who worked at a coolant company in the Deep South before enlisting, passes around the extraordinarily explicit letters sent to him by his girlfriend back in Jackson. In them, she details how she would like to jump on him, and what her tongue would do to his sensitive parts and for how long, just the way he likes it. The recruits read the steamy missives eagerly by flashlight under their blankets.

Recruit Gay, the former New Hampshire welder who was chewed out by Sergeant Carey this morning for swatting at a sand flea while drilling, dreams at attention and loudly sounds off in his sleep: "Yes, sir . . . no, sir . . . aye, sir." Recruit Nathan Manczka, an earnest nineteen-year-old who used to work as a clerk at a Toys 'R Us store in Edinboro, Pennsylvania, performs a drill in his sleep, holding his pillow above him and at an angle for rifle inspection. Down at the end of the barracks, Andrew Lee, who is tense even when unconscious, worries in his sleep about keeping the platoon on track, mumbling, "C'mon recruits, get on line."

Prish is on firewatch for one hour tonight. Essentially, the job is barracks security duty, watching for recruits out to steal, commit suicide, or run away. He uses the time to study his "knowledge." When Jumal Flow, an older recruit who came here from working in a nursing home in Cooperstown, New York, awakes to go to the head, Prish stops him. "Ask me the first general order," he says. Flow does.

With the platoon asleep, Staff Sergeant Rowland goes home to his wife and two daughters, who live in a small ranch house on the base just a few blocks away, across from the field where 3086 took its initial strength tests. The only drawback to the location, says his wife, Nancy, is being awakened at five o'clock every Saturday morning by a fresh batch of recruits shouting as they are tested. The dining nook of their comfortable house is chockablock with Marine Corps memorabilia. The living room is dominated by a big screen Hitachi television and a personal computer. Few books are evident. "We're simple people, with simple tastes," Rowland says neither apologetically nor proudly, but as a simple statement of fact.

Among Marine wives, Parris Island has the reputation of being a rough tour of duty, with husbands serving terribly long hours. "If your marriage is rocky coming down here, you are in big trouble," says Maj. Stephen Davis, director of Parris Island's Drill Instructors School. "There was a lot of infidelity going on a couple of years ago. We had two battalion commanders relieved. And homosexuality—I don't want to get into it, but it's naive to think that it doesn't occur."

But for Nancy Rowland, Parris Island has been a relief. Her husband is happy, and he comes home two nights out of three. (The third is his turn to sleep in the DI house near the recruits.) But having a DI for a father has been harder on his two daughters, now ages eleven and seventeen. At one point during Rowland's first cycle as DI, his senior drill instructor sat him down and ordered him to go home, talk softly, and play with his kids. Confirming the senior's suspicions, one night his teenage daughter, Brandy, brought him up short: "Dad, I'm not one of your recruits. Don't talk to me like that."

Two years later, the family seems to have found a balance. "Most of the things he does in the military, we have no idea what he's doing," says Brandy, a pretty girl with searching eyes and a way with words. "Here, we can see pretty much just about anything he does. I've looked out the window and seen him running with his little troops." But she says that having a father who is a DI still sometimes scares boyfriends.

Nancy Rowland will show up toting a video camera to record most of the platoon's major events—close combat hitting, pugil stick fighting, final drill inspection, graduation. "It's the only time in his career that I've had a chance to get involved, and I really like that," she says.

There is no typical DI. But, aside from his advanced age—he is about ten years older than most DIs—Staff Sergeant Rowland is about as close as they come, in physical size (DIs tend to be surprisingly small, perhaps because the incessant running of boot camp erodes the knees and ankles of heavier men), in background (rural Southern, with a major in adolescent hellraising) and in outlook on life (the Corps *is* life).

After some hesitation, Staff Sergeant Rowland finally agrees to discuss his personal history. "We fit in the 'poor' category," he begins. "We moved from Tulsa to a small little town, Marvel, Arkansas, when I was about three. Then moved to Memphis— Lamar Terrace, rough neighborhood. My father was always a laborer, no career orientation. My mother was a nurse's aide. Lived in Memphis 'bout till I was thirteen or fourteen. Kind of had a little run-in with the law. I had this thing for motorcycles, couldn't afford one, so got one the best way I knew how. So my family decided to move to Searcy, Arkansas, partly to save me."

In 1977, the eighteen-year-old Rowland had one of the ugliest jobs in one of the hardest lines of work available: working the clean-up shift at a meat processing factory, getting up at seven at night, spending nine hours shoveling guts and hosing blood, and coming home in the morning with nothing to say. "Life was going nowheres, just a dead end." So he went down to the recruiting office to ask about the Navy. But the Navy's man wasn't in, and the Marine sergeant was, and that made all the difference.

Rowland thrived in the Corps, graduating near the top of his communications class at Twenty-nine Palms, California. His new wife, burdened with a newborn and away from home from the first time, didn't: "She said, 'It's me or the Corps.' " So in 1980, having made sergeant in just three years, he reluctantly left the Corps and moved back to Arkansas.

Working in a factory making stainless steel sinks, he says, he felt like part of him was missing. "I'd think, 'Damn, if I'd stayed in I'd probably be on the drill field right now.' " So in 1986 he gave Nancy an ultimatum: She could come with him if she wanted, but he was going back to the Corps. He reenlisted as a corporal, and was sent first to Okinawa, then to Camp Lejeune. During the Gulf War he served in Saudi Arabia and Kuwait with the 6th Marines.

Today, says Nancy Rowland, "I done gave up on him getting out of the Marine Corps. I don't talk about it anymore." She would still like to be back working at the pharmacy in Arkansas.

The other major type of DI, the bookend to Rowland's rural Southerner, is the tough city kid, usually black or Hispanic, but still sometimes a Northeastern steel mill ethnic white. This group tends to be as talkative as Rowland is taciturn.

Take Staff Sergeant Phillip Johnson, the starched senior drill instructor of Platoon 3080. He grew up in the streets of Belize City, in the tiny Central American country of Belize. He illustrates the wilder side of some drill instructors—something that may be lost as the Marines raise recruiting standards and insist on high school diplomas as a requirement for enlisting. He also illustrates the deep commitment of the good drill instructor.

At age thirty-four, Staff Sergeant Johnson has spent exactly half his life in the Marines. Much of the prior half was spent hustling, first in Belize and then in Los Angeles. Third-World deployments have been no shock to him, but rather a journey back to the tin-roofed shacks, cooking fires, and banana trees of his youth. His journey into the Corps began with a hurricane in Central America. "Me and my buddy left right after that. I was sixteen. We came up through Mexico. We had no money. We had a couple of loaves of bread and jars of peanut butter and jelly—that'll take you a long way.

"In Mexico City, we were out of money, so we went to the Belize Embassy, and an assistant counselor gave us some money to get closer. Then my uncle wired us enough money to take a Greyhound into Los Angeles.

"I enrolled in the Manual Arts High School, one of the worst schools in LA. Kids had their feet up on the desks. So I went out on the street and hustled, just like I did in Belize. There was a lot of weed, a lot of gambling.

"One day my mother saw me counting my money, and she figured I wasn't going to school, so she stopped buying food for me. Then one day me and a buddy was making a food run for the gamblers at McDonald's. We saw a guy in the Marine 'deltas'—tan shirt, blue pants with a red stripe. I thought he looked cool. I said, 'Who's that?' My buddy said, 'He's a Marine.' I said, 'What do they do, feed the dolphins at Sea World?' 'No,' he said, 'they're like soldiers, but they're not. They jump out of helicopters, do attacks from the sea.'

"I was sick of what I was doing, coming to LA and doing the same things I did in Belize. The recruiter showed me about boot camp—running, jumping, and sliding. I said, 'I've been doing that my whole life.'

"So I took the test, and I failed. I couldn't do fractions, long division. So every evening, I'd go over to the recruiting station and he'd teach me division and fractions. So after three weeks I passed. I just wanted to get away. I didn't know I was going to get paid. I thought I'd get a place to sleep, something to eat, and a uniform.

"When I got there, my first thought was that the Marine Corps must have hired criminals, or people out of the insane asylum, and dressed them up as drill instructors. They were screaming, frothing at the mouth. Other kids in boot camp probably thought I was retarded. I'd only lived in America six months. People would talk about Vietnam, and I didn't know what they meant. When I was in Belize, there was no TV, and just one radio station. I never got no letters the whole time. My drill instructors would ask me, Do I know anybody who knows how to write?"

Today, he says, "I look at the Marine Corps as a home. The Marine Corps did something for me that church and schools didn't. I was a filthy kid, bad temper, very very violent. The Marine Corps taught me values—not just words. Honor, courage, commitment. Fidelity. Integrity. Not just using them, but actually practicing them. Out in the civilian world, those words don't even get mentioned. I'll say, 'Integrity,' and they'll say, 'What kind of shit you talking? You done got brainwashed in the Marine Corps.' Guys I came up with in the streets of Belize, guys I love, and will love till I die, we can't sit down and hold a fricking conversation. We speak two different languages now."

Being a drill instructor, he says, "isn't a job, it's a way of life." He cites the case of a friend of his who, while working as a DI, suffered a hernia. "He didn't tell anyone," Staff Sergeant Johnson says approvingly. "He worked until the day the platoon graduated, still didn't tell anyone, and then checked into the hospital and got it cut."

Staff Sergeant Johnson is especially good at working with recruits from the inner city. "You get the gangbangers and the drive-bys, I can look at them and say, 'I've been there. And you're not so bad as you think. And if you think you're *baaaad,* make it through boot camp.' I can identify with him, teach him my way."

The first thing that a Parris Island drill instructor—a "PI DI," as some of the decorative red and gold license plates on their Jeeps and pickup trucks read—is likely to tell a visitor is that drill instructors are drawn from the top 10 percent of sergeants in the Marine Corps. Most believe this fervently. The quiet little secret of the Corps is that it isn't true. The DIs are good—but they generally aren't the cream of the NCOs. The very best are shipped off to recruiting duty, where they troll for new Marines and operate in the civilian world as ambassadors of the Corps, unsupervised for long stretches of time. The DI is generally from the second tier—somewhere in the top 20 or 30 percent of his cohorts. To make a twenty-year career in the Corps, an enlisted Marine generally must either do recruiting duty or a tour as a DI. The difference is that the DI is far more closely watched. Indeed, the main function of officers on Parris Island is to be watchdogs, ensuring that DIs rigidly adhere to the all-important *Standard Operating Procedures* manual, and resented for it. "Once I learned to fold my arms and nod, I made a great series commander," remembers one lieutenant on Parris Island.

Unlike military music, military architecture has never been good enough even to be mockable. Perhaps the ugliest building on Parris Island is the Drill Instructors School, a froglike one-story building that squats near the office of the commanding general. Inside it are a charmless group of offices wrapped around a large windowless lecture hall. This is where Marines learn how to be drill instructors. Essentially, they go through boot camp again, but now are held to impeccable standards so they can be walking models of Marinehood. Like boot camp, DI school lasts eleven weeks. Its students arrive with an average of nine years in the Corps. Almost all have been rated as above average. Yet one in five drops out—an attrition rate higher than boot camp itself.

One theme dominates the teaching at the school: The drill instructor holds in his hands the future of the Corps. Sgt. Maj. Philip Holding tells a seminar on leadership, "Don't ask a recruit to do something you wouldn't do. Think of them like your sons and daughters. Change the way they think about life. Do your best or get out of the Marine Corps. And don't hurt my bunnies, or I'll stomp you." The sixty-seven young sergeants in the class look at one another: Did the sergeant major call the recruits "bunnies"? Yes, he did. The gravelly sergeant major continues: "We want a warrior who thinks, like those down in Somalia that held babies one day and had to kill the next day, and knew the difference between the two."

The oddity of DI school is that it is very threatening, far more so than boot camp is to the actual recruits. Its official motto is "The future of the Marine Corps begins here." But it should be "Don't mess with my Marine Corps—and God help you if you do." Across the corridor from the lecture hall, the student lounge is decorated with framed newspaper clippings about the Ribbon Creek incident in which six recruits died. "If you do something stupid, or I do something stupid, it could give the Corps a black eye," another visiting griot, Sgt. Maj. Ronald Fetherson, tells the leadership class. "This is the Corps, which I love. It is all we have." The message is repeated in a dozen different ways: If a choice has to be made between saving a DI's career and protecting the Corps, the DI will be thrown overboard in a heartbeat. Every allegation made by a recruit is investigated. (The recruit, in turn, will be labeled by the DIs as an "allegator.") That is the price of being entrusted with the job of transmitting the culture of the Corps. One of Sgt. Carey's closer friends on Parris Island, another drill instructor named James Humphrey, will be reminded of that message a few months later.

Just a few days before this class of sixty-seven students is set to graduate and become junior drill instructors, retired Master Sgt. Vic Ditchkoff delivers a lecture that really is a very pointed piece of performance art. But first the gray-haired sergeant, now a deputy in the Beaufort Country sheriff's office, establishes his standing. He tells them how he served five tours as a DI, for an astonishing total of fifteen years and eight months on the island. Then he tells them that was the easy part. Before he came to Parris Island, he was a "tunnel rat" in Vietnam. "Weighed one hundred forty-seven pounds. Used to go down with a forty-five in one hand, a grenade in the other, pin pulled out, so if the other guy got me—and my head was going down first—then my body would be blocking the tunnel and the grenade would roll downhill and take him with me."

He strides back and forth across the stage in his light brown uniform, pistol holstered on his hip, and tells them the true tale of a crackerjack drill instructor. This DI graduated fourteenth in a class of fifty-five out of ninety who began the class. He reads the glowing fitness reports from DI's battalion and company commanders, chief drill instructor, drillmaster. All found him to be smart, conscientious, and possessing initiative. "He was very squared away. He was a Marine's Marine," concludes Ditchkoff.

He faces his audience. "Pretty good DI, huh?" Then he throws it in their faces: this was Staff Sgt. Matthew McKeon, the DI responsible for the darkest mark in Parris Island's history. "Staff Sergeant McKeon had everything going for him—just like you."

Without warning, he reenacts the Ribbon Creek incident in an almost trancelike way, quoting dialogue from the subsequent court of inquiry. McKeon and a fellow DI "had not one, not two, not three, but four shots of vodka. Then they go to the Staff NCO Club and have a few more drinks. He decides he wants to play games.

"He marches his platoon into the swamp. It seemed like it was going to be a normal night swim, and the high tide was coming in, and he was smart enough to know it. But there was a 'trout hole' twelve feet deep in the creek. And his tallest recruit was six foot, three inches."

Ditchkoff acts out the death march. "Keep to the right, recruits!" he shouts at full blast.

He pauses and resumes his narrative. "Six recruits drowned

that particular night, eight April nineteen fifty-six. And the whole image of the Marine Corps changed that day. We almost lost our own training in nineteen fifty-six. His court martial was conducted on this spot."

Ditchkoff's verdict: "He marked his destiny with a deceitful and disloyal act. He took the DI pledge—and he failed the DI pledge. It was a willful, wanton intent to deceive, deceiving not only the commandant of the Corps, not only the families of the six recruits, but his God, his Corps, his country, and himself, when he marched his platoon into the swamp."

In the wake of the Ribbon Creek disaster, the Marines fired the commanding general of Parris Island and more than a hundred drill instructors. They also instituted a set of boot camp reforms, most notably introducing a new level of supervision, the series commander and gunnery sergeant, putting an officer and a senior NCO over each group of three platoons. Army basic training doesn't have that level of supervisors. But the Army, experiencing its own version of Ribbon Creek with its sexual abuse scandal that began with charges in November 1996 that trainers at its base at Aberdeen, Maryland, raped and sodomized female soldiers, is likely to be forced to institute similar reforms.

Drill instructors are acutely conscious that the NCOs are the backbone of the Corps. And the keepers of the NCO culture are the drill instructors. Parris Island is where the culture is passed on, where recruits are given a new set of aspirations in life. On the other side of the island, Staff Sergeant Johnson stands in the shade of a live oak tree and watches 3086 drill. He sees before him the future of the Corps. "Someday, a few of them may become sergeants, and one or two drill instructors, and they'll pass on the things they learned from their drill instructors."

The end of Week Three brings the actual tests.

Physical testing, held on a dewy field near the Third Battalion on the morning of March 22nd, is predictable. Gary Moore Jr.

looks unhappy. At the other end of the platoon, Andrew Lee, in his usual Terminator mode, burns through ninety-nine sit-ups in two minutes and then does thirty pull-ups. "Every time we did PT, I wanted to be Lee," Jumal Flow will later say. "He went through the obstacle course with a smile. He was just hard."

Sergeant Carey runs three miles in eighteen minutes, forty seconds, ahead of all but three members of the platoon. Standing at the finish line to exhort those who follow, Sergeant Carey congratulates a recruit who stumbles across the line, staggers to the grass, drops to his knees and vomits. "That's the effort we're looking for," he says. "But don't eat so much breakfast." He stands in the middle of the ring of recruits walking to cool off and instructs with his personal mantra. "You got to test yourself everyday. If you don't test yourself, that day is wasted." By the time they graduate, they will be able to recite those sentences word for word, no matter if they are so bushed they can't remember how to count off. They also will grow accustomed to another of his admonitions, one they hear as he gives them extra PT on the quarterdeck, as if bestowing a present rather than punishment: "Pain is just weakness leaving the body."

The minimum performance in today's physical test is three pull-ups, forty sit-ups, and three miles in twenty-eight minutes. The platoon averages ten pull-ups, sixty-six sit-ups, and a run time of 23.30. That totals to an average PT score of 188, out of a possible 300. "That's pretty good," says Staff Sergeant Rowland, nodding at Sergeant Carey as if to remind him that not everyone is Force Recon. But there are two failures. One is a recent pickup named Stephen Torchia, who did only two pull-ups and also failed the run by half a minute. The drill instructors distrust his attitude and have been waiting for an opportunity to move him on. And Shawn Bone, a cautious black college student from Birmingham, Alabama, came in dead last in the run, at 28.39. A "WNOD"—that is, "Written Notice of Deficiency"—is placed in his file, but he isn't dropped.

Sergeant Carey marches the platoon back to the barracks for a shower. "Nice and easy," he yells in cadence with the march. The platoon shouts back: "Nice and slow!"

But after he takes them to the mess hall for noon chow, the heavy hat paces uneasily. The inspection of uniforms, rifles, and appearance looms, and he is more troubled by the prospect than are his unwary recruits. He knows something they don't: they will be inspected by Sergeant Humphrey, a DI from 3085 who became Sergeant Carey's friend at drill instructors school. The two men are intensely competitive with each other. "It's a good thing they didn't put the two of us with the same platoon, 'cause we'd burn it out," says Sergeant Carey. "Me and Humphrey, we're action guys." That is a euphemism for being a hard-charging, in-your-face, Type Triple-A Marine NCO. This is not good news for Platoon 3086.

Conscious of their impending doom, Sergeant Carey works after chow to clean up his recruits. "I want you to get those stinkin' gas masks out of the footlocker NOW. Ten, nine, eight, seven, . . ." After a weak "Aye, sir," he cracks the verbal whip: "I don't like that little monotone belligerent attitude," he says. "I'll take you to the freaking pits." Those are the giant sand boxes just outside the barracks windows in which recruits suspected of recalcitrance are made to run—a taxing effort in the deep, squishy sand—and then do push-ups, offering their faces and forearms to the eager jaws of the thousands of sand fleas that thrive in the boxes.

Charging up and down the line through the barracks, Sergeant Carey pulls a hanging thread—what the Marines call an "Irish pennant"—from the starched camouflage uniform of Tony Wells, a twenty-five-year-old recruit who came here from a Du Pont chemical factory near Rocky Mount, North Carolina. "You accept substandard performance," shouts the agitated DI. "That's why America will fall one day, just like the Roman Empire. But not me, understand? BUT NOT ME!"

At 2:19, Doom himself appears at the end of the barracks: Sergeant Humphrey, a black fireplug of a man from Columbia,

South Carolina, with arms so muscled they appear difficult to bend. He conducts the inspection with the heated language of an evangelist running a revival. But he dismisses the failures with the cold heart of a soldier machine-gunning a charging enemy. He begins with Recruit Shelton, who appears almost cocky. "You're lazy," he hisses in a voice that sounds like it carries a poisonous sting. "Did you clean that rifle? Oh, I'm *sure* you did. Did you shine those boots with a brick?"

Recruit Shelton doesn't know what hit him. Short Sergeant Humphrey cocks his head and gazes up the tall recruit's nostrils. "Your hygiene is unsatisfactory. Did you shave? No discipline. NO DISCIPLINE!" For all that, Recruit Shelton passes a tacit part of this test: He doesn't lose his bearing.

Sergeant Humphrey has the next recruit in line recite the Marine equivalent of The Lord's Prayer: "This is my rifle. There are many like it but this one is mine. My rifle is my best friend. It is my life. I must master it as I master my life. My rifle without me is useless. Without my rifle I am useless. I must fire my rifle true. I must shoot him before he shoots me." Sergeant Humphrey nods and moves on.

Anthony Randolph, a nineteen-year-old former construction worker from Cookeville, Tennessee, doesn't know the name of the battalion sergeant major. Sergeant Humphrey rasps: "The most important people in your life is your chain of command." He cuts the guts out of Recruit Randolph: "Rifle manual—below average. Rifle—below average. You don't know anything about this weapon, which you sleep with every night. Poise—average. Hygiene—unsatisfactory. Knowledge—average. Overall—below average."

So it goes with the rest of the platoon. Recruit Moore, who believes his white DIs are racists, finds he fares no better with this black DI. "Below average," he is labeled by Sergeant Humphrey.

Landon Meyer, a thin, pimply former short order cook from Long Beach, California, also loses his way on the chain of command question. "Sir, this recruit was confused," he says.

"How old are you?" asks Sergeant Humphrey.

"Nineteen, sir."

"You've been confused for nineteen years," says the sergeant, utterly dismissing the recruit's life before Parris Island. Part of the message is that whatever you were or did before your life in the Marines is absolutely, entirely, irrevocably irrelevant. What matters is what you do here, in a ruthless meritocracy. Invariably, you aren't doing enough.

Johnny Thomas smiles at Sergeant Humphrey's judgment of Recruit Meyer—and once more is betrayed by his gold tooth. The sergeant swings over to him. "You have gone *insane* here," shouts Sergeant Humphrey. "The only thing funny is you thinking there's something funny here!" Recruit Thomas is unable to name most of his chain of command. "You will meet standards, or you will fail," hisses Sergeant Humphrey. Recruit Thomas fails.

Even forewarned, Sergeant Carey is a bit stunned by the demolition job his friend performs on the platoon. Back in the DI house, he complains that Sergeant Humphrey just shredded them, ripping them down when the first inspection should be used to lift them up. The platoon looks as dazed as it did during the first hours of the forming, as if it had been hit by a truck.

The results of the physical testing are recorded. Torchia gets the big boot. Sergeant Carey sarcastically dismisses him from the barracks: "'Bye, have a nice life." Then he takes aside Bone, who is being sent for retesting on the run: "Stay hard. Stay motivated." Bone goes out, trims his time, and returns to the platoon.

The next morning brings hours of drill practice, followed by 3086's first close order drill inspection. It goes only slightly better than Sergeant Humphrey's demolition job.

Even more than in the regular Marine Corps, power on Parris Island resides with the senior NCO's—staff sergeants, gunnery sergeants, first sergeants, and, above all, sergeants major, before whom even captains and majors are deferential. A powerful lineup arrives to cast a cold eye on 3086: 1st Sergeant Tucker, Kilo Company's senior sergeant; Gunnery Sergeant Camacho, the sergeant for 3086's group of platoons; Staff Sergeant Pabon, who had been acting in that capacity until Camacho returned from a temporary duty off Parris Island; and Staff Sergeant Balenda, the battalion drillmaster. They watch as Sergeant Zwayer, 3086's junior drill instructor, wheels the platoon through an intricate series of moves: presentation of arms, about face, forty-five degree turns as a unit. The platoon moves with surprising intensity for the entire fifteen minutes. But the senior sergeants grading them grimace at a myriad of flaws invisible to the civilian eye. Watching from the sidelines, an agonized Sergeant Carey vows under his breath to take the platoon to the pit for punishing push-ups among the sand fleas.

But the inspectors blame the lack of crispness not on the recruits but on Sergeant Zwayer's handling of them. Gunnery Sergeant Camacho, disappointment hanging across his hound-dog face, takes Staff Sergeant Rowland aside. That was a near-disaster, he tells the senior drill instructor. He knows the fault lies not in the platoon, he says, because he has seen Sergeant Rowland lead them before. "*You* can drive this bus." Sergeant Zwayer didn't. The gunny isn't going to give the junior DI quite as low a grade as merited, but only, he says, because "I don't want to ruin the rest of his tour on the island."

That night, the word comes down to Sergeant Zwayer that he must "improve his command presence." "It's not something you want to hear, but you have to accept it," he says. Privately, he believes he has been undercut by Sergeant Carey's competitiveness. "Sergeant Carey had wanted to drill them to perfection, so I hadn't gotten a lot of hands-on time," he says. "It was minimal."

For all that, at its core the Marine Corps is about fighting, not marching. The biggest test of Week Three isn't even listed as a test. It is the third round of pugil sticks, which will take the entire afternoon of March 23rd. Much more than in the past, the Parris Island training schedule today emphasizes pugil fighting. The reason, the Marines say, is that the video game generation is arriving at boot camp overflowing with passivity. "A lot of these kids have never done any fighting except in Nintendo," says Gunny Marrero, the chief instructor in close combat training. Alarmed by that trend, Parris Island's administrators made pugil fighting more elaborate, adding to "the Bridge" two more rounds, "the Octagon" and "the Pit," which isn't to be confused with the sandbox "pits" where the recruits perform punishment exercises.

All three DIs are present for this third round of pugil fighting, partly because it is an enjoyable high point in the training cycle, but mainly because the pugil events are seen as a test of the fighting spirit of each recruit. This event will go a long way toward determining the pecking order in the platoon—who will lead squads and who will be labeled a sad sack.

They march to "the Octagon," a padded wooden enclosure in the piney woods on the edge of the swamp, not far from Ribbon Creek. "Elbows tight," yells Staff Sergeant Rowland. They respond, "Rifles right!" They stop near the two wooden chutes that lead into the corral-like center of the Octagon. Pugil sticks simulate bayonet fighting in general. Today's session will teach the recruits to kill blindly and without hesitation. Running through the chutes is meant to evoke the experience of clearing an enemy-infested trench in World War I. The 3086 recruits are sent charging down each chute, only to meet in the arena a member of 3084 coming down the other chute. Their duels are short and violent, rarely lasting more than two or three seconds. Though bloodless, they suggest how horrible trench warfare must have been.

Shane Logan, the upstate New Yorker who wants to be a social worker, pounds his opponent into the sawdust. "That's what I'm talking about, death and destruction," says Staff Sergeant Rowland.

Joshua Parise, the graphic artist from Pittsburgh who misses his mother, is crushed sideways against the olive drab wall and falls to his knees.

Recruit Shelton confidently charges through the arena and up the other chute, where he pounds with his padded stick on a pugil instructor's back three times before being whistled to a stop. He finally has realized the urge he conceived during the "Forming" to slam a DI. But hitting a sergeant here isn't considered a screwup, because he is being so aggressive, and because the attack was judged to be an accident. "Awesome!" applauds Staff Sergeant Rowland.

Blind aggression doesn't always work. Legs churning, Recruit Anderson, the perpetually scowling kid who trusts no one and suspects his drill instructors are racists, sprints at full speed into the other recruit—who simply holds out his pugil stick and lets Anderson impale himself.

Johnny Thomas charges in and takes a swing. The other recruit gets turned around—but blindly swings back over his shoulder and lands a solid blow, "killing" Recruit Thomas. Recruit Randolph, the Tennessean who didn't know his chain of command in the previous day's inspection, bats his oncoming opponent backward into the chute where he came from. Staff Sergeant Rowland smiles. In sharp contrast to his clumsy first pugil outing, Recruit Armstrong, the slow-moving, storklike Floridian, confidently beats his opponent around the head, whacking him on one side and then another as he works the stick like a kayak paddle. He leaves the Octagon with an improved standing in the platoon. Altogether, 3086 scores thirty-one victories, versus twenty-six and twenty-four for its companion—and today, competing—platoons.

Finally, the platoon moves to "the Pit," a adjacent arena that is far larger—about thirty feet long by twenty feet wide. Here the recruits are sent in for multiperson matches, which result in brawls so intense that three instructors stand in the pit and, because shouting can't cut them off, end the matches by grabbing the combatants from behind and wrestling them to the ground. As with the Octagon, each match begins with the recruits charging blindly through the woods and around a curve. But here the running recruit meets not one but two or more recruits coming at him from the other direction just as fast—and just as intent on "killing" them.

Recruit Shelton, still pumped, employs a powerful uppercut home-run swing to the kid's stomach that lifts his opponent's feet off the ground. "Nice kill," says an admiring instructor.

But it is Mark Beggs, a small, quiet recruit who came here from working on a farm and at a Wal-Mart near Pittsburgh, who becomes the pupil star. In the final round, five recruits are sent into the Pit for a free-for-all. Weighing just 140 pounds and looking like a younger version of his two bantamweight DIs, Rowland and Carey, he jumps from spot to spot, popping his stick, jumping, hitting, and moving—until all four adversaries are sprawled in the dust. When he finishes, his eyes are bulging and his mouth is wide open in an inarticulate roar. His booted feet continue to jump around. Sergeant Humphrey, the demon of yesterday's inspection, watches with deep approval. "That little one has the barbarian in him," he rasps.

But not all the DIs present are pleased. Staff Sergeant Frasier, the lean, intense senior drill instructor for Platoon 3085, believes his unit has been slighted in the scoring. He begins to argue vehemently with the pugil instructors. Gunnery Sergeant Camacho, his boss, quickly steps in—and finds Frasier so angry that he is willing to argue with him as well. Camacho barks: "Staff sergeant, don't lose your bearing." This remark is cutting, even insulting, for it is what drill instructors continually tell wavering recruits. Later that day, Camacho will order Staff Sergeant Frasier to apologize to his platoon for nearly losing his head.

The platoon assembles on the edge of the marsh for a casual awards ceremony. Staff Sergeant Johnson, the DI from Belize and LA, surveys the platoons. "They come here and they're empty," or are emptied by the first few days and weeks, he says.

"They want to be Marines. They start walking like you and talking like you." A few moments later, as the platoon douses itself with bug juice to fend off the fleas, Chris Anderson grows impatient waiting for his turn. Unconsciously adopting the language of his drill instructors, he says, "Any day, Ruiz," to Jeffrey Ruiz, a former JC Penney clerk from Wilmington, Delaware.

Larry Maner, an Army warrant officer from North Carolina who is chaperoning a group of Junior ROTC kids from high school, comes away from the pupil event awed. "This is superior training," he says.

"We had good violence and intensity in there today," Gunny Camacho says, bestowing the honorary pugil stick on 3086. Recruit Beggs is given the honor of carrying it back to the barracks, where it will hang near the door of the "DI house." For the rest of 3086's time on the island, Beggs will be seen as a top recruit. Staff Sergeant Rowland writes that night on his evaluation card, "Displays a mature disciplined attitude, extremely motivated."

The senior drill instructor is less impressed with the perpetually lagging Paul Adriaan Buijs, the youngest member of the platoon. "Appears to be a timid, shy type who never had a lot of demands placed on him," he writes.

Despite his youth, Buijs remains his own man. Other members of the platoon feel continually harassed by the dictates of the DIs; Recruit Buijs takes his own sweet time. "Being out of the civilian world, I don't have to worry about job security," he confides. "Now that I'm in the military, I am mainly the one who decides how my life runs—whether I work hard or not." Of course, that's not the view of his drill instructors. But Recruit Buijs has his own opinions. "This recruit used to be part of the alternative lifestyle," he says. Among other things, he maintains even now, in the midst of Marine boot camp, that he is still a pacifist.

One afternoon, Andrew Lee is running up the recruits' stairwell at the back of Building 420 when he is stopped by a drill instructor from a companion platoon, a man he admires. The sergeant tells Lee to hand over to him 3086's guidon—something he has no right to ask for. Recognizing that he is being tested, Lee hesitates for a moment: Can he refuse an order? Yes, he decides. "No, sir," he says, quickly explaining, " 'Cause you don't give up the colors." The sergeant tenses: "Give me the fucking guidon." Then he shoves Lee in the chest, grabs the guidon pole, stands back, and hurls it at the startled recruit. The point of the pole jabs into Lee's leg, drawing blood.

No one else sees the incident, and Lee won't report it. "I never said anything about it," Lee later recalls with pride. "Some of the chumps would have gone to an officer, 'I was assaulted.' I think he felt a little bad about it, 'cause he talked to Sergeant Carey about it." Lee bears no grudge. "I thought it was great. I thought he was a pistol before, and I thought he was a pistol after." Even as he relates the story of the incident, he asks that the offending sergeant's name not be used, for fear of hurting the man's career.

The results of Week Three's other major test, the written examination of knowledge, arrive. There is one surprise: Recruit Shelton, who had thought of himself as one of the leaders of the platoon, fails. A few days later he will be "recycled" back to a following platoon, leaving 3086. Almost alone in the barracks, he packs his seabag slowly, as if he is being kicked out of his family and shipped to an orphanage. He leaves notes of encouragement under the pillows of a few buddies.

Week Three has performed its function, sorting out the platoon and letting it members know where they stand. They have shed their old civilian selves. They aren't yet Marines, but they are moving in that direction. "I'd say they're thirty percent, forty percent there," Staff Sergeant Rowland says, sitting at his desk in the DI house. "The concept is there, and they see it and breathe it every day, but it's not embedded in them."

* * *

The end of each week brings one hour of relief: church. Under such sustained pressure, the recruits find new meaning in Sunday services. "Never missed it," Lee later says. "It was salvation. You lived meal to meal, rack time to rack time, and church to church. Salvation. We sung 'The Marines Hymn' and 'The Battle Hymn of the Republic' in Mass. That was the balls."

It also is one of the few places where 3086, generally in the dark about upcoming events, can get the word from more seasoned recruits. "You could lean over and say, 'What's the gas chamber gonna be like?' " one recruit later recalls.

"Good morning," the chaplain says, beginning the Protestant service one Sunday morning. Today's chaplain is Navy Lt. Aaron Jefferson Jr. The Marines have no chaplains of their own, but ones assigned to them from the Navy may wear the Marine uniform, as does Lieutenant Jefferson.

"Good morning, sir," respond the packed pews of recruits, who even here in the recruit chapel give off two distinct odors: a veneer of soap and, underneath it, a reek of sweat held in their fatigues through repeated washings. The drill instructors who have been bustling around the rear of the chapel retreat as the service begins. Some stand watchfully near the back wall's stained glass windows depicting the flag-raising at Iwo Jima, and featuring two strafing aircraft and a Marine flamethrower, his weapon's flames billowing out in a red, orange, and yellow mass illuminated beautifully from behind by the morning sun.

"Hey man, give God praise," shouts Lieutenant Jefferson, then sings,

> *Soon and very soon*
> *We are going to see the King*

He points to the recruits, members of the platoon about to graduate, sitting in the chapel's place of honor. These men are distinctly dressed not in recruits' green fatigues but, like him, in Marine olive drab wool—"service bravo with the service sweater."

No more crying then
We are going to see the King

The graduating recruits shout back: "Four days!"

Lieutenant Jefferson calls up a recruit to the altar microphone to give testimony. The recruit reads the parable of "The Footprints in the Sand," the point of which is that when in your hour of need you only see one set of footprints, they aren't yours, they are the footprints of God carrying you.

"This means a lot to me because about three weeks ago, this recruit was almost dropped for failing a drug test," says the testifying recruit. "I didn't know what to do. For the first time in my life, I was completely lost. I started talking to the Lord. Then, the next thing you know, my drill instructor comes up to me and said, 'I just want to let you know I'm going to bust your heart until you graduate.' It was the most exciting day of my life.

"So I just want to let you know," he continues, his voice beginning to choke as he begins to weep. *"I'm . . . going . . . to be . . . a Marine."* The response comes back: an intense "Amen."

A sextet of four blacks and two whites from the platoon about to graduate comes up to sing in an uneven dirge:

I know I've been changed
I know I've been changed
I know I've been changed
The angels in heaven have signed my name

Then the lead singer steps out: *"When I'm alone I can call on you."* The other five sing back: *"I know I've changed."*

"Back when I was in BWT, Lord!" the lead sings, referring to

117

basic warrior training—the eighth week of training, more generally called "Warrior Week" by the recruits, who eagerly look forward to it.

The backups respond: *"I know I've changed."*

A recruit reads Proverbs 6:23, which in the plain English translation used here reads: "For these commands are a lamp, this teaching is a light, and the corrections of discipline are the way to life." It could be Parris Island's motto.

Another recruit leads a prayer, his words rolling over the bowed and shaven heads of the congregation. "Father, when we gave up, you stood by us. Father, when we were all down and we were out, you stood by us and told us to keep going." In this service, God has become the most Senior Drill Instructor of all. "Father, there has been times when we couldn't take another step, and you gave us a push."

A black recruit with a powerful baritone is called up to sing "Amazing Grace." For these wretches, it is deeply moving: They once were lost, but now are found. In most church services, a handful of those attending might be in crisis. Here, nearly every single person present is in the midst of a life-changing moment; many of them feel more isolated than at any other point in their lives.

Lieutenant Jefferson invites prayer requests.

"Sir, this recruit's uncle is in the hospital, getting heart surgery."

"Sir, this platoon is going to BWT." And so on, nine more times.

The lieutenant wraps it up with an open prayer. "These struggling recruits in BWT and on the A Line,"—the advanced round of firing on the rifle range—"we pray that you help them. We pray that you touch broken bodies and heal them. We ask in Jesus' name, and for Him we pray. Amen."

The recruits say back: "Amen."

Strolling back and forth across the stage, he sermonizes on answering the call from Jesus. "Now, when your bunkmate tells you to come, you might be there in three minutes. But when your DI tells you to come, you're there immediately." The point is clear: You've got to run when you're summoned by the Big DI in the Sky. "There ought to be footsteps, there ought to be a commotion, when God says, 'Come.' The time is NOW to walk with God, not to wait until it's all hunky-dory and peaches and cream." As he reaches this emotional peak, recruits break out in ripples of applause.

He concludes: "You've got to march to the drumbeats and commands of our Father in heaven."

The service has lasted precisely one hour. The recruits face the American flag and turn to page five of the *Recruit Songbook* to sing "The Marine Corps Hymn." The graduating platoon stands at attention correctly. The drill instructors descend to fix the backward-facing palms of some newer recruits.

Lieutenant Jefferson surveys the chapel. "Dismissed," he says.

The drill instructors reclaim their wards: "Let's go." After noon chow, two hours of close order drill await them on this Sunday afternoon.

For Weeks Four and Five, the platoon moves out to the rifle range barracks for basic rifle training. The gospel according to Parris Island is that shooting accurately is a matter of discipline: Even the clumsiest recruit can do it well if he follows the prescribed steps, from sighting and aiming, to proper positioning, to trigger control and sight adjustment. "Any person in the world can be a marksman if he applies himself," preaches Capt. Patrick Stefanek, operations officer for the weapons battalion. Staff Sergeant Rowland worries that instead, the recruits of Platoon 3086 are getting lax and lack the discipline of mind they will need on the range.

Parris Island is a world of its own, but the rifle range area is doubly isolated, a world apart from the rest of the boot camp. Located behind some woods in the southwestern corner of the island, the range has its own barracks, mess hall, chapel, officers, and atmosphere. Far away from the prying eyes of the brass at headquarters, and the parents who come to the island every Thursday to see their graduating Marines, the range feels a bit rougher, more like the boot camp of old. Platoon 3086's march out to the range with packs and rifles makes the range feel even more distant: Though the range is only a mile from its barracks, their route winds for five long miles around the island before looping over to the weapons area.

For 3086, the primary emphasis of boot camp has been on drilling. Now their attention will be shifted to shooting. "You can drill and have a perfect thirty-inch step," comments Warrant Officer Anthony Carbonari, a range supervisor, moving his left boot forward exactly thirty inches. "But I've never seen the enemy killed with a thirty-inch step. It's the rifle that does it. This is where it's at. If a recruit can't shoot, he can't be a Marine."

Moving into their temporary barracks at the rifle range, Recruit Benjamin Read deposits a seabag near the senior drill instructor's feet. Staff Sergeant Rowland asks, "Where did you get this?"

"Carey's Jeep, sir," replies Read, who tried one semester of studying forestry at North Carolina State before enlisting. Getting wind of Read's lèse-majesté, the heavy later says to Read, "So, we're drinking buddies now, you call me 'Carey'?" Then he has Read patrol the barracks "duckwalking" in a moving squat. Johnny Thomas laughs at this, so he is ordered to fall in behind Read, on his knees also. The two squatters move behind Carey like baby ducklings as he surveys their temporary home.

Week Four, "Grass Week," tests the limits of the platoon's mental discipline. It can be stupefyingly boring, with hours of almost theological discussions on how to hold and fire a rifle. The recruits spend their days in an old white shed open on two sides, sitting on six rows of backless wooden benches while an instructor stands at a blackboard. It is a scene out of a backwoods nineteenth-century one-room schoolhouse. At 6:00 A.M., they begin with 110 minutes on "Weapons Handling," a safety brief that boils down to four commonsense rules: treat every weapon as if it were loaded, keep your finger off the trigger until ready to fire, keep the weapon on safety until you intend to fire, and never point a weapon at anything unless you intend to shoot it. Then come classes on "Introduction to Marine Marksmanship," followed by "Fundamentals of Marksmanship," then lunch, then "Introduction to Positions," then "Shooting Positions." There are three common elements to any shooting position, the marksmanship instructor insists, over and over again: relaxing the muscles, using the bones of the body (rather than the muscles) to support as much of the weight of the rifle as possible, and firing at the "natural point of aim," the point on which the rifle sights settle when the first two conditions are realized. When more than a few recruits' heads begin to nod and jerk back up from their chests, the drill instructors take the platoon to the pit for a little wake-up call. At 3:30 they go out for a two-mile jog wearing boots and carrying rifles.

The next day follows the same pattern: First a talk on different shooting positions, because the recruits will have to qualify by shooting while sitting, standing, and prone. Then a talk on "Zeroing Procedures"—essentially, how to adjust a rifle to the individual recruit's arm length and hand strength. Then lunch, and eighty minutes on how wind and other weather conditions affect riflery, especially accuracy. Finally, they actually get to shoot—just five rounds into a target a mere thirty-six yards away, simply to see if they can group their shots. This tests whether they have absorbed the fundamentals of "BRASS-F," for "Breathe, Relax, Aim, Stop, Squeeze—and Follow Through." At three o'clock, a three-mile run, followed by exercises.

Most of Wednesday morning is dedicated to learning how to use the *Entry Level Data Book/Rifle 5.56 mm, M16A2*. From now on, each recruit will log every round he fires—not only where it hits, but also how he was sitting, how his rifle was adjusted, and where the wind was blowing and how hard. The spring afternoon drones on with a mix of more time in the pits and more lectures about shooting positions. A Marine C-130 propeller plane circling overhead as part of an exercise is more interesting.

Taking the platoon to the pit for some refreshment push-ups, Sergeant Carey half-jokingly challenges Andrew Lee. "You hard, Lee?" The tough Bostonian, who knows he is hard, but that Carey is harder, replies, "Yes, sir, harder than chewed gum." It is a phrase that will stick with Lee for the remainder of his time on the island.

In midweek, word arrives that Recruit Thomas has failed academic testing, and then failed the retest. He must leave boot camp. The new ways fall away from him with surprising swiftness: A day or two later Staff Sergeant Rowland sees Thomas playing cards in "Casual," the dismal holding pen for those being shipped home, the 14 percent the Marines throw back to society. The rejects are categorized in a variety of ways: "FTA," for "failure to adapt to the Marine Corps way of life," or "LRE," for "lack of reasonable effort," or "CoG," for "convenience of government," which covers problems like continual bedwetting. But all the acronyms boil down to the same message: You can't be a Marine. Staff Sergeant Rowland says hello to Thomas, who casually returns the greeting from the table at which he is playing cards. "He didn't even get up when he spoke to me," the senior drill instructor reports with a mixture of dismay and surprise. Recruits are flown to Parris Island, but the washouts are bussed home, unworthy of any additional expenditure by the Corps.

Thursday, the day 3086 "zeroes in" its weapons, begins like most others, with Sergeant Zwayer calling Prish onto the quarterdeck for extra push-ups, sit-ups, and jumping jacks. "Every morning, he'd drop the ball," the drill instructor would later say. "One morning he'd have his belt in, but not buckled. The next day he'd have his belt buckled—but his boots had been polished and weren't laced."

During an exercise session that day, Prish repeatedly requests permission to make a head call. "Shut up, Prish," Sergeant Zwayer repeatedly responds. Finally, Prish gets tired of asking. "Just screw it," he thinks to himself—and he urinates in his pants.

Seeing the dark splotch on the recruit's pants, an arriving drill instructor says, "Why didn't you ask?"

"This recruit didn't want to waste his breath," says Prish.

"Some people felt I was picking on him," Sergeant Zwayer later explains. "But what I was trying to do was expose him to what was going to happen to him in the Fleet, because he was a little bit slower, the last to get the first-phase knowledge. His mentality would cause him to catch a hard time, and they'd use the tattoos on top of that. He was always going to get stuck cleaning the commode unless he got better."

On Friday morning, Prish reports as usual to the end of the barracks. But as he begins his jumping jacks, his pants fall to his knees. He hadn't yet buckled his belt. Zwayer has him do his extra exercise—and then has him stand on the quarterdeck sucking his thumb. Prish later will say that this taught him a lesson. "I thought I was a badass when I first got there. I found out on the quarterdeck and in the pit that I wasn't."

Zwayer uses the rest of Friday, essentially a day of riflery review, to pull Prish out of the instruction shed for hours in the pits. In midafternoon, a groggy, flea-bitten Prish looks up from his push-ups, and stares at Sergeant Zwayer from the sand. Holding his push-up position, he says evenly, "You can't break me. You can't make me quit." It is exactly what the drill instructor wants to hear.

But the recruit with the toughest life nowadays is Trujillio, a pick-up from the 2nd Battalion. He will be watched closely by the drill instructors. His first move in his new platoon also sends a worrisome signal: The loud New Yorker shows up and almost immediately begins running down 3086 as "nasty." Recruit Winston, who takes pride in 3086, decides that has to stop. At evening chow, as Trujillio is running to open the rear "hatch" of the rifle range mess hall, Recruit Winston's clenched fist swings into the point of his chin, dropping him cold. "It was the most well-timed punch I've ever seen," Andrew Lee later marvels. "Hit the ground like a piece of wet meat."

As Trujillio lies on the floor and regains consciousness, Winston leans over, extends a hand, and says, "Wha' happen, you trip?"

Winston later explains, "He badmouthed us. He also said, 'Don't mess with me, 'cause I'll mess you up.' " Where Winston comes from, you pay attention to such threats—and you get the other guy before he gets you or you risk ending up dead, like Anton, Taurus, Darlwin, Fish, Rick, and Tarzan.

Of course, that's not the way Winston tells it to the drill instructors. According to a subsequent "Recruit Incident Report," "Rct. Winston told Sergeant Zwayer that while going into the chow hall, Rct. Winston waved his arm to swat away a sand flea and poked Rct. Trujillio in the eye. Rct. Trujillio then tripped over his own feet and fell to the deck." Lieutenant Richards, the series commander, notes at the end of this report that Trujillio "has shown little or no discipline."

The weekend brings a 7.5 mile march, plus more classes.

After the eternal week on the grass, "Firing Week" is a relief. They move from the teaching sheds to the range, a huge area on the edge of the tidal marsh. Earthen berms hem it in on three sides, leaving only the entrance open. In the distance, just before the marsh begins, the numbers one through fifty are painted on signs about six feet high, marking the targets above them. At the top of the berm are the target holders, 6 x 6 feet on white frames. Some holders bear targets that are twelve-inch black circles, others twenty-six-inch high outlines of a man's head and shoulders. Two huge red pennants flutter from flagpoles at either end of the line of targets, indicating to the world that the range is "hot"—that is, has live firing going on—and telling the recruits how the wind is blowing near the targets.

Aside from the noise of rifle fire, the most notable quality of the range is how closely the recruits are watched. For every two recruits shooting, there is one coach—usually a private first class or a corporal. Each group of twelve coaches in turn is watched over by a sergeant. Supervising all this is a range instructor, an experienced sergeant. And, of course, 3086's three drill instructors hover, making sure that the coaches know which recruits to observe especially closely. Every recruit with a loaded weapon in his hands is tracked at all times by several pairs of eyeballs. "Recruits are an unknown entity," explains Captain Stefanek. "A stable recruit might get a letter from his girlfriend saying, 'You joined the Marines and left me.'" The result of all this monitoring is that accidents occur rarely on the range. Instructors say they aren't aware of anyone ever being shot and killed on the range.

The first four days of the week are a blur of waiting, firing in one position, then waiting and firing in another, then moving to a new distance and repeating the process.

The last day on the range, Friday, April 7th, is Qualification Day, the culmination of their two-week visit to this side of the island. It begins badly. The day is overcast, drizzly. Sergeant Zwayer marches the platoon across the road from the range barracks toward the actual firing line. It begins to rain, and he stops them to have them don their ponchos. Everyone finishes but Joseph Parker, a recruit from Corbin, Kentucky, who was picked up by the platoon just before it came to the range. Parker is tangled in his poncho, which he can't get over the top of his rucksack. "We're waiting on you, Parker," says Sergeant Zwayer, "waiting on you."

Parker glares at the drill instructor. "This recruit requests permission to speak frankly," he says. Sergeant Zwayer nods permission. Parker rips off his poncho, lays his rifle on the grass, flings his rucksack in the air, and then looks at the drill instructor: "Sir, you can take your Marine Corps and shove it up your ass." Sergeant Zwayer orders him to sit down on the grass, tells Lee to watch him, and heads back across the road to fetch Staff

Sergeant Rowland. This is senior drill instructor business. Parker is soon riding a bus home.

The rest of the platoon goes out to shoot to qualify. First it shoots sitting, kneeling, and standing at 200 yards; then sitting and prone at 300 yards. Finally, it shoots prone at 500 yards. This last group of ten rounds at about a quarter of a mile makes the Marines unique among the world's military services: No one else makes basic recruits fire at such a distance. As 3086 fires, the range sounds like a huge snare drum.

After each round of shooting, the big targets are marked by recruits working down behind the berms. Shots into the black of the target are marked with white spindles, which at this distance appear as distinct dots. Shots outside, in the background white, are marked with black.

Thirty eighty-six does well: Everyone but Recruit Campas qualifies on the first try. The success rate is evidence that 3086 is relatively happy, as platoons go. An old boot camp trick is for a platoon to dump its "shitbirds" at the range by secretly adjusting the sights on a disliked recruit's rifle, so he won't qualify. Though 3086's one initial failure, Campas, can be a whiner at times, he is generally liked. Sergeant Zwayer takes him aside at midday Friday. "Campas, we really want you back in the platoon," he says. "Do what you have to do." Campas qualifies on the next try and is back in good standing in the platoon within twenty-four hours. Overall, the platoon scores an average of 214, in the middle of the "sharpshooter" category, and takes the honors in Kilo Company.

By the end of Week Five, the platoon is starting to take on a new, more confident feel. "It was almost like we finally could do something right," Andrew Lee recalls. "You could see it in the drill instructors' eyes: 'Oh, you ain't a bunch of fuckups.'"

They march another looping ten miles back to their old barracks on the Third Deck of Building 420. Recruit Manczka, who performs drills in his sleep, is rewarded for high marksmanship by being allowed to call home to Edinboro, Pennsylvania. "Hi,

Mom," he says in a voice hoarsened by shouting responses to orders seventeen hours a day.

"Who is this?" she asks.

Lees, another new "expert" on the range, also calls his mother. The shock of hearing her voice triggers tears in him. She listens, then chuckles over the phone, "Big tough Marine."

Week Six is a routine round of drill, interspersed with a dental call, haircuts, and the first hint of graduation: They are issued real Marine uniforms that they will wear at that ceremony in five weeks, and they sit for their graduation photos. Even Buijs tries to look grim for the photographer, but he still comes off more Bambi than Rambo.

They plunge into "Mess and Maintenance Week," an odd break from the military routine of boot camp. It is a surprisingly intense period in which the platoon simply does the scut work of Parris Island, from mopping floors to cutting grass to washing pots in the mess hall sculleries. Those assigned to mess duty awake at 3:30 A.M., leave the barracks at four, and get back at about seven that night, fifteen sweaty hours later.

"Recruits always tell us that this is the week that they really came together as a team," notes Lieutenant Colonel Becker, Third Battalion's commander. "For the first time, everything depends on everyone pulling their load. The mess hall is a terrific test, because either the chow is served or not, either the place is clean or it is not."

Buijs pulls his load in his own way. One day he is sleepily scrubbing trays in a mess hall. With his head in the clouds, he doesn't even notice that a drill instructor is standing on the other side of the huge tray, eyeing this odd, slow-moving recruit. The water ricochets off the tray—and accidentally sprays the DI. Buijs still isn't aware of his offense when the DI walks up, reaches for the nozzle, and hoses Recruit Buijs's front. "There, recruit, how do *you* like it?" asks the DI.

Winston, the violent son of the inner city, is intrigued by the pacifistic Dutchman. The two talk while scrubbing pots. "He was more of a man than some of the older ones in the platoon," Winston concludes. "He didn't bite his tongue to fit in with the Marines. And he never gave up—and he was stressed out more than most of the guys who dropped out."

At one of the senior drill instructor's paternal evening meetings with the platoon sitting cross-legged around him on the quarterdeck, Recruit Buijs says, "This recruit wouldn't mind Parris Island if people just didn't yell so much. Why do we have to scream all the time?"

Sitting on a wooden footlocker, Staff Sergeant Rowland looks down at Buijs in amazement. He can understand most recruits, rich and poor, black and white, smart and stupid. This young Dutch-American pacifist is somewhere beyond his ken. Finally, he just shakes his head, grins, and says, "Where do you think you are, recruit?"

Recruit Linsky, the hearty, loud-talking carpetlayer from southern New Jersey, is amused by the exchange: "He wanted people to say 'please'—sure, when the enemy's coming in, 'Will you *please* shoot them?' "

For most of the platoon, Week Seven's "Mess and Maintenance" is a welcome change. "It was a familiar setting," James Andersen, the Taco Bell veteran from Pittsburgh who is the "juice recruit," fetching the milk, soda, water, juices, and soup, would later remember. "It was also nice to get away from the drill instructors for awhile."

And vice versa. During this week, each of 3086's drill instructors takes off for at least two days, their first real break in weeks. "It feels so good," says Staff Sergeant Rowland. "You really need it—that first phase is so demanding, that's really your money-making time."

Far from their DIs, 3086 gorges on ice cream and doughnuts in the mess hall when no one is looking. They become casual about it, until one day a cook catches a group scarfing doughnuts in the back of a walk-in refrigerator. "Someone better 'fess up to this," the cook warns. Weber, a quiet recruit who always does exactly what he is told, and so never encounters the wrath of the DIs, is nominated to take the rap. He does. When Sergeant Zwayer is informed of the offense, he presses Weber to give up other names. Weber refuses, even though it means taking on an enormous amount of punishment PT. He wins the grudging respect of Sergeant Zwayer. Nevertheless, the DI announces to the platoon, "I'm going to sweat those doughnuts out of you, thirty eighty-six." Over the next three days, he does.

A mess sergeant makes a crack one day that upsets several of its black members. That night, Anderson, Bone, and others sit up and whisper well after lights out. Lees, who is on firewatch, comes by at midnight. "Okay, guys, I'll give you ten minutes," says the big Samoan.

Anderson gives him a dour look. "That's the problem, I'm really tired of you white guys ordering me around."

Lees wishes Anderson would drop the race thing and start thinking like a Marine. Lees himself comes from a mixed background. His father was born in Samoa and came to Massachusetts to be a mechanic and to box. Lees draws himself up and quickly lists four reasons why they should listen to him: "First of all, that's not what matters. Second, I'm only half white. Third, I only open my mouth when I know I'm right. Fourth, if you don't go to sleep right now, I'm going to go knock on the senior drill instructor's door"—just at the other end of the barracks, in the DI house. They go to sleep.

Week Seven also brings Trujillio's brewing troubles to a head. No wiser from his run-in with Winston, he rags Linsky, another strong recruit, while they work in the mess hall kitchen. Linsky waits until that night, then retaliates by grabbing Trujillio in the latrine and holding his head out the third-story window to scare him.

Trujillio's blowup comes at the end of the week. It will prove to be the one day at boot camp that Andrew Lee doesn't enjoy. While others are out working in the mess hall or raking leaves, Lee is in charge of a work party of eight left behind to clean the barracks, make everyone's beds, and wash their clothes. This is dull work, but unusually important, because several members of the platoon somehow picked up crabs at the rifle range barracks. The entire barracks must be scrubbed down, and the mattresses and pillows steam-cleaned and then hauled out to dry in the sun.

As usual, Trujillio is complaining. Barrows, the quiet kid with the brother at Camp Lejeune who sends the envelopes that intentionally provoke the DIs, tires of listening to Trujillio. "Shut up, you fucking pussy," he says, "before I smack you." Others second that emotion. Trujillio yells, "Fuck you, I'll fight you all!" Lees, always level-headed, yells at everyone to "Stop it!" Trujillio runs into the latrine crying. He walks in and out of the latrine door, looking back across the quarterdeck at his antagonists. Lee yells at them: "What are you doing, the guy feels awful!"

A minute later, Lees, who despite dropping dozens of pounds still weighs in at 220, decides to follow Trujillio into the latrine to see what is going on. Trujillio is sitting on a toilet in one of the doorless stalls. He has broken open a plastic safety razor and is jabbing his wrist with the corner of the razor. Lees slams Trujillio against the wall and calls for help. Lee runs in to find big Lees facing little Trujillio, holding the other recruit's wrists. "Drop the razor or I'll punch you in the face," Lees yells. To emphasize the point, he places a big booted foot on Trujillio's crotch. "Drop it," he repeats.

Plenty scared, Lee runs downstairs to look for a drill instructor. He slaps on the door of another platoon's DI house. A lazy voice responds: "Recruit, why are you pounding?" Lee shouts, "There's a suicide attempt on the Third Deck, sir." Drill instructors come running from all directions. There are few things that so quickly will get the attention of Parris Island's power structure.

After all the commotion is over and Trujillio has been sent packing, never to be seen again by 3086, Staff Sergeant Rowland calls Lee into the DI house. "Guide, talk to me," he begins. Lee can't look at him. His eyes moisten as the strain of the day catches up with him. "Sir, they were picking on him." He stands at attention and weeps, heels at a forty-five degree angle, fingers curled. It is the only time he will cry as a recruit.

Chris Anderson, perhaps the most cynical member of 3086, is less impressed by Trujillio's display. "To me, he was really just trying to make a show," he remembers dismissively.

"We were happy when it happened," Linsky later says. "He was just a nasty little asshole. It actually kind of brought the platoon together, because he was going to try to fry the drill instructors, say they hit him." That night, Staff Sergeant Rowland jots a three-letter epitaph on Trujillio's evaluation card: *"FTA."*

Week Seven fells another, better-liked member of 3086. Landon Meyer feels sick and is diagnosed as having pneumonia. He is shipped to Beaufort Naval Hospital, where he will spend a week before going to the Medical Rehabilitation Platoon for a month, and then to the Physical Conditioning Platoon for nearly three weeks. Throughout that period, Sergeant Carey brings him his mail and encourages him to hang in there. "That impressed me, because he no longer had any responsibility for me," Meyer says later.

CHAPTER FOUR

WARRIOR WEEK

Week Eight, "Warrior Week," is the fulcrum point of Platoon 3086's boot camp experience. They enter it still more civilian than Marine. They will return from the woods more Marine than not, with a new hard-eyed confidence and sureness in their bearing: After "Warrior Week," they know they will make it.

The infantry training is the kind of crawling-in-the-woods fun that most recruits envisioned when they joined the Marines. It is the big payoff after the sweat, grease, scum and drudgery of Mess and Maintenance. It is also the last big hurdle to becoming a Marine. "After BWT, all that's left is inspections and drill and administration. BWT is really it," says Staff Sgt. Frasier, Platoon 3085's whippetlike senior drill instructor.

To understand how "Warrior Week" came to be, and why it goes to the heart of today's Marine Corps, it is necessary to step back from Parris Island and look at the stories of two men instrumental in the remaking of today's Corps: James Webb and Al Gray.

In a quiet, air-conditioned corner of the Pentagon, where the seventh corridor meets the E Ring, two oil paintings hang a few feet from each other. One portrait, displayed above the model ships in the Navy's bright wainscoted hallway, is of a noticeably young man, face still boyish, wearing a suit. The other, around the corner in the Marines' dimly illuminated churchlike corridor, lined by portraits of the commandants of the Corps, is of an old man in camouflage fatigues.

The two portraits are very different, yet they are of a piece in how sharply they stand out from their peers. The young man portrayed in the Navy corridor is half the age of the string of white-haired gentlemen on either side of him. Unlike those plain, dull images of men in suits on chairs, his portrait is a busy mess of reminders of the Vietnam War, slyly including on its left edge even a red and blue sliver of a Vietcong flag. He stands leaning back against a table. Painted on the table next to him in the picture are two books, their titles clearly legible in the middle of the canvas: *Fields of Fire* and *A Sense of Honor.*

Around the corner, the gruff old Marine general also stands out: He is wearing fatigues, sleeves rolled above the elbows, in contrast to the other commandants who were painted wearing dress blues with medals on display, or even wearing a cape and holding a sword, as is Randolph Pate, one commandant from the 1950s. Portrayed in the field, a Light Armored Vehicle poised behind him, the painting of the old general in fatigues almost seems to challenge the staff weenies scurrying through the cool halls of the Pentagon, reminding these chairborne troops that their neat uniforms and dry briefing papers are a far cry from the hard, muddy, sweaty, confusing, sometimes bloody work of the real military.

The younger man in the Pentagon portraits is James Webb, who briefly served as secretary of the Navy late in the Reagan administration. The old general in the reverse snobbery fatigues is Alfred Gray, who because of Webb's tenacity became twenty-ninth commandant of the Marine Corps. Between the two of them, Webb and Gray had an enormous impact on the Marines in the 1980s, arguably making the Corps what it is today. Indeed, Platoon 3086 will march into the piney woods for a week of "Basic Warrior Training" because of the changes General Gray made in an effort to refocus the Marines on fighting. They will emerge from these piney woods hard-eyed, tanned, and calm. They will consider themselves almost Marines. Drill instructors say that of the eleven weeks recruits spend on Parris Island, this is the one that makes the biggest difference.

As a fairly recent innovation, "Warrior Week" stands out in a place dedicated to preserving and transmitting a tradition and a culture. Its origins can in part be traced back to Webb's thoughts as he sat in a Georgetown University Law School classroom late in 1973, confused and angered by the attitudes of his classmates and stunned by his nation's handling of the Vietnam War and its veterans. His stewing led to the book that would influence a generation of Marine officers, shaping their views of what they should be and what they should expect of the society they defend. It also would help propel Webb to become Navy secretary fourteen years later, where he would fight the Marine Corps' leadership to install as commandant General Gray, who reinvigorated the Corps' warrior culture.

As Robert Timberg tells the story in *The Nightingale's Song,* a wonderful account of the parallel lives of Webb and four other Naval Academy graduates (Oliver North, Robert McFarlane, John Poindexter, and John McCain), Webb returned from Vietnam with a distinguished combat record and shrapnel lodged in his head, back, kidney, left arm, and left leg.

In April 1969, less than a year out of Annapolis, he had exposed himself to enemy fire while rescuing a wounded Marine, an action for which he was awarded the Bronze Star. A few weeks later he had won the Silver Star for repeatedly exposing himself while rescuing casualties and leading a counterattack. Two months after that, he led an attack on three bunkers, and used his own body to shield another Marine from a grenade blast. He then destroyed one bunker with his own grenade. For this, he was awarded the Navy Cross. By the time he arrived at law school, he had lost a host of friends, with his platoon alone suffering fifty-six killed or wounded in just one eight-week period. Webb was shocked to find that his law school classmates knew few, if any, people who had gone to Vietnam. Adding insult to injury, they considered themselves morally superior to those who had.

It wasn't just the students who struck him as morally obtuse. Timberg writes that Webb's criminal law professor, Heathcote Wales, who himself was opposed to the war, offered in a final examination question on search and seizure a hypothetical vignette about a Marine sergeant named "Webb" who tries to smuggle jade in the bodies of dead comrades. The professor knew Webb had been wounded in Vietnam.

"That night," recounts Timberg, Webb went home and "went through some of the bleakest hours of his life, repeatedly bursting into tears as he tried to study for the other finals."

One day in constitutional law class, Webb ignored a discussion of the War Powers Act and began jotting on a yellow legal pad a short story that ultimately would become *Fields of Fire,* a powerful novel based on his experience as a Marine infantry lieutenant in Vietnam. It is an unusual war story. By its end all its heroes, including the Webb-like Lt. Robert E. Lee Hodges Jr., have been killed. What's more, the book's quasi-villain—not a Vietcong, but a kid from Harvard who joins the Marines and dangerously bumbles his way through Vietnam—gets the final word. That villain, transparently named "Goodrich," realizes only as he prepares to speak to demonstrators at a Harvard antiwar rally that all the talk of a "generation gap" pales in the face of the huge "culture gap" between the Ivy League kids and their working-class contemporaries who went into the military. "HOW MANY OF YOU ARE GOING TO GET HURT IN VIETNAM?" the crippled Goodrich shouts in the novel's final paragraphs. "I DIDN'T SEE ANY OF YOU IN VIETNAM. I SAW DUDES, MAN. DUDES. AND TRUCK DRIVERS AND COAL MINERS AND FARMERS. I DIDN'T SEE YOU. WHERE WERE YOU?"

In the novel, Webb effectively commemorates the Vietnam War by declaring cultural war at home. He claims the moral high ground for those who went to Vietnam, arguing that they were right to go—and that those who refused, and especially those who fled to Canada, were wrong. The book's first section, introducing his Marine platoon, carries the title "The Best We Have." Coming just a few years after the war ended, the book constituted an in-your-face challenge to the prevailing wisdom about who "the best and brightest" were, and where they were during the Vietnam War. It is a question that still hangs over America during the presidency of Bill Clinton, with his murky record of sidestepping military service. "The major theme of *Fields of Fire* is the abandonment by elites," Webb says in a conversation.

Webb wrote *Fields* during the mid-seventies, arguably the lowest point in the history of the Marines and the U.S. military generally. "From the end of the Vietnam War until 1978, soldiers were murdering their officers and destroying their equipment, drugs were rampant, weapons and facilities were neglected and poorly maintained," military journalist Arthur Hadley wrote a few years after that nadir.

The Marines arguably were the most devastated of all the services. Calling the early part of the seventies a debacle for the Marines, Jeffrey Record noted in *Proceedings* that, "the Corps registered rates of courts-martial, non-judicial punishments, unauthorized absences, and outright desertions unprecedented in its own history, and, in most cases, three to four times those plaguing the U.S. Army. Violence and crime at recruit depots and other installations escalated; in some cases, officers ventured out only in pairs or groups and only in daylight."

Those abstract statistics were lived on a painful day-to-day basis by some of the sergeants now serving at Parris Island. Staff Sergeant Rowland remembers smelling marijuana smoke in the head of his barracks at Camp Lejeune in 1978. "Drugs and race were big then," he says laconically. One reason today's DIs display such an edgy determination to keep standards high is that most remember the bad old days when the Marines came close to being a broken family. It isn't just the drill instructors who carry this feeling. "The people who are now generals, at my level, and what we went through, . . . the late sixty-nine and seventies experience," says General Krulak, the current commandant of the Marines, "If you can get through that, you carry in your heart and soul: Never again. Never again."

Even as Webb was writing and rewriting his novel—seven times in all—the counterrevolution was beginning within the Corps. Procedures for discharging troublesome Marines were eased, and soon 4,000 of those deemed "losers" by their commanders were kicked out. Enlistment criteria were altered— rather than pursue IQ, the recruiters were directed to pursue prospects who had shown the gumption at least to earn a high school diploma. DIs were ordered to make boot camp less of an initiation rite and more of a training process. To ensure that the change actually happened, additional supervisory officers and senior sergeants were added to the structure that oversees DIs. Platoon sizes also were reduced by about two dozen to ease the load of the DIs.

After recruit quality improved, the Corps in the early and mid-eighties begin rebuilding its non-commisioned officers— the sergeants who are key in any good American military organization, but who are absolutely essential to the Marine way of pushing responsibility to the lowest possible level. Retired Lt. Gen. Bernard Trainor, who was the Marines' operations chief back then, recalls watching an appalling exercise early in the decade at the Marine base at Twenty-nine Palms, California. The riflemen didn't even know what area they were responsible for covering, he recalls. He and others agitated for more and better training. By 1987, that work began to pay off—and the Corps once again had an NCO corps it could lean on, just as it got a commandant who wanted to do that: Al Gray.

The administrative changes reflected a larger philosophical shift about how the Corps, a wounded institution, needed to

heal itself, to restore its sense of honor. In his writings, Webb provided the cultural manifesto needed especially by younger
Marines, those with no memories of the pre-Vietnam Corps—and
perhaps a bit tired of hearing from those whose pasts did reach
back to Korea and World War II. (As Webb has often observed,
the Marines suffered more casualties in Vietnam—a total of
103,453—than they did in World War II, in which they had
90,709 casualties, a figure that includes all those killed, wounded,
or lost to accidents and disease. The difference is that 6,660
more Marines died in World War II.) Essentially, Webb states that
he and his comrades have nothing to apologize for. It is the other
side, those who avoided service, and saw service as dishonorable,
that is at fault. "Vietnam sowed the seeds of a class selfishness that
still exists," he argues. "The problem of the eighties and nineties
isn't that corporate America abandoned the people, but that
elites have decided to pick up their pieces and protect each other
at the expense of everyone else. The greatest problem in this
country is the lack of a sense that we're all sharing the problem."

In *Fields of Fire,* he has the statement made by Goodrich's
father, a liberal lawyer who nonetheless summons the police to
arrest Goodrich's roommate Mark, a draft dodger who has come
back into the country from Canada. "To my mind, he committed
the ultimate crime, son," the father explains to Goodrich. "He
rejected the society that nourished him."

The father continues:

> These people have no sense of country. They don't look
> beyond themselves. . . . We've lost a sense of responsibility,
> at least on the individual level. We have too many people
> like Mark who believe that the government owes them
> total, undisciplined freedom. If everyone thought that way,
> there would be no society. We're so big, so strong now, that
> people seem to have forgotten that a part of our strength
> comes from each person surrendering a portion of his indi-
> vidual urges to the common good.

That, in a nutshell, states the ideology that the Marine Corps tries to inculcate today at Parris Island. Pulled by Webb and others, and pushed by the trends of American history, the Marines effectively went into cultural opposition—where they remain today. As a matter of survival, if nothing else, they had stopped viewing themselves as a better version of society, and began acting as a dissenting critique of it. The Marines' cultural sensitivity isn't surprising: unlike the other services, they are built on an ethos, a culture, an attitude. That foundation makes them conscious of the role that traditions, manners, and beliefs play in a given society, and sensitive to changes in those values.

In subsequent novels and in opinion journalism, Webb would sharpen his indictment of American political, economic, and cultural elites. It was they, he argued, who during the 1960s abdicated their responsibilities and betrayed the working stiffs who, left holding the bag, labored on. Even today, he knows by heart the number of Ivy Leaguers who died in Vietnam. Over lunch at a Vietnamese restaurant outside Washington, where the waiter is a former Vietnamese Army Ranger, he recites them: Just twelve from the 12,595 who graduated from Harvard College between 1962 and 1972; six from Princeton; two from MIT. In an opinion piece in *The Washington Post,* Webb noted that the predominantly Irish working-class neighborhood of South Boston, by contrast, produced about 2,000 draft-age men, and lost twenty-five of them in Vietnam. This class resentment lingers over the entire U.S. military, but is most concentrated in the Marines. In this world view, for example, the three most salient charges against Bill Clinton are that he protested against the Vietnam War as a Rhodes Scholar, that he evaded military service while doing so, and that upon becoming president he sent his daughter to private school in Washington, D.C.

Fields of Fire and, to a lesser degree, Webb's three subsequent, equally fierce novels, have had a quiet but pervasive effect on the Marines. To be sure, some of Webb's contemporaries in the officer corps—especially those who have experienced his stubborn

and abrasive side—seek to marginalize him as a zealot, somewhere out there in the ozone with Webb's boxing rival in the
Annapolis class of '68, Oliver North. Indeed, Commandant Krulak argues in an interview that overall, Webb's influence on the
Marine Corps has been "minimal" when compared to, say, that of
Al Gray. But to younger officers, those leading infantry platoons, companies, and battalions today, Webb is a huge and
trusted figure. When a guest at a mess night at the Basic School,
the Marine officers' equivalent of boot camp, mentions that he
knows Webb, heads swivel up and down the long formal table.
"We've all read those books," enthuses a young Delta Company
second lieutenant, fresh out of Annapolis. Indeed, across the
base at Quantico, stacks of Webb's novels are on sale at the
Marine Corps Association's bookstore.

"That book influenced a generation of Marine lieutenants,"
says Capt. John Church. "My generation, as we went through
the Basic School, was told you *will* read *Fields of Fire,* and you *can*
be a sensitive leader like Robert E. Lee Hodges."

"There are probably very few Marines who read who haven't
read *Fields of Fire,*" says Brig. Gen. Terry Murray, an Annapolis
classmate of Webb's who later served in the same regiment in
Vietnam. He is talking over chicken Caesar salad and iced tea in
the Navy's "flag mess," or lunchroom for admirals—just a few
steps down the Pentagon hallway from the anomalous portraits
of Webb and Gray. "All of my contemporaries, and most of the
younger guys, know it. It really is about what the Marines are all
about, the rifle squad. For Marines, it really resonates, because
that's what it is all about, from day one of boot camp, OCS, or
the Basic School: Being a cohesive small unit that fights."

Asked if he has read *Fields of Fire,* Staff Sgt. Michael Marti, the
head of the Marine recruiting station in Boston, replies, "I've
read *all* his books."

With his novels alone, Webb would have left a mark on the
modern Marines. But the books also helped catapult him to a posi-

tion of influence in the Reagan administration that permitted him to shape the Marines more directly. As Robert Timberg tells it in *The Nightingale's Song,* Webb was on a San Francisco radio talk show, plugging his novel. The host asked Webb what he thought of Jane Fonda. "Jane Fonda can kiss my ass," Webb replied. "I wouldn't go across the street to watch her slit her wrists."

One of Webb's listeners that day, Timberg continues, was John Herrington, a former Marine and California lawyer who a few years later, as White House personnel chief, would remember Webb and recruit him into the Reagan administration's Pentagon as an assistant defense secretary. In 1987, Webb became Navy secretary, the top civilian overseeing both the Navy and the Marines. At age forty-one, he was the youngest Navy secretary ever. At his swearing-in, Webb introduced twenty-three members of his old rifle platoon, noting that among them they had collected twenty-seven Purple Hearts.

The uncompromising Webb wouldn't last long as Navy secretary, where one must constantly work with deal-oriented congressmen and bureaucrats. But he made one personnel selection during his short tenure that would have a huge impact on the Marine Corps. As he moved into his new job, he met individually with most of the senior admirals in the Navy and top generals in the Marines, seeking their opinions in long conversations about what needed to be done in their services. The Marines were in a rough patch. In December 1986, Lt. Col. North had taken aback many in the Corps by appearing before Congress and invoking his Fifth Amendment right to avoid self-incrimination—while wearing a Marine uniform. In April 1987, a murky scandal surfaced involving allegations that Marine guards had compromised the security of the U.S. embassy in Moscow. Underlying these blows was an unsureness of mission—just what was the post-Vietnam role of the Marines? Some defense intellectuals argued that there really was none.

Most of all, hugely looming over the Corps like a wrecking ball there was "Beirut." To Marines, that word means one thing—an event largely forgotten by the rest of America that looms in the collective memory of today's Corps perhaps as large as the Vietnam War. On October 23, 1983, a terrorist drove a truck laden with TNT into a building full of Marines executing a hazy peacekeeping mission. Some 241 Marines and other American soldiers died in the bombing attack, marking one of the worst days of the history of the Corps. To make matters worse, Gen. P. X. Kelley, then the commandant, sent a shudder through the Corps when he testified before Congress that he was out of the chain of command on the Beirut mission and so not responsible. Though in fact an accurate statement—the service chiefs don't have operational control of deployed troops—the newspaper accounts of his testimony made him look cold, as if the leader of the Corps wasn't watching the backs of his men in the field. Was the commandant someone you'd want on your flank?

"Critics of the Corps say it suffers from a lack of leadership at the top," reported *Time* magazine in an April 1987 piece typical of the scathing reviews the Marines were collecting that year.

"The Marine Corps was really reeling," Webb remembers. In his long conversations with the admirals and generals in the winter of '86 and the spring of '87, one Marine officer struck Webb as understanding the Corps' malaise. Webb had known Al Gray since 1984, when as a Pentagon official for reserve affairs he had gone to watch a Marine reserve brigade perform an amphibious landing. Marine aides had tried to corral Webb, provide him with an escort, keep him on the beach. Instead, Webb went aboard ship the night before and landed in a Light Armored Vehicle, ordering it to charge across the beach past Webb's designated keeper. "Finally, around noon, I surrendered," he recalls, and went to lunch with General Gray, notorious for just the same sort of get-with-the-troops antics.

The soul-searching conversations in the winter of '86 to '87 struck Webb. "I brought Al Gray back three times, not to interview him for commandant, but because he had such a grasp on the spiritual problems of the Corps."

Among the problems, Webb thought, was the current commandant, General Kelley. "After Beirut," Webb argues, "P.X. Kelley basically killed off many of the real combat leaders of the Marine Corps," mainly, Webb further argues, because he resented their critiques of his handling of the incident. "The people around Kelley hadn't made their reputations as combat leaders. The man he wanted to be commandant had been forced for medical reasons to turn down command of an aviation squadron in combat. In the two years before I became Secretary of the Navy, they had turned down nine [winners of] Navy Crosses and two [winners of] Medals of Honor for [promotion to] brigadier general." (Gen. Kelley responds, "I don't know who he's talking about. I think that's an outrageous statement.")

Gray, a fifty-eight-year-old ex-sergeant on the cusp of retirement, struck Webb as the general most likely to "make Marines feel like the Marines again." In May, Webb set up a secret meeting with General Gray in Jacksonville, Florida, to ask him to become commandant. A native of New Jersey who dropped out of Lafayette College in Easton, Pennsylvania, and enlisted in the Marines in 1950, Gray fought in Korea and was commissioned as a second lieutenant. Throughout his career he seemed to be a person the Marines turned to with tough jobs. He was one of the first Marines on the ground in Vietnam, going there in 1962 for special operations work. ("We really don't talk too much about those tours," he says, declining to elaborate.) He also was one of the last, commanding the Marine ground troops in the evacuation of Saigon in April 1975. As the Marines assigned to the U.S. embassy collapsed their defensive perimeter toward the helipad on the embassy roof, Gray directed the placement of demolition charges in the defense attache's office at Tan Son Nhut Airport. A few years later, as a division commander, he once "secretly arranged for a unit of the 82nd Airborne to make a parachute landing in the rear of one of his own battalions and attack it," noted military analyst William S. Lind. "The result was good training."

One thing the barrel-chested, tobacco-chewing general didn't have was a college degree, but that didn't bother Webb. "He knew how to fight, he knew how to lead, and he knew how to remember," Webb says from his office overlooking the Iwo Jima Memorial. Those were the three characteristics Webb believed were essential for anyone leading the Marine Corps. "The Marines were shook up by Beirut. I never saw a memorial go up, anywhere, in some small town that lost a Marine in Beirut, that he didn't go to. He knew that you never leave behind your wounded and you never forget your dead."

But, recalls Webb, "When I brought his name up, shit flew everywhere."

General Kelley, who had his own candidate to succeed himself, fought the brash young Navy secretary over the selection of Gray. Webb says he was told Kelley went to Vice President George Bush to protest, but that Bush deferred to Defense Secretary Caspar Weinberger. "Weinberger called and said, 'Nobody's covered with glory, but I'll back your guy,' " Webb recalls. (Underscoring the intensity of feeling that still divides the two men ten years later, General Kelley flatly denies ever contacting Bush in an attempt to block Gray's promotion. Asked directly for his opinion of Webb, General Kelley simply says, "I'm not going to talk about that.")

When the news leaked out of the Pentagon that Al Gray would be the next commandant, Gray remembers, Marine Corps headquarters at first put out the word that the leak was incorrect. Gray and Webb would expect nothing less of the staff of top headquarters. There is a perpetual tension in military life between field types and staff types. Webb and Gray thought that the staff officers, especially those who worked successive tours of duty at Marine headquarters in Washington, had grown far too influential. Gray grabbed the pendulum and swung it back toward the warriors.

He set the blunt tone of his term during his first moments as commandant. "We're warriors, and people who support warriors, and we must always keep that focus," he lectured at his induction. "Some people don't like to hear about war—people who fight don't like to have to do it, but that's what we're about."

Gray also took pains to demonstrate his personal responsibility for the Corps, an important move in the wake of the Beirut bombing. Most strikingly, recalls Major Davis, director of the Drill Instructors School at Parris Island, after nineteen Marines were badly burned in a collision between two helicopters, Gray flew to the military hospital in San Antonio, Texas, where they were hospitalized. Without any introduction, the general walked into the waiting lounge of the hospital where the parents of the burned Marines had gathered and said, "I'm Al Gray. I'm the commandant of the Marine Corps. I'm responsible for your sons being in the burn ward. I'm here to answer your questions."

Emphasizing that a new era had begun in Gray's first year as commandant, "we got eighteen retirements out of the sixty-seven" generals then in the Marines, recalls Webb. "Over the course of nine months, he went to each guy personally."

The new commandant also went out of his way to encourage an independence of thought, both in preparing for war and in actually fighting. "One neat thing about Marine Corps culture is that it swings between being knuckle-dragging knuckleheads and flexible intellectuals—and Gray managed to combine the two," observes Larry Cable, a combat Marine in Vietnam who now teaches national security studies at the University of North Carolina at Wilmington, just down the road from Camp Lejeune. (The Corps is a small world: Cable's unit at Parris Island was Kilo Company of the Third Battalion, the same as 3086's.)

Soon after assuming the commandancy, General Gray introduced a formal reading list, not just for officers but for all ranks from corporal up. Staff sergeants and first lieutenants, the men who run platoons, were told to read, among other books, Webb's *Fields of Fire*. First sergeants tackled Sun Tzu's *The Art of War*. Captains, who run rifle companies, were assigned Tom Peters's *Thriving on Chaos*. Majors, who typically are mired in staff jobs, had to look at life differently by reading Mao Tse-tung's *On Guerrilla Warfare,* for which the author was listed, in typical Marine style, as "Mao, T.," as if he were one more shavehead recruit. Lieutenant colonels were asked to look at the very big picture: Solzhenitsyn's *August 1914,* Thucydides's *Peloponnesian War,* and Tolstoy's *War and Peace.*

Most pointedly, colonels were yanked back to reality by having their noses rubbed in a library of military failure: Neil Sheehan's *Bright and Shining Lie,* about the U.S. effort in Vietnam; General Giap's *How We Won the War,* a view from the victors' side of that conflict; Paul Kennedy's *Rise and Fall of Great Powers,* about how military spending can undercut national security; and C. S. Forester's undeservedly obscure *The General,* a gloomy meditation on how good but unimaginative officers could lead a generation of British youth to slaughter in World War I.

Gray also imposed a major departure on the Corps' approach to fighting, which, after all, is the purpose of the organization. He emphatically settled a long-running debate about whether it would pursue attrition warfare or maneuver warfare in favor of the latter. As the proponents of "manueverism" put it, the issue was whether to pile up dead Marines in front of enemy machine guns, or find ways to "hit them where they ain't." William Lind, one of the major theorists of maneuverism, defined it thusly: "In maneuver warfare, you always try to avoid the enemy's strength and hurl your strength against his weaknesses. You want to use judo, not fight a boxing match."

General Gray made even the raw recruits in boot camp think about how to be warriors. In November 1987, he explained why he was reviving combat training in boot camp, rather than simply having the minority who would be grunts get their training later, at infantry school. Parris Island still offered some basic infantry training, but it had slacked off over the years to allow time for classes on check-writing and other matters. Grass covered the grenade range, which had been closed in 1985.

"Everyone is going to be a rifleman," the new commandant vowed in *Sea Power* magazine. "So that from now on, no matter where you are, when you see a Marine, no matter what he does, you will be able to say that guy has been through at least 160 hours of Basic Warrior Training—hand-to-hand combat training, combat shooting, and all the other things that are going to make him a pretty good gunslinger." Recruits were to fire all weapons used by the infantry, including machine guns and grenade launchers. Two years later, Gray added "Marine Combat Training" as a follow-on course after boot camp, to ensure that all noninfantry Marines knew the basics of infantry work. Gray's man at Parris Island, Maj. Gen. Jarvis D. Lynch Jr., sent a memorandum to the Recruit Training Regiment assuring it that, "I don't mind bloody or broken noses." He signed it, as he did most of his memos, "No prisoners, J. D. Lynch Jr."

Gray's effect on the Corps was enormous. He continues to loom over the Corps today—which, one suspects, doesn't make the current leadership altogether comfortable. It is as if the current pope had to deal with an influential predecessor looking over his shoulder, and occasionally offering commentary. Even now, well into his first decade of retirement, Gray looks and talks like a senior officer. His tie clasp carries the eagle, globe, and anchor of the Corps. His watchface displays the flag of a four-star general. Speaking to new officers at a mess night at the Basic School, he begins by saying that he is retired, so of course he has no influence over the Corps. It is clearly a joke. What bothers him most about today's military, he goes on to say, is careerism. It has eroded the other services, he warns, and is creeping into the Corps. The only thing you should worry about, he tells the assembled second lieutenants, is taking care of your people. In fact, he recommends adding one new little box to the officer evaluation reports: It would say, Does this officer care more about his career than about his troops? A "yes" mark would terminate that officer's career.

To many, especially to the sergeants who are the soul of the

Corps, Al Gray remains the real commandant. Walk into the Marine recruiting station in Boston, and the only officer honored with a photograph is Al Gray, in a poster. In it, he is wearing combat fatigues. At the bottom is a quotation: "I'm looking for warriors to follow me.—Al Gray." Sgt. Alfonso McNeil, who despite his Italian-Irish name is a black Marine from New York City, points at the poster: "Al Gray, he's the icon—he's the one who brought back the warrior spirit."

Most of all, Gray lives on in the hearts of the Corps' sergeants. It is striking how, in an organization of nearly 200,000 people, he managed to reach down into the lives of the enlisted ranks. Every Marine NCO seems to have some sort of story about an encounter with Al Gray, generally along the lines of the time he showed up without advance notice to inspect a unit at quitting time, when all the snafus happen. One story retold throughout the Corps is about the sergeant who walked up to Gray at a base and said he was being unfairly discharged because he was officially "overweight," yet could run at the required times. Gray said, "Okay, show me"—and had the sergeant run right there. When he passed, Gray cleared him to stay in the Corps. It all illustrates a favorite theme of Gray's: Don't look good, *be* good.

Even 3086's DIs have tales of Gray's encounters. Staff Sgt. Rowland recalls that a friend of his was serving on the U.S.S. *Blue Ridge* and was due to be promoted to sergeant when General Gray arrived. "Gray said, 'Let's do it right now,' " and pinned the chevrons on Rowland's friend on the spot.

Sergeant Carey recalls an even more direct connection to Gray: He remembers the general fondly from the days when Gray commanded the Fleet Marine Forces, Atlantic, one of the top jobs in the Corps. Carey was a young lance corporal in Force Recon. Gray would speak directly to Carey's platoon, asking about equipment and training. "He came up to a short stocky guy, slapped him on the shoulder, and said, 'Hey, how ya doin', sergeant?' " recalls Sergeant Carey. "It was probably the guy who looked most like him when he was a sergeant." Even more impressively, Gray in an interview remembers Carey: "Good man, with Force Recon when we were creating Special Operations Capable forces."

"I like him for what he did for the Marines," says Sergeant Carey. "He held us to the concept of every Marine being a rifleman. Everyone always said it, but he held us to it. Also, he implemented Basic Warrior Training in boot camp, so even cooks got some combat training."

By the beginning of Week Eight, almost all of 3086's "overweights" have reached their weight goals; the last three will meet their targets during this week. The platoon is tanned, muscular, and a bit cocky. Their hair has grown out into a short brush on top, but is still shaved on the sides, giving them a look resembling the distinctive "high and tight" tonsure worn by their DIs.

They no longer think about quitting. On a beautiful spring afternoon in late April, with fresh honeysuckle blossoms scenting the air along the side of the dirt road, the platoon marches along a causeway through a salt marsh. Platoon 3086 mocks its dropouts with its own "Casualty Cadence," written during a quiet moment of Mess and Maintenance Week by Joshua Parise and some others. The cadence commemorates 3086's two most spectacular washouts, Joseph Parker and Ivan Trujillio.

> Hope you like the sights you see
> Parris Island casualty.
> As for you, it's still a dream
> On May 19th we are Marines.
>
> See ya later Tru-jill-i-o,
> It's off to Disneyland you go.
> Place for fun, games, and rides—
> Follow Parker, he's your guide.

They are growing comfortable with the Marines' culture of self-sacrifice, of seeing suffering as a good in itself, of managing violence.

They assemble on benches for an introduction to "The Marine Rifle Fire Team." "A fire team is four guys who beat up on one guy," lectures Sgt. Paul Norman, an infantry instructor. "That's what it's all about. Your job is to learn how to kill people."

The instrument of their chosen occupation, he continues, is the M-16 rifle. "An M-16 can blow someone's head off at 500 meters," he teaches. "That's beautiful, isn't it?"

"Yes, sir!" shout the 173 voices of 3086 and its companion platoons.

"*What* is the mission?" he asks.

The platoons chant in rollicking unison: "The mission of the Marine rifle team is to locate, close with, and DESTROOOOOOY the enemy!"

"Isn't that a beautiful thing?"

"Yes, sir!" they respond in a roar.

Sergeant Norman walks them through the Marines' trinitarian structure. There are three fire teams per squad, three squads per platoon, three platoons per company (plus a headquarters platoon, where all the shitbirds are dumped so they don't screw up patrols), three companies per battalion, three battalions per regiment, three infantry regiments per division (plus artillery and support units), and three divisions in the active-duty Marine Corps.

He finishes and steps outside the metal shed. Over the sergeant's head, a passenger aircraft descends into nearby Hilton Head Island, famous for golf and for Bill Clinton's twelve years of introspective Renaissance Weekends. Sergeant Norman clearly prefers the spartan ways, and the lack of introspection, that is characteristic of Parris Island. "Being a Marine," he muses in a conversation, "is the greatest thing in the whole frigging world."

"I love the Corps," Norman waxes on as another instructor teaches a session on the hand signals used by a fire team. "It is the only place I fit. I did nothing with my life until I was twenty-four. Then I joined the Corps. When I got in, I told them I was staying twenty years. I loved it. I wake up every morning and I can't believe someone is paying me to play in the mud and blow up things and be a drill instructor at Parris Island."

Unsolicited, he offers one final thought: "Homosexuality will never be accepted in the Marine Corps, even if it is accepted in American society." Indeed, the Corps has been the most resistant of all the armed services to adopting the new, purposefully ambiguous policy of "don't ask, don't tell." In that policy, homosexuality is simply taken off the table as a matter of discussion: Service members aren't supposed to reveal their homosexuality, and their superiors aren't supposed to ask about it. This policy had the politically brilliant effect of driving a wedge between the interests of gays in the military and gay activists with a larger agenda. Gays in the military generally wanted the security of knowing their sexual orientation wouldn't be used to terminate their military careers. But some gay activists wanted to use the military as a model for integration, as happened with blacks in the military during the 1950s, following President Truman's order on military desegregation. The new policy may comfort gays in the military—but it deprives the gay community of the possibility of acquiring a new symbol, a gay Colin Powell.

There certainly are homosexual Marines. The extreme macho posture of some Marines evokes nothing more than the Village People, the unabashedly gay-positive 1970s disco singers. But partly because the Marine identity is culturally based, the Corps has had difficulty with "don't ask, don't tell." In a 1995 review of the implementation of the policy, the Service Members Legal Defense Network accused the Marines of conducting a "witch hunt" among Marines in Okinawa, Japan, questioning over twenty-one members of the U.S. armed forces "about the sexual orientation and activities of themselves and other service members."

The platoon marches to a class on rappelling and assembles at the base of the metal tower. It is only forty-seven feet high, but looks taller, perhaps because it is bigger than the surrounding pine trees, but probably because of the imminent prospect of dropping off it holding nothing more than a thin rope. Perhaps because "Warrior Week" is such a rite of passage, such a time of cementing new identities as Marines, the subject of homosexuality again surfaces in this class.

"Now, on your wrist there is a strap. This is called a 'fag strap,'" begins Sgt. Christopher Robinson's class on rappelling. "But we know that at Parris Island there are no sissies or fags, right?"

The three platoons shout: "Yes, sir!" Heads tilted back, squinting into the warm spring sky, they watch as Sergeant Carey ascends the tower and then demonstrates the safety of the rappelling system by doing an astonishing "dead bug" leap. He jumps backward off the side of the platform—without holding onto the rappelling rope, but with it loosely looped around his waist. About twenty feet down, he jerks to a stop, face to the sky, waist high, arms and legs and head all hanging down. It is a classic example of "leading from the front." If he can leap from the platform without holding the rope, the platoon quickly reasons, they can easily go off the platform while holding on to it. They climb up the stairs, line up, and do it with ease, each letting loose a "Hoorah!" as he steps backward into space, taking a leap of faith into the Marine Corps.

The platoon has a class on "Camouflage, Cover and Concealment," and then another on "Field Sanitation," and then bivouacs in the woods along Page Field, an abandoned World War II airstrip. A sign made by Parise, the Pittsburgh artist, portrays a crab in a canteen cup and says 3086/ SEAFOOD PLATTER PLATOON, commemorating the crabs the platoon acquired at the rifle range. Their fifty-seven rifles are propped above the dust in the handles of their entrenching tools. They place their helmets atop the pole at the end of each tent. Out on the runway, Porta Potti graffiti reflect Parris Island culture: There are no names or profanity, just platoon numbers and a few plaintive scribbles, such as "21 DAYS MORE." The DIs don't give the recruits much time to leave longer thoughts in the latrines. Lingering recruits are roused with a flat palm slapped on the plastic potty door, producing a sound within like a rifle shot.

On sentry duty, Recruit Bourassa, the former Ernst & Young accountant, finds a sharp contrast between Sergeant Carey and the murky ways of the business world. "He's an impeccable Marine," he observes. "There's a purity in that."

He has wondered about the sergeant's history. "You see those scars on Drill Instructor Sergeant Carey when he's on line, screaming, and you wonder, 'Jesus, what the hell happened?' " says Bourassa as he walks under the pines. "When you've gone sixteen hours, and you're wiped out, and you see him motoring, you say to yourself, 'I've got to tap into whatever he has.' "

Sergeant Carey, whose father founded the Nassau County bias crime squad, the first such unit in a U.S. police force, and commanded it for thirteen years, uses this time in the woods to assign Earnest Winston Jr., the gang member from Washington, D.C., to share a pup tent with Jonathan Prish, the former white supremacist from Mobile, Alabama, whose racist tattoos have been noticed by several of the black drill instructors. The implicit message is that if these two are going to be Marines, they are going to have to overcome their prejudices and learn to look at each other as comrades, even brothers. The experiment produces an unexpected side effect: The two happily find common ground in anti-Semitism. "It was weird. Winston was raised as a Black Muslim, and we were surprised" to be put together, Recruit Prish later recounts. "We both agreed that the Jews owned the first slave ships."

"Prish was pretty cool," Winston later concurs. "He told you the truth, so you knew where he stood. We agreed that a race war is going to come." Back home in inner-city Washington, he says dryly, "the National Guard comes out sometimes. They got M-16s. We got AK-47s."

From then on, the two would-be racists, black and white, become almost buddies. "We stuck up for each other after that," Prish says. "He's really just a straight-up homey-g thug." He means that as praise.

Prish also develops another unexpected friendship, with Paul Buijs, the seventeen-year-old Dutch-American pacifist who is the weakest member of 3086. Not only are both favorite targets of the drill instructors, but in a unit dominated by lovers of rap and country music, they also share tastes in alternative and screeching "industrial" music—Rage Against the Machine, Smashing Pumpkins, the Cranberries, Nine Inch Nails.

Platoon 3086 forms for dinner on the old runway, metal trays held in the prescribed manner, with arms flush at the sides, bent ninety degrees at the elbow. A truck arrives from the mess hall. "Sit down and eat. We ain't got time for formalities," orders Staff Sergeant Rowland. Then, in the next breath, he contradicts himself, yelling at Recruit Prish: "Take that cover off! What's the first thing we do when we sit down?" The recruit doffs his utility cap. The senior drill instructor takes a moment to review the hand signals used in combat patrols. Then the platoon eats silently in rank-and-file formation, the only sounds the wind whistling in the pines and their collective munching on chicken.

And they are almost all happy.

Most of the recruits have addressed their shortcomings in fitness, marksmanship, drilling, and knowledge. But in each platoon, three or four lag, and are hammered for their faults by DIs and recruits alike. In Parris Island's manifestly unfair system, the group suffers for the sins of its individual members: Every time a slow recruit messes up, the entire platoon is punished with additional exercise. They begin to sound likes DIs themselves, shouting at the end of a warm-up jog to the laggards behind them, "C'mon, run it out!"

"The ones who are getting harder are getting mad at the ones who are slower, 'cause when the slow ones slow down, we take it out on the whole platoon," observes Sergeant Carey as the platoon settles into bleachers under live oaks for a lesson on hand grenades. White smoke from a detonated illumination grenade hangs in the small shiny leaves of the trees.

Behind him, an instructor lectures. "You don't roll it. You throw it in the room to make it bounce off the walls and corners so they can't pick it up." Then he drops an incendiary grenade into an old metal ammunition box. The grenade flares to 4,000 degrees. The metal turns red, then white, then burns, leaving a fist-size hole in the side of the box. "That's a motivating grenade, is it not?" he asks in the distinctively precise patois of the Parris Island teacher.

They march to the live grenade range, where they will crouch in cinderblock "throwing pits" and hurl live M-67 fragmentation grenades at two enemy dummies in foxholes in a dusty field. Next to Throwing Pit One, "Safety Pit B" is pockmarked from where a nervous female recruit dropped a grenade four months earlier. "No one was hurt, except pride," reports Sgt. James Watson, one of the instructors on the live grenade range.

"There ain't no friggin' room for error out here," begins Staff Sgt. Kevin Crandall, warning recruits beginning to nod in the warm southern morning amid the buzz of mosquitoes. "So if you're in such nasty shape that you can't keep your eyes open, you better pack your trash and go home, 'cause you're in the wrong line of work."

As the platoon lines up at the base of the berm to wait its turn, the distinctions among the stronger and weaker recruits become clearer. Those who are lacking are being pushed hard by the DIs. But the DIs are easing up somewhat on the better ones—not treating them as equals, but bantering with them a bit, giving them a taste of what it will be like to be considered a Marine.

Sergeant Watson asks Jumal Flow where he is from. "Sir, Cooperstown, New York, sir," responds Recruit Flow, jumping to attention.

"That's where that baseball place is?"

"Yes, sir," says the recruit.

Sergeant Watson draws himself up. "That place should be the Hall of Shame for Sore Losers. Bunch of babies, understand, crying over getting paid $1.5 million to do something I'd do for free." Sergeant Watson makes about $1,600 a month.

"Sir, this recruit thinks that too, sir," says Recruit Flow. He smiles at the unexpected civility of the exchange.

A few feet away, Recruit Buijs, the perpetual laggard, is receiving far rougher treatment. "You just want the uniform," Sergeant Carey snarls at Recruit Buijs, who stands at attention before him. *Bang!* A fragmentation grenade explodes on the other side of the berm. Recruit Buijs flinches. "You don't want to earn it."

Bang! Another grenade explodes, shaking leaves on the nearby oaks and kicking up a fifty-foot-high column of dust. "You want everything on a silver platter," the heavy hat intones. *Bang!*

"This recruit is often classified as a screwup, sir," Recruit Buijs observes later, while walking sentry duty in the woods. His delicate, observant face scrunches in thought. He wants to be precise. "But this recruit respects what they're doing here. This recruit used to bitch about stuff that this recruit now understands doesn't matter." Nevertheless, he is sticking to his pacifistic guns. As he explains why, he slips back to the first person, perhaps because, as his drill instructors suspect, his individualism still lurks just under the surface. "I still don't believe in killing, really." Why, then, did he join an organization where people shout "Kill, kill, Marine Corps" three times a day? "Love of America, the mentality of Americans—the good Americans," he shrugs enigmatically. The answer goes deeper, but he isn't willing to get into it.

But the sorriest member of the entire series of platoons—3084, 3085, and 3086—is Platoon 3085's Recruit Waldron. The drill instructors are ready to give up on this skinny nineteen-year-old with a lingering acne problem. So, in the shade of a live oak near the grenade range, he is being worked over verbally by the company commander, Capt. Jeffrey Chessani, who left the high plains oil fields of western Colorado in 1986 and enlisted in the Corps, going through boot camp before being selected for Officer Candidate School. A tight-lipped, gray-skinned man whose face is chiseled in a way that makes him appear older than his thirty-two years, the captain wants to see if the young recruit really is hopeless. Recruit Waldron has been stuck on the island for months with one simple problem: He cries nearly every time someone shouts at him. And the United States Marine Corps doesn't want to have a weepy Marine on its hands, so it won't graduate him.

The DIs and officers think Recruit Waldron's problem is that he lacks an emotional "shell." "You better issue yourself a mental helmet and flak jacket," says Captain Chessani, gesturing at the protective gear worn by recruits preparing to throw grenades, "because if you don't, I'm going to send you home. *And you've got nothing to go home to, do you?*"

"No, sir," says the quivering recruit, standing at attention and looking miserable. Grenades bang in the background.

Other drill instructors gather to watch the instruction. Behind them, recruits lined up to throw grenades watch impassively. "It's unfortunate, but sometimes you use the negative example," shrugs Sergeant Carey.

Gunnery Sergeant Camacho, the gunny for the series, takes over working on Recruit Waldron. He orders the recruit to do "mountain climbers," a kind of running in place while in the push-up position. "You want to cry, we're going to give you a reason to cry," vows the hawk-nosed Texan. Tears stream down the recruit's face, which is scrunched up as if to squeeze them off. "Aye, sir!" Waldron shouts. Then he sobs.

The observing DIs are strikingly unsympathetic. "He's just full of water," laughs Sgt. B. K. Jones, senior drill instructor for 3084, the recruit's platoon.

"Where's momma?" taunts Staff Sgt. Marvin Frasier, 3085's tightly wrapped senior. The next day, he says, Recruit Waldron will be shipped over to the Drill Instructors School, where he will be displayed as an example of the sorry material with which DIs sometimes must work.

But even before that happens, Sgt. J. J. Pettis, the junior DI for 3084, sounds a note of caution. In a few hours his platoon will be out in the piney woods practicing "night combat movement." That remote exercise will present a perfect opportunity for the other recruits to beat up on the deeply resented weakest 10 percent. "We better be out there tonight, because otherwise West will get out there and catch Waldron and pound him," says Sergeant Pettis. West is a hard-charging, valued recruit, so they will be careful to prevent him from doing something that could get him thrown out of boot camp.

Captain Chessani later says that Recruit Waldron is a bit of an oddity. "Most of the guys like that who aren't going to adjust, you usually lose up front," in the first few weeks. "I felt bad for him, and I think they done him wrong," concludes Recruit Daniel Keane, a soft-spoken, observant community college dropout whose father is a bond trader for Merrill Lynch. "But I wouldn't want him next to me in combat." And that, they have been taught here, is the ultimate measure of a man.

But Waldron somehow combines vulnerability with a persistence that eventually wins the grudging admiration of the DIs. Indeed, although dropped from Captain Chessani's Kilo Company, Waldron eventually graduates from boot camp and goes on to become a specialist in military intelligence.

Platoon 3086 spends the entire next day learning how to read maps, or at least pretending they are learning.

The day after that brings the gas chamber, which provokes more worry than it turns out to merit. In keeping with the Marine Corps bias for simplicity, the squat cinderblock building is identified by a plain sign: GAS CHAMBER. (Other U.S. armed services would be more inclined to call it the "Nuclear-Biological-Chemical Warfare Training Facility.") The recruits file in at the gray door bearing the

Marine Corps emblem. The DIs set two canisters of tear gas on the cement floor. The recruits' faces begin to sting. Lee, following the instructions, scrunches up his face to hold his breath. Each recruit must take off his mask, put it back on, then take it off again and hold it at his waist for thirty seconds, then don it again. This would be difficult in any circumstance, but they must do it while the gas soaks into their raw sand flea bites, making each bite feel like a needle pricking into the skin.

The chamber isn't the terror some had imagined—except for Jonathan Prish, who thinks his mask isn't working and panics. He breaks for the door, but is held against the wall by a drill instructor from another platoon. "I'm getting out of here!" shouts Prish. The DI says, "No, you're not." Sergeant Carey isn't cutting anybody slack even in the chamber: When Anthony Randolph mumbles a response, the heavy shouts, "When I talk to you, sound off!" So Randolph shouts, "Yes, sir!"—and gets a hacking blast of gas.

They file out of the building into the sunny day, arms held out straight. Tears stream from their squinting eyes, mucous from their noses, vomit from the mouths of some. Platoon 3086 shows more spirit than most platoons, attempting a few weak "hoorahs." "Shut your mouth and open your eyes," shouts an instructor, in another one of those reflexive phrases that could be a Parris Island motto.

"It was kind of scary," concludes James Andersen, one of the Pittsburgh recruits. "But it wasn't as bad as everyone made it out to be."

The most fun they have during "Warrior Week" is their night crawl through booby-trapped woods. At 7:00 P.M. one evening, they settle into a warehouselike room on the edge of the swamps for a class on "The Principles of Night Movement." It is the essence of Marine training: precise, commonsensical, and rooted in experience. "If the enemy has few flares up, that's telling you he has a lot of patrols out," the instructor says. And to suppress a cough while on patrol, Marines press two fingers against the Adam's apple. The second part of the class is held outside in the dusk, to permit the recruits' eyes to adjust to night vision. It also tests the recruits' discipline as they try to pay attention while the sand fleas come out in force. Recruit Gregory Tenhet, running as fast as he can while wearing his helmet, combat pack, and rifle, cuts behind a drill instructor and shouts, "By your leave, sir!"

For the actual night movement, Sergeant Carey and his friend Sergeant Humphrey, the demon of 3086's first personal inspection, plant themselves in the pitch-dark woods. Starting on the edge of the runway, recruits try to crawl along booby-trapped paths toward the two drill instructors. Illumination flares rocket overhead and then swing down on parachutes. As the flares descend, they create a deeply disorienting visual effect: "moving shadows" cruise through the woods, making it seem that the trees and bushes have come alive in some boot camp version of *Macbeth*.

As each flare arcs overhead, the recruits melt slowly into the ground, averting their eyes from the bright light to preserve their night vision. When darkness—and visual sanity—return, they again begin crawling with Kabuki-like deliberateness, trying to sense the strings that run to the traps.

There is a flash and firecracker bang as Recruit Linsky, the determined carpet layer from New Jersey, trips the first trap. "Dear Mr. and Mrs. Linsky," Sergeant Carey begins dictating into the flare-crossed night. "We regret to inform you that your son was killed *because he was stupid!*" This parody of the standard Defense Department notification to the next of kin of a casualty strikes closer to home than the platoon can know: In 1985, Sergeant Carey's own mother and father received a telegram that began in a very similar way, after their son was critically injured by an Evinrude 35 while on scuba exercises in the Mediterranean.

Recruit Parise, the Pittsburgh artist, is next to blow off a booby trap. Sergeant Humphrey ghoulishly rasps across the woods: "Guess what? *Mail me home!*"

The flag-raising on Iwo Jima is probably the most famous image of World War II. It also captures the essence of Marine Corps culture in a single image—of a faceless team of men struggling to achieve a larger goal. (Joe Rosenthal photo, Associated Press)

The front gate to Marine boot camp at Parris Island. The recruits of 3086 passed through here during the middle of the night. The best of them didn't leave the island for another eleven weeks, until they had become Marines. (USMC/Cpl. Mark J. Harmon, USMC)

(Left) Sgt. Darren Carey, the perfectionist drill instructor who dominated the lives of the members of Platoon 3086 for eleven weeks. His history as a Marine is visible here: The "scuba bubble" and parachutist's wings on his chest show him to be an elite "Force Recon" scout Marine. The vertical scar alongside his mouth marks the time in 1985 when a speedboat ran him down in the Mediterranean, breaking his jaw, fracturing his skull, and knocking out several teeth. (USMC PHOTO)

(Right and below) Sgt. Carey leading from the front. At age thirty, he still scores a perfect 300 on the Marine physical fitness test—though now he aches for a day or two afterward. (USMC PHOTO)

Welcome to boot camp: The first major event in recruit training is "combat hitting skills," a boxing match held in a ring not much bigger than a telephone booth. First straight punch to the head wins. (Both photos: USMC PHOTO/Cpl. William M. Lisbon, USMC)

(Above) Daily life on Parris Island: Each recruit is nearly anonymous in a group, yet faces a constant stream of tests as an individual. A new platoon wearing the "shaveheads" of newly arrived recruits cooks in the sun of Parris Island's Leatherneck Square. (USMC PHOTO/Cpl. William M. Lisbon, USMC)

(Left) A more experienced recruit leaps through the island's obstacle course. (USMC PHOTO/Sgt. Pete Trujillo, USMC)

Marine boot camp instruction is given the old-fashioned way: loud and in your face. Here a "close combat" instructor prepares a recruit for pugil stick fighting. (USMC PHOTO/Cpl. William M. Lisbon, USMC)

(Above) "Without my rifle I am useless. . . ." So says part of the Marine equivalent of the Lord's Prayer. Every Marine, whether cook, clerk, or infantryman, is expected to be a rifleman. This is the core of the Marines's cultivation of a warrior culture. (USMC PHOTO/Cpl. J. R. Lewis, USMC)

That includes women as well. The Marines train female recruits separately but hold them to equal standards on the rifle range. In the Parris Island view of the world, marksmanship is the ultimate test of individual discipline: Anyone who can follow orders can learn to shoot accurately. (USMC PHOTO/Cpl. William M. Lisbon, USMC)

There is a reason that the sergeants who run boot camp are called "drill instructors" rather than "military instructors." Drill is where individual discipline comes together with unit discipline. Boring and repetitive, the sixty-two basic movements of drill are the heart of boot camp—morning, noon, and night. (USMC PHOTO/Cpl. William M. Lisbon, USMC)

Two of the more unusual paintings hanging in the Pentagon. Above, James Webb's official portrait as Navy secretary. Webb's novel, *Fields of Fire,* is next to his left hand. (Artist: Richard Whitney) Below, Gen. Al Gray's official portrait as commandant of the Marine Corps. (Artist: Peter Egeli) Together, the two men helped remake the Marine Corps in the late 1980s.

"Warrior Week" events: Out of the gas chamber (above), and down the rappel tower (right). (Both photos: USMC PHOTO/Cpl. William M. Lisbon, USMC)

A band of brothers. Above, Platoon Guide Andrew Lee sits at the front of Platoon 3086 during its "Warrior Week" in the woods. Below, members of 3086 assemble after graduating. For many, this moment will be the high point of their entire lives. (Both photos: Personal collection of Cpl. Charles H. Lees III)

Graduation: Staff Sgt. Ronny Rowland, the little Arkansan drill instructor, welcomes Charles Lees III, the big Samoan-American recruit, into the Marines. (Personal collection of Cpl. Charles H. Lees III)

Lees with Sgt. Leo Zwayer, the junior drill instructor, who was transformed into a leader by his experience of training recruits. (Personal collection of Cpl. Charles H. Lees III)

This page and page 14 following: Six shots of 3086 members, posing in dress blues. (Credit for all six photos: USMC PHOTO)

Charles Lees III

Andrew Lee

Mark Beggs

Gary Moore, Jr.

Chad Shelton

Paul Buijs

In the Marines: Two recruits who barely made it through Parris Island went on to thrive in the Corps. Jonathan Prish had once been a white supremacist teenager living in Alabama; Paul Buijs was a pacifist living in the Netherlands. They became friends in boot camp. Above, Prish strolls on a street near the U.S. Embassy in London. (USMC PHOTO/PH2 Guy T. Noffsinger, USNR) Below, Buijs works on the internal equipment of an EA-6B Marine electronic jamming aircraft. USMC PHOTO/LCpl. Jon Wilke)

Two of the happiest graduates of Platoon 3086 were Prish and Jonathan Crigger, who both wound up as guards at a U.S. military installation near the American embassy in London.

An illumination grenade ignites near a bush. A knot of recruits prone behind the bush begins squabbling in whispers about who is at fault. Sergeant Carey detects the identity of one recruit by the voice. "Why are you giving me excuses, Warren?" he says almost bitterly to Recruit Robert Warren, the quiet former grocery clerk from Murfreesboro, North Carolina. "What excuses am I going to give your parents when you're dead?"

The stronger recruits feel they are finally in their element. This is what they joined the Marines to do. "The first time I got the feeling of being a Marine is when I was lying in the dirt when the illumination grenade when off," Recruit Donald Campas later relates. "It lit up the whole forest. Then I heard Sergeant Carey yell. A feeling came over my body of actually being in a war."

Earnest Winston, the gangbanger from Washington, D.C., crawls through the woods with tree branches jabbed into the slits of his helmet cloth, effectively blending his dark head into the shadows and bushes under the pine trees. "Awesome—that is *motivated,* Winston," says an impressed Sergeant Carey. Winston stares back at him, saying nothing but suppressing a smile.

By eleven at night, the platoon is out of the woods, exhausted but elated. All told, 3086 and its companion platoons tripped six of the fifteen traps set on the night movement course. As the platoon assembles in the heavy, warm South Carolina night, Sergeant Carey runs them through his favorite rote: "Every day you've got to do what?"

"Test yourself, sir," the weary voices respond.

"And if you don't?"

"It's a wasted day, sir." They happily march back to their tents near the runway, bringing to an end a seventeen-hour day of classes, marching, and crawling through the woods. Recruit Mickeal Perkins, a former fireman from Rockingham, North Carolina, is feeling very much like a Marine. Dealing with booby traps, he says, "is better than having the drill instructors screaming in your face about how you didn't pack your trash right."

"It was intense," he says of the night combat movement course, adopting Sergeant Carey's vocabulary. "Intense" and "motivated" are the highest praise. Their opposites are three synonyms: "nasty," "undisciplined," and "civilian." For example, at mail call held at dusk one night in the woods, Sergeant Carey denounces a recruit's package of brownies from home as "nasty civilian food."

Civilian life seems remote to the platoon. "People outside military life are repulsive," says the platoon's top member, Andrew Lee, as he sits cross-legged under a pine tree and cleans his M-16. "I don't like civilians. I get on the T in Boston and, *ugh.*" He makes a sour face. "I think America could use a lot more military discipline. Outside of South Boston, I feel it's gotten pretty pathetic. No one strives to be their best."

"Some of it has its benefits," adds Benjamin Read, the former forestry student from Charlotte, North Carolina, who is the platoon's top marksman. "But for the most part I believe America's teenagers and city life are disgusting."

Lonnie Christian, a former construction worker from Stroudsburg, Pennsylvania, who eventually will score a perfect 300 on the Parris Island physical fitness test—matching Sergeant Carey—and who also is 3086's Protestant lay reader, says that "civilian life is 'nasty.' " Without being asked, he explains. "The reason for that is simple: The Marine Corps is a band of brothers who live by the motto 'Semper Fidelis' "—that is, "always faithful."

Charles Lees, the Holy Cross graduate who is regarded as the smartest member of the platoon, goes whole hog in deploying Sergeant Carey's phraseology. Civilian life, he says, is "nasty, too much 'me-ness' and selfishness, lazy, undisciplined."

Tough little Mark Beggs, the king of the pugil pit, says that civilian life is characterized by "so many undisciplined and unmotivated people who bring the country down."

Lesser recruits agree. When recruits are asked to fill out a questionnaire about their views of civilian life, almost all use the language of their drill instructors. Eric Didier, who came here from the wealthy Washington suburb of Potomac, Maryland, criticizes civilian life as "lazy and unstructured." Another three recruits call it "nasty." And seventeen more term it "undisciplined."

The only member of the platoon expressing reservations about this general indictment of civilian life is Craig Hoover, the detached Maryland suburbanite who just isn't buying the Marine Corps' vision of life. He looks at Parris Island as a kind of goofy summer camp; he is strong and smart enough so that it never pushes him into the kind of transforming experience that many recruits will experience here. He won't fail boot camp, but boot camp will fail him. "Society today lacks discipline, but there has to be a yin to every yang," Hoover says. "For every disciplined person, there will be an undisciplined one." He isn't sure which he will wind up being.

Despite Parris Island's reputation for brutality, even sadism, the platoon's members generally find it a more courteous place than the neighborhoods they left behind. James Andersen, the former Taco Bell shift manager from Bethel Park, Pennsylvania, outside Pittsburgh, describes the civilian world as "rude, uncaring." Jonathan Crigger, who worked in a grocery store in Oakwood, Virginia, complains that in civilian life, "nobody helps each other, they're all just one person."

The black and Hispanic recruits especially welcome the relative racial toleration they find on Parris Island. Luis Polanco-Medina, who used to work at an Olive Garden restaurant in northern New Jersey, says military life is "a healthier, safer environment." If America were more like the Marines, he says, "There would be less crime, less racial tension among people—because Marine Corps discipline is also about brotherhood." Jumal Flow says that a dose of the Marine approach could help people "*respect* each other more."

This element of trust may be the biggest difference between the Marines and civilian life—and the biggest attraction the Corps holds for today's youth. For years, the University of Michigan has surveyed the opinions of high school seniors. One of the questions it puts to them is, "Generally speaking, would you say that most people can be trusted or that you can't be too careful in dealing with people?" In 1975, 40 percent of high school seniors agreed that "you can't be too careful." By 1992, the figure had shot up to 59 percent.

For all that, racial tension still slips into the platoon. Parise, the Pittsburgh artist, grows tired in the woods of what he considers to be tough-guy posturing by Winston, the D.C. thug. "You ain't as tough as you act," Parise mutters. Winston regards the other recruit from under lidded eyes. Shawn Bone, Winston's friend from Alabama, replies, "I've shot white boys for less." So, Parise later recalls, "I get stupid, and I said, 'It's been a long time since I've hung a nigger.' It was stupid. It wasn't really a racial thing, but I used the words."

The incident blows over without escalating—partly, Winston says later, because Parise "said a lot of smart stuff," but never used quite that language. "It wouldn't have been tolerated."

At end of day, mail call again goes badly for Recruit Barrows. Sitting cross-legged in the dust with the platoon, he doesn't even wait for the order. When he sees his brother's envelope in Sergeant Carey's hand and hears a sharper tone in the heavy hat's voice, he sighs, stands, and walks to a tree. (It says on the outside: "Don't worry, my DI was a dickhead, too.") Barrows begins doing "Ranger push-ups"—hands on ground, booted feet about two feet up the trunk, so that his body is parallel to the ground when his arms are extended. He exercises for the remainder of the mail call. After a short break to clean rifles and straighten up gear, the platoon counts off down the tents in the gloomy woods. At the end Recruit Lee shouts, "Sir, the count on deck is fifty-six rough, tough, can't-get-enough United States Marine Corps recruits, sir!"

At night, James Peters sneaks out and lies on his back on the old runway, looking at the sky, enjoying the simple things in life. For the last eight weeks, few members of the platoon have had a chance to gaze at the stars.

Well before dawn the next morning, 3086 is again sitting in cross-legged formation, this time with its companion platoons. Today they must take the combat conditioning tests: climb up a twenty-foot rope, run three miles in formation, and perform the fireman's carry, as if they were rescuing a wounded buddy. All three tests must be done in modified combat dress—carrying a rifle and two full canteens, and wearing a helmet. This is also the day when Gary Moore Jr., always close to the edge, comes close to punching his ticket off the island.

The other platoons go first up the ropes, climbing up into the darkness, where bats dart among the swarming bugs. Recruit Waldron manages to make it to the top—but forgets to follow the instruction to shout out his name when he gets there. He is told he has failed. He slides down the rope, silently weeping.

Failing recruits ignite a slow burn in Sergeant Carey. He tells his DI colleagues that he would just as soon kick them off the island right now, for the good of the platoon today and the Corps tomorrow. But regulations inexplicably force him to give the laggards another chance. "It almost degrades me," he hisses in genuine anger.

At 6:50 A.M., the platoons take off on a three-mile run. It must be performed in thirty-four minutes. Sergeant Carey's voice rings out from a half mile down the old runway: *Sound off/ Here we go/ Tighten it up/ Suck it up/ Marine Corps shuffle!* He leads the platoon across the finish line at 7:21:47 A.M., leaving the slow runners two minutes to follow him in.

Sweaty and red-faced, most of the platoon paces under the outdoor showers, then stands in an open field, steam rising from their bodies in the cool morning air. But Recruit Buijs seems amused by something, and he is pulled aside by Sergeant Zwayer: "Buijs, you laugh because you want attention. *But you never want to do anything!*"

The laggards begin crossing the finish line. Gary Moore isn't among them. The weary recruit has dropped out, unaware that casualties of the run must receive what the DIs laughingly call "the silver bullet"—a rectal thermometer, to ensure that their body core isn't dangerously overheated from the run. He is taken into a military ambulance, where a corpsman tells him to drop his shorts. Moore pushes him away and tries to scramble out of the vehicle. A nearby DI shouts at the recruit to do as he is told. Moore looks for a moment as if he is willing to fight him rather than follow the order.

Moore emerges from the ambulance looking shamefaced. Sergeant Carey shouts at him in disbelief: "You copped an attitude with a drill instructor?"

"No, sir," says the hangdog recruit. "I copped an attitude with myself."

Sergeant Carey drops his voice. "You're killing yourself, Moore."

Looking pained, Recruit Moore whispers, "This recruit can't hack it, sir."

Sergeant Carey isn't looking for that sort of answer. "I'm sick of motivating you, Moore. Today you spaz out and start pushing corpsmen and drill instructors when they're trying to help you and make sure you don't freaking die. That makes me feel *real* good. I guess we're just lip service to you." Moore listens in silence, his clothes drenched, his bootlaces, belt, and pants undone. Sergeant Carey delivers his order: "Let me tell you, Moore, face the music like a man."

The platoon assembles to march to the third test. Recruit Buijs is a few inches out of "alignment"—that is, not marching exactly behind the person in front of him. Sergeant Carey wearily says, "Mommy's not around and we need attention, right, Buijs?" The heavy hat is becoming genuinely and deeply aggravated with Buijs, Moore, and the others in the bottom 10 percent of the platoon.

At the fireman's carry, each recruit must run fifty yards across a field, pick up a "casualty"—a fellow recruit lying limp on the ground—and then jog back, carrying the recruit and both men's rifles. Most stumble through but succeed in the allotted forty seconds. Tough little Beggs eats it up. He shoulders Shane Logan, who weighs 200 pounds to his 140, and actually sprints the fifty yards back across the field. Even the DIs from the other platoons stop to watch and nod their heads in approval. Andrew Lee also notices. "He doesn't shout," the guide says of Beggs. "He doesn't strive to impress people. He just does his job."

Wet and dirty, the platoon stands in formation on the intersection of two runways, strips naked, and there on the cement changes to dry, clean fatigues. Andrew Lee scans the platoon and then "squares away" a recruit who has failed to properly stow his gear inside his pack. Sergeant Zwayer orders them to drink an entire one quart canteen. Recruit Buijs, who is having a bad day, fails to completely drink his. When the DI orders them to hold their canteens upside down over their heads, to demonstrate they have all replenished their bodies with water, a trickle runs out of the young recruit's canteen and drips off his head, across his face, and onto his fatigues. Sergeant Zwayer, normally the least showy of the platoon's three DIs, watches in disbelief. "I'm tired of your mother's boy attitude," he shouts. He knocks the canteen from Buijs's hand, then kicks it skittering down the runway. A detonation erupts at a nearby mine warfare class, as if in sympathy with the DI's mood.

Aside from the laggards, the platoon looks and talks like Marines. They don't yet have the technical skills they will need "in the Fleet," but they are indoctrinated into the culture. To the Corps, that is by far the most important thing. They are nearly ready for the Corps.

CHAPTER FIVE

READY

Week Nine, the week after "Warrior Week," is taken up by several days of "A Line" firing. The platoon marches back out to the rifle range to fire its M-16s at moving targets, to fire while wearing gas masks, to fire in low-light conditions, and to fire M-60 machine guns, which sound like giant woodpeckers hammering away at the air. Even this late in boot camp, young Paul Buijs continues to lag. At night, after lights out, Sabella, Bone, and some other members of 3086 whisper that the young recruit should be given a secret "blanket party"—that is, wrapped in a blanket and beaten with soap bars in socks. It is a punishment they know from the war movie *Full Metal Jacket,* which most rented from video stores and viewed before leaving for Parris Island. (In using Hollywood to shape their approach to the real military, they are unconsciously falling into a long American tradition. One of the best lines out of the Vietnam War was the young Marine who, when wounded, shouted, "I *hate* this movie!") A majority of the platoon appears to favor going after Buijs. Arguing against the party is the worry that their DIs will get in trouble if Buijs becomes an "allegator."

Also, some in the platoon point out that the most vehement advocates of the blanket party come from the weaker end of the platoon. This is natural—those least able to bear the extra physical training are those most provoked by Buijs's laggard ways. "We were getting close to graduation," Sabella, the would-be ringleader, later explained. "Everybody was doing what they were supposed to be doing. He just kept screwing up and screwing up. He was real slow, he didn't know what to do in close-order drill. Always talking to someone else. So we thought it might make him learn." Interestingly, Sabella will make it through boot camp, but then desert a few months later—while Buijs will go on to thrive in the Corps. Little Frank DeMarco agrees that Buijs is the biggest screwup in the platoon, always the last to get dressed or get out of the shower. But he objects to beating him by invoking the golden rule. "I say, do unto others what you want done to you," he argues. Also, he dislikes Bone and his buddies because they call him "Shorty."

The strongest members of the platoon get wind of the talk and squelch it. Andrew Lee and Charles Lees don't much like Buijs, whom they consider a whiner. But the seventeen-year-old reminds Lee of his younger brother of the same age. "Pat would have a hard time of it, too," he says later. Lees uses his firewatch duty that night to put out the word: "There will be no blanket party. We're not beating up a member of the platoon. And I pack a big punch."

Buijs appears oblivious of the talk about him. On the fourth day of "A Line" firing, he twists his ankle. He is put on light duty, meaning he will accompany the platoon but simply sit on the sidelines when it does anything requiring exertion. So he stands on his crutches and watches mutely as 3086 navigates the combat assault course, crawling through mud puddles under barbed wire, then running across a field and bayoneting enemy dummies.

Buijs's inflammation worsens overnight. The next day he is put on "no duty"—a status, which, if it continues, will result in his being recycled out of the platoon just two weeks short of graduation. Faced with the prospect of being thrust among strangers, Buijs begins to reconsider his nonconformist approach to boot camp. "During those days, I realized what it felt like to not be part of the platoon," he explains later. "So I thought about being like everybody else. I wasn't fighting it anymore. I wasn't scared anymore. I all of a sudden got the drive I needed, that some guys had the whole time."

The next day, even though he is on crutches, Buijs strains and manages to do twenty pull-ups for the first time in his life. Two days later, on training day forty-eight, he returns to full duty. Other recruits sense the shift in the platoon's youngest member. "In that last couple of weeks of boot camp," John Hall says later, "I noticed a difference with Buijs—he dropped his light voice, started sounding off like a man." Andrew Lee takes advantage of Buijs's new attitude to try to improve Buijs's sloppy drill skills. He wakes the younger recruit at night and tries to show him how to march without bouncing up and down. He has little success, but Buijs is trying.

The platoon quickly falls into a new routine in this last phase of training. On May 9th, they run four miles, then perform nearly three hours of close order drill, then go to chow, then sit through an afternoon of instruction on how to deal with Marine Corps paperwork. The following days follow the same pattern: exercise, drill, and then a brief on how to travel as a Marine, how to behave on leave, how to pursue educational benefits.

The platoon also uses the time to sort itself out. One night during Week Ten, it gives Sabella a kind of nonviolent blanket party. He has never really bonded with most members of 3086, mainly because (correctly, it turns out) they don't believe the stories he tells them about his father being a sergeant major in the Marine Corps and various other stretchers. Lees, on sentry duty, notices that Sabella is sleeping with his eyes open. He shines his flashlight in Sabella's eyes and gets no response. So he wakes up some other recruits to show them this oddity. They in turn wake others. "We all stood there and looked at him, about twelve of us," Lees says. Sabella never awakens.

The next morning, Sergeant Zwayer calls Prish to the quarter-deck for extra exercise. The bedraggled recruit marches up. But this time he is followed by Lee, Lees, Beggs, and other leaders of the platoon. Then the rest of the platoon comes up. Sergeant Zwayer watches, arms folded, in silent approval of this show of solidarity. "It was good for Prish," he later comments, "because it helped him realize the team concept—that he may be a little weaker, but he has the Marines behind him."

Recruit Warren has a simpler explanation: "We just got tired of Zwayer fucking with him."

On May 12th, the platoon runs through the barriers, ropes, and towers of the confidence course one last time. Andrew Lee achieves boot camp nirvana. Pitted against recruits from the two companion platoons in a race over several barriers and then up the hanging ropes, he makes it to the top of his rope and shouts "Lee, 3086," before the other two even make it to the bottom. As he is walking back to the platoon, arm sockets aching a bit, Sergeant Carey takes him aside. "There isn't much else you could beat me at," the heavy tells the startled recruit, "but you beat me at that obstacle course." It is the highlight of Lee's eleven weeks on Parris Island: "The day the perfect machine told me I could beat him at something. I'll never forget it. God, he was tough." That night he writes a letter to his little brother Pat about his feat.

If 3086 were an Army basic training platoon, Lee would not have had his triumph. In the Army, Buijs would have graduated on Day 48—the day he really stopped being a civilian and started becoming a Marine. Army boot camp is only eight weeks long; by this point in 3086's journey, Army recruits are back home on the block showing off their new uniforms. But the differences between the Marine approach and the Army's run much deeper than simple duration.

The Army's boot camp at Fort Jackson, South Carolina, is just 145 miles to the northwest of Parris Island, but it seems like a parallel universe in a *Star Trek* episode. The military of the same nation is doing essentially the same thing with a similar group of young people—but there is a world of difference. It is immediately noticeable at the front gate: This is an "open post," so there is no guard at the gate. Overall, Fort Jackson's handsome new buildings, sprawling across a slight roll in the wooded South Carolina upland, look nicer than Parris Island—much more like a state university coming off a building spree than like Parris Island, with its ambience of a prison camp in a small southern state not inclined to spend much money coddling criminals.

But the biggest difference is human. Army basic training is intentionally "user friendly." All units at Fort Jackson, which trains support personnel—clerks, cooks, truck drivers, nurses, and mechanics—are gender integrated. Men and women sleep in separate barracks, but do everything else together—and, recruits there say quietly, don't always sleep separately. And the recruits are treated as Army soldiers—indeed, they are referred to not as recruits but as "soldiers-in-training." New recruits getting off the bus at receiving are welcomed in informational tones, rather than verbally assaulted. Then they are shown an eight-minute video about what to expect in the receiving process, given a meal, and sent off to bed for a night's rest before beginning basic training. The next day they are given haircuts, but not shaved bald. Rather than emphasize the culture of the service, as the Marines do, the nine buildings in the Fort Jackson receiving complex emphasize the United States, displaying the flags of the fifty states and portraits of the presidents. Similarly, the rifle ranges at Fort Jackson are named after states, not great battles.

Nor does the tone of training change when they move from receiving to their units. There is no shock theater "Pick-up." "We do not try to intimidate," explains Lt. Col. Mark G. McCauley, commander of the receiving area. "We do not try to strike fear in their hearts. We conduct the handoff in a calm, quiet, professional way. We want the soldiers in training to have a sense of comfort. You can treat somebody with dignity and respect and still get a good performance out of them."

Once assigned to a training unit, they can use the PX, make unlimited telephone calls, and occasionally watch television. There is no training after 3:00 P.M. on Saturdays, and none on Sundays. After two weeks, relatives can visit on Sundays. Once or twice during their training, the soldiers-in-training can attend a pop music concert on base at which pizza and sodas are served.

In some ways, being an Army drill sergeant appears more difficult than being a Marine DI. The Army drill sergeants have to do a similar job with fewer tools and more problems. They wear the same uniforms and exercise clothing as their trainees. They address their troops respectfully, without shouting. Most strikingly, the drill sergeants wishing to give their platoons punishment exercises must themselves do the exercises they assign. The maximum punishment exercise that can be given an individual soldier is ten push-ups. "You've also got the hygiene and emotional issues to deal with—PMS, for example," notes Capt. Matthew Orenstein, commander of Bravo Company, First Battalion of the 28th Infantry. It is a far cry from the life of 3086's DIs.

"Fun" isn't a word one hears on Parris Island. Here it comes naturally to the lips of trainees. "They teach us, but they also make it fun," says Eric Escamilla, a soldier-in-training from Lubbock, Texas. Spec. Sheila Suess, his comrade in Delta Company, agrees as they eat breakfast in their mess hall. At other tables, trainees chat in conversations. No drill sergeants hover, and there is no shouting anywhere in the building. "It isn't always, but it can be fun," says Suess. A recent graduate of Oregon State College, she was given a rank of E-4—that is, just one level below 3086's Sergeant Carey—as part of her enlistment package.

Out on the bayonet assault course, Alpha Company of the Third Battalion, 13th Infantry Regiment, is going through the paces. The platoon sergeant—the Army equivalent of senior drill instructor—addresses them. "Soldiers, please be interested in what I have to say," begins Staff Sgt. Ron Doiron. "This is the only time in your military career you get to do the bayonet assault course. Make the most of it. Let's have some fun out here." Indicating the targets to be bayoneted, he adds, "You're going to make these tires sorry they were ever born tires."

Alpha Company responds to the drill sergeant with a "Hooah"—not the hypercharged, guttural Marine shout, but a polite, semi-loud yell. Then it takes off on the course through the piney woods, climbing over low obstacles, sticking the tires and rubber dummies with bayonets. Jumping down into a trench, Pvt. Tralena Wolfe's knee pops. She comes off the course, sits on a log, and cries.

Out on the range, another unit is firing M-60 machine guns. Four of the guns hammer away simultaneously, making conversation nearly impossible. "It hurts my ears," complains one female soldier in training.

"I don't subscribe to the 'tear 'em down and build 'em up' school," says Lt. Col. James Helis, commander of the 1st Battalion of the 28th Regiment. "We're training them to go into the field Army. There isn't a lot of yelling and shouting there. And there shouldn't be a disconnect between basic training and the field experience."

Essentially, the Army seems to be trying to accommodate itself to changes in society, while the Marines try to separate themselves from those changes. "I wouldn't say we coddle our soldiers," explains Douglas Cook, Fort Jackson's public affairs official. "But we do try to adjust." He says he used to complain about the slack discipline of some new soldiers, "But I realized I was complaining about the state of society, failing to adjust to an ever-changing environment."

Over at Fort Benning, down in the red clay and sand of central Georgia, the drill sergeants roll their eyes when Fort Jackson is mentioned. Benning, where all Army infantrymen are trained, is a far tougher course than Jackson. It is, first and foremost, all male. Benning's trainees march where they need to go, instead of riding buses. They don't take off Saturday afternoons. They aren't allow to talk in their mess halls, and the only eating utensil they are permitted is a spoon, the better to shovel in the food.

Yet where Parris Island is almost theatrical, Benning is simply serious. Drill sergeants, for example, eat in the same mess hall as the trainees. The barracks are kinder, gentler versions of Parris Island, featuring wall lockers and doors on the latrine's toilet stalls, and even private shower stalls. Benning's thirteen-week course for basic infantrymen provides far more military training than does Parris Island. (Marines going into the infantry proceed from the eleven weeks on the island to seven weeks of training at the School of Infantry.) Strikingly, the attrition rate for the Benning basic infantry course hovers at about 14 percent, almost exactly the same as that of males at Parris Island.

Col. Johnny Brooks, commander of Benning's infantry training brigade, says the major difference between Parris Island and Benning is that the Army focuses on training, while the Marines focus on indoctrination. "I think Parris Island does exactly what the Marines want it to do," he says. "It instills discipline, the values of the Corps, and how to wear a uniform, which is very important to the Corps—they have a lot of uniforms.

"But they don't train infantrymen at Parris Island," he continues. "What they do is turn a civilian into a Marine."

Strikingly, Benning virtually refuses to let anyone leave during the first few weeks. That first phase was when 3086 experienced its big rush to the door—most notably, Campbell, Bayless, Maletesta, Torchia, and Poynor. At Benning, some of those washouts would have been told to sit back down. "The first four weeks of training, we won't separate anyone," says Capt. Louis Mayo, watching his Bravo Company, 2nd Battalion, 58th Infantry Regiment, run through the woods during a laser-tag firefight, faces striped in green and black, laser-equipped M-16s at the ready. "Eighty percent of them don't want to be here: 'This wasn't in the commercial.' " Drill sergeants say that if a soldier-trainee tries to wash out by failing to qualify on the rifle range, his instructor will take the rifle, fire it at the target for the trainee, and then say, "There, you're qualified."

As Captain Mayo talks, a soldier lying in a nearby ditch looks up at him. Staff Sgt. Todd Christopherson leans over and shouts at him: "Get behind cover, numbnuts."

At the top of a sandy ridge, Pvt. Charles Day lies sprawled in the pine needles. His laser receptors emit a low whine, indicating that he has been "shot" in the assault on the ridge. "I love it," he says. "I have more discipline now. I'll never take nothing for granted again, sir."

The ubiquitous Sergeant Christopherson looks down at the private: "Hey, dead man, get up when someone's talking to you."

The military training at Benning is good, often far more realistic than Parris Island's. In one training session, two-man "buddy teams" crawl 250 yards down a rifle range. One soldier lies behind an obstacle while the other rushes forward for five seconds. The soldier doing the covering fires live rounds past his buddy to make the "enemy"—pop-up targets at the end of the range—keep down. Reaching the end of the range, they throw practice grenades into an enemy foxhole and a bunker. If they expose themselves too long, or rise too high, they will be hit with a laser by a drill sergeant and declared "dead."

Ultimately, though, Benning seems to lack the rock-hard esprit that distinguishes Parris Island. "The Marines can be choosier," concludes Sgt. Maj. Philip Hafler, the senior NCO of Benning's 1st Battalion of the 38th Infantry Regiment, who joined the Army twenty-nine years ago when a Miami judge gave him the choice of jail or enlisting. "They're smaller, so they're selective. They get the cream of the crop. We get the leftovers. When you're smaller, you can produce quality. We produce quantity." When "prior service" former members of the Navy and Air Force sign up for Army infantry, he notes, they are required to start boot camp at day one. Former Marines are allowed to skip basic training and go directly to infantry training, he says. "They stand out for their professionalism, their manner, the way they attack the job."

If the drill sergeants of Benning had tried to reach into Prish and change him as Sergeant Zwayer did, they might have ended their military careers in disgrace. "If you do something that singles out an individual, if you degrade him, that is a violation of TRADOC policy," says Capt. Michael Moline, commander of the 1st of the 38th's C Company, referring to the Army's Training and Doctrine Command. Sergeant Zwayer's ritual quarterdeckings of Prish likely would have resulted in the dismissal of the DI. "Depending on how bad the abuse was," the captain says, "you could counsel him, remove his hat—which is career-ending—or court-martial him."

The Army approach shouldn't be dismissed out of hand. It may seem lax compared to the Marines, but it produces a military that is extremely good. "Believe it or not," insists Sgt. Yolanda Rose, a thirty-two-year-old drill sergeant at Fort Jackson, "you get the same or better results by not demeaning the soldiers, by not tearing down their egos." Also, there are benefits from being responsive to society, especially in a democracy. Of all the services, the Army has the best record on racial integration. As sociologists Charles Moskos and John Sibley Butler note, its 10,000 officers who are black form the largest group of black executives in the country. For all its harassment and sexual abuse problems, the Army also has taken the integration of women more seriously than have the Marines.

The test of training is how a military performs in the field. The Army did extremely well in the Gulf War. Then, after posting mixed results in Somalia and Haiti, mainly because of uncertain leadership at senior levels, it again performed marvelously in Bosnia, bringing peace in a way that European militaries were unable to do. The main difference between UNPROFOR, which presided over a continuing war, and IFOR, which kept the peace, was the presence of 15,000 American troops. The American troops were noticeably more disciplined than most other militaries—which is a major reason U.S. casualties were so low in the Bosnian mission. American troops, as a rule, don't drink and drive, don't play with their rifles, and don't pick up unexploded mines as potential souvenirs.

For all that, the Army today appears to be drifting into an identity crisis, no longer sure of who it is and what it does. Should it answer the call of Somalia, Rwanda, Haiti, and Bosnia and remake itself into a benign version of an imperial police force, dominated by light infantry? Or should it leave that to the Marines and focus on remaking itself into a twenty-first century force that will be so powerful, so technologically advanced, that it will deter the Russians, Chinese, and Iranians from thinking about tackling it? Or should it try to straddle those two missions, even as it shrinks?

Platoon 3086's recruits were powerfully indoctrinated into the Marine culture. In the Army, by contrast, "We . . . don't make as much sense anymore—we keep on taking on new missions, doing different things," worries one thoughtful officer who has studied the morale problems of Army troops deployed to Somalia and Haiti. "If something makes less sense, it's harder to belong to it." In a trend that appears to reflect that confusion, the propensity of male Americans aged sixteen to twenty-one to enlist in the Army has steadily dwindled for years. In 1989, the Defense Department's *Youth Attitude Tracking Survey* found that 17 percent of those asked were inclined to enlist in the Army. In 1995, the figure had dwindled to 12 percent—the level at which the Marines have held steady for almost a decade. The problem for the Army is that it needs almost twice as many recruits as the Marines every year, and so, unlike the Marines, must recruit people who really aren't very interested in becoming a part of something bigger than themselves. Indeed, Fort Jackson alone—just one of the Army's five basic training camps—trains as many new soldiers every year as does the entire Marine Corps.

Strikingly, the Army's malaise about its identity comes as it finds itself, for probably the first time in its history, with the possible exception of the fifteen years preceding the Spanish-American War, being asked to justify its existence. Self-justification is old hat to the Corps, which is long accustomed to attempts to minimize it or fold it altogether into the Army and Navy. Every new Marine learns at boot camp, as 3086 did, that the Marines are America's "911 force." The Marines' skill at explaining themselves is proving especially useful during an era when many Americans, especially the governing elites, know little and care less about the military. It is a skill the Army is only acquiring slowly and painfully.

To the Marines, the end of the Cold War meant a return to center stage after decades of being a sideshow. One president, Harry Truman, had tried to abolish the Marines. He was succeeded by Dwight Eisenhower, another former Army man with almost as little use for the Corps. Then came Vietnam, where the Marines were discouraged from applying their knowledge of counterinsurgency operations and instead were used in a way they disliked. Retired Marine Lt. Gen. Victor Krulak, father of the current commandant, later wrote that under the command of Army Gen. William Westmoreland, the Marines were forced to disregard all the lessons they had learned in fighting in Central America and the Caribbean, and instead were pushed into waging static, defensive warfare in "a self-punishing, self-defeating cycle brought on by a faulty attritional strategy." The military historian Allan Millett once partially summarized the Marine critique of Vietnam this way: " 'Search and destroy' and 'body count' were created at MACV, not at the headquarters of the III Marine Amphibious Force. Holding Khe Sanh was not a Marine idea, but a requirement from General Westmoreland." Aside from the Vietnam War, during the four decades of the Cold War the Marines never acquired a significant role in the nuclear chess game that dominated the thinking of the Air Force and much of the Navy. "We never were a Cold War force," says Marine Maj. Gen. Carol Mutter.

The end of the Cold War meant a return to another kind of

history, to the messy multipolar world the Marines had thrived in before World War II. In the public mind, the Marines are still associated more often with World War II and *The Sands of Iwo Jima*. But for most of its history, the Corps was the force that fought the nation's small wars—the often ambiguous, usually messy, sometimes undeclared fights that stretched "From the halls of Montezuma/To the shores of Tripoli," as the Corps' hymn puts it. In the 140 years preceding World War II, the Marines made 180 landings in 37 countries, including much of the Caribbean and Central America: Cuba, the Dominican Republic, Puerto Rico, Honduras, Nicaragua, Mexico, and Haiti. It is these sort of places in which the members of Platoon 3086 are likely to spend the most interesting parts of their careers in the Marines.

When the Cold War ended, and the other services began shrinking, the Marines argued that since they hadn't lost any core mission, they shouldn't shrink as much. The Bush administration and Gen. Colin Powell, then the chairman of the Joint Chiefs, didn't buy that. The Bush "Base Force" plan, the first effort to plan a post-Cold War U.S. military, scheduled the Marines to be cut to 159,000 troops. But the Clinton Administration, which subsequently proved itself more inclined to use force in a "gunboat diplomacy" fashion, was persuaded. Its "Bottom-Up Review" plan, completed during the short tenure of Defense Secretary Les Aspin, gave them 174,000 troops, where they stand today. They have been used heavily: In the six years after the Berlin Wall came down, the Marines carried out fifty-five operations—that is, everything from invading northern Haiti to evacuating the U.S. embassy in Liberia—compared to fourteen such operations in the six years preceding the fall of the wall.

In May 1989, even before the wall came down, Al Gray reminded the Senate Armed Services Committee that the end of the Cold War promised a new emphasis on "low-intensity conflict." And, the commandant continued, the Marines had written the book on it. "Before the term 'low-intensity conflict' existed," he observed, "Marines published the *Small Wars Manual*—a publication as applicable today as it was during the 1930s." It was a book after the commandant's own heart, stating that, "the policy that every man, regardless of his specialty, be basically trained as an infantryman has been vindicated time and again, and any tendency to deviate from that policy must be guarded against."

The *Small Wars Manual* is a brilliant little book that deserves a wider audience. It accurately describes the world of the 1990s, even though it was written half a century earlier. It distills many of the lessons the Corps learned before World War II. But it is also interesting because it manages to capture and preserve a sense of the Marine culture, an unusual feat for an official manual. It is primarily that culture, that deep sense of how to behave that is rooted in tradition, that seems to have made the Marines so much more comfortable in the post-Cold War world than the other branches of the U.S. military. With the exception of Bosnia, which few in the U.S. military wanted to touch, the Marines have shown a genuine eagerness to carry out the same missions that the Army has engaged in so reluctantly. As Lt. Martin Nevshemal wryly put it in an article in the *Marine Corps Gazette* about guarding Cuban refugees at Guantanamo Bay, "The Marine Corps will prove that it is up to any task, no matter how 'humanitarian.' "

Stephen Rosen, a Harvard professor of government and author of *Winning the Next War,* an influential study of military innovation, keeps a copy of the manual on his office bookshelf, and makes it required reading for several courses he teaches— one on war and politics, another on the Vietnam War, and a third on the future of war. "For my money, the *Small Wars Manual* is the best book on the subject, period, for any power that wants to engage a guerrilla force," he says.

"Small wars represent the normal and frequent operations of the

Marine Corps," the manual states in its opening paragraph. It goes on to describe with alarming accuracy the sort of operations the American military has found itself performing in the 1990s—dealing with anarchy in Somalia, tribal warfare in Rwanda, tinpot dictators in Haiti, and treaty enforcement in Bosnia. To be sure, some of it is sharply anachronistic. It assumes, for example, that all Marines are white—which was the case when it was written. And it offers an involved discussion of the procurement and employment of horses, including a cross-section diagram of a horse's incisor. It also contains several photographs illustrating how to load a Browning machine gun and accompanying ammunition onto a pony, with shots from the front, side and, yes, the rear.

For all that, much of the manual offers insights that the Army has only slowly and painfully replicated through its own experiences. A major controversy arising out of the Army's disaster in Somalia was that, well before the October 3, 1993, firefight in Mogadishu that left eighteen Americans dead, the commander in the field had asked for armor—tanks or Bradley Fighting Vehicles—only to have that request sat on by top Pentagon officials. That was an omission the manual warned against. "The morale effect of tanks and armored cars is probably greater in small wars operations than it is in a major war," it states. "Tanks are particularly valuable in assaulting towns and villages, and in controlling the inhabitants of an occupied hostile city. Armored cars can be employed to patrol the streets of occupied cities, and to maintain liaison between outlying garrisons." Perhaps with that sort of lesson in mind, the Marines went into Somalia expecting a near-combat experience, and they weren't wrong. They brought their Light Armored Vehicles—a pet project of Al Gray before he became commandant—and used them effectively, surrounding warlords' compounds with them and negotiating the other guy's continued existence. The Army, by contrast, landed in the seeming expectation of carrying out a quasi-diplomatic mission akin to traditional United Nations–style peacekeeping.

The diverse approaches of the Army and Marines to the use of force in the Somalia mission caused the two services to inflict casualties in ways that are counterintuitive. Marines begin to learn to be aggressive in the pugil pits and rifle ranges of boot camp. Don't point your weapon at someone unless you intend to shoot him, 3086 was taught. (And, it was implied, don't let anybody point a weapon at you.) The Marines went into Mogadishu wielding firepower for all to see. The Army tried to act more diplomatically. Paradoxically, the Marines probably wound up killing fewer than 500 Somalis, most shot by Marine snipers who were using force precisely, mainly to protect fellow Marines. The Army was initially far more restrained, but then, as its mission fell apart, retaliated with great firepower, using attack helicopters to fire on mobs in the alleyways of Mogadishu. By some estimates, these tactics killed more than 5,000 Somalis.

The contrasting approaches of the Marines and Army were noted by others on the ground, friend and foe. Robert Oakley, the veteran U.S. diplomat who was the Bush administration's special envoy to Somalia, observed that "the departure of the heavily armed, aggressively patrolling Marines from south Mogadishu obviously had a much greater psychological effect on the Somalis, especially the SNA (Mohamed Farrah Aideed's Somali National Alliance) than the continued presence of the QRF (Quick Reaction Force) from the (Army's) 10th Mountain Division."

Significantly, when the Army occupied Port-au-Prince, Haiti, less than a year after the Mogadishu firefight, it brought with it light tanks—not particularly useful in warfare, but very good for deterring surging mobs and generally keeping the capital quiet. And in 1995, the Army went one step further and used its tank-heavy 1st Armored Division to lead the way into Bosnia.

Another lesson the Army absorbed in Somalia, and now teaches in peacekeeping exercises at its Joint Readiness Training Center in Fort Polk, Louisiana, is that the U.S. military commander in a deployment may find himself reporting to a civilian

U.S. official. This is no great revelation to the Marines. "In small wars, diplomacy has not ceased to function and the State Department exercises a constant and controlling influence over the military operations," the old manual warns. "In certain cases of this kind the State Department has even dictated the size of the force to be sent to the theater of operations."

In the missions of the nineties, it has become commonplace for the U.S. military, led by the Joint Chiefs—whose last two chairmen have been Army officers—to demand that it be given a clear mission, with a defined end state, a deadline for completion, and an "exit strategy" that shows how the American military will get out. Such demands sometimes have helped clarify policy, but also may hobble it by minimizing what the U.S. military will do. The *Small Wars Manual* dismisses the entire idea of seeking predetermined clarity and well-lit exit ramps. "Small wars are conceived in uncertainty, are conducted often with precarious responsibility and doubtful authority, under indeterminate orders lacking specific instructions," it instructs. Then, in the next breath, it adds: "Formulation of foreign policy in our form of government is not a function of the military."

Nor does the manual support Gen. Colin Powell's formulation that operations should only be conducted if they enjoy the clear support of the American people. It doesn't exactly welcome domestic criticism of a mission, but rather simply accepts it as inevitable. "An ordinary characteristic of small wars is the antagonistic propaganda against the campaign or operations in the United States press or legislature," it states. As for a congressional declaration of war, the manual tartly tells the concerned Marine commander: "Whether his government has declared war is no concern of his—that is a diplomatic and international move over which he has no control."

After dealing with four major new "small wars" missions— Somalia, Rwanda, Haiti, and Bosnia—in four years, the Army awakened to this new sort of mission. Look on the bookshelf of

Col. Michael Thompson, the smart young commander of the U.S. replacement brigade that went into Bosnia late in 1996, and there sits *Small Wars*. Today the Army seems to be edging onto Marine Corps turf as it learns how to do the fast, small, difficult jobs, like evacuating embassy personnel from chaotic Third-World capitals. In an iconoclastic new book, *Breaking the Phalanx: A New Design for Landpower in the Twenty-first Century,* Army Lt. Col. Douglas Macgregor argues that the Army should reorganize itself into "mobile combat groups positioned on the frontiers of American security, ready to act quickly and decisively, primed to move with a minimum of preparation." That is, of course, a good summary of exactly what the Marines say they already do. (The differences are that Lt. Col. Macgregor would transport his troops by air, not by sea, and also would send more tanks and artillery and attack helicopters.) It is what 3086 was told from day one would be its eventual mission in the Corps.

But the Marines are also on the move. As the Army edges more onto the Marines' turf, culture can only become more important to the Corps. As one smart Marine officer puts it, the Marines will be forced to think more about their "Marineness"—what it is that sets them apart. More than anything else, they are distinguished by their culture, which shapes how they treat one another and how they fight. If the Army declares that it, like the Marines, is willing to do windows, then the Marines can up the ante: Yes, and we're willing to take casualties when we do. There is now some discussion within the Corps about whether to issue a new manual—*Small Wars II*. More broadly, says Harvard's Professor Rosen, the Marines are thinking in novel ways about "infestation tactics" that might radically change ground warfare. "They've really thought about tearing themselves down and doing something new, much more than the Army has," he reports.

Even the Army has taken note of how the Marines are moving smartly into the twenty-first century. "The Marines are doing a brilliant job of reinventing themselves while retaining their essence, and their achievement should be a welcome challenge to the Army," notes one of the most insightful officers in today's Army, Lt. Col. Ralph Peters, in *Parameters,* the journal of the Army War College.

Probably few U.S. officers have as good a grasp on the nature of today's and tomorrow's U.S. military missions as does Marine Lt. Gen. Anthony Zinni, who worked in the post-Gulf War relief mission to the Kurds in northern Iraq and later in helping get the U.S. out of Somalia. He also is being talked of nowadays as a possible future chairman of the Joint Chiefs of Staff. Interestingly, among his supporters are some Army officers who have heard him speak or worked with him on missions in Iraq and Somalia. He is a commonsensical sort who has been known to follow other senior military speakers with opening remarks such as, "I don't know what the hell that was about, but it sounds like a disaster to me." In Somalia, he recognized the key role that political cartoonists play in Somali politics, and so began to meet and talk with them—"every day," he later wrote.

In the last five years, he said in a 1995 speech, "I have trained and established police forces, judiciary committees and judges, and prison systems; I have resettled refugees, in massive numbers, twice; I've negotiated with warlords, tribal leaders, and clan elders; I have distributed food, provided medical assistance, worried about well-baby care, and put in place obstretical clinics; I've run refugee camps; and I've managed newspapers and run radio stations to counter misinformation attempts."

Lt. Gen. Zinni has distilled his experiences in a talk on "twenty lessons learned" that feels like a modern appendix to the *Small Wars Manual.* The earlier you go in, the better, he argues. Start planning as early as possible, and coordinate it with organizations like the United Nations and private relief groups. Assess the differences between your views of the situation and theirs. Coordinate everything, but decentralize execution. Know the culture. "Who makes decisions in this culture? What is the power of religious leaders? Of political people? Of professionals?" Zinni argues that this is probably where the American military fails most often, as it unconsciously seeks the levers of power that exist in its own society. "Truly, the decision makers are at the back of the tent. You have to find them." Restart a key institution, probably the police, as soon as possible. But don't offer well-intentioned help, such as extensive medical care, that you can't sustain. Don't set high expectations. "Don't make enemies, but if you do, don't treat them gently." Give faction leaders a forum in which to gripe. "Everybody that has a gun, you better have a way of talking to them." Be flexible and open to new approaches, such as using nonlethal weapons—that is, gear that disables or inhibits without killing. "Nonlethals" were first used in a large-scale, open way by the Marines under General Zinni during the U.S. and UN evacuation from Somalia in early 1994. Finally, understand that in this sort of operation, the military may not be the centerpiece of the operation.

Much of this, of course, is common sense—which the Marines like to rely on, but which doesn't always wash with other parts of the precedent-oriented, hierarchical U.S. military establishment. As the sociologist Ann Swidler has observed, "common sense" is really just deeply embedded culture: "the set of assumptions so unselfconscious as to seem a natural, transparent undeniable part of the structure of the world." Some of Zinni's rules are straight out of the *Small Wars Manual.* Others are key parts of the Marine Corps' own culture, most especially the one about avoiding making enemies, but not treating them gently if you do. Some of Zinni's findings are over the head of the typical member of 3086. But the entire platoon was sufficiently steeped in Marine culture to be capable of helping implement his rules.

Overall, Zinni's rules read like an updating of how to apply the Marine Corps culture to today's conflicts: Stay loose. Stay focused. Keep it simple. And be honest. Similar messages can be heard in many parts of the Corps, wherever there are good officers willing to seize the initiative—that is, who care more about their mission and their Marines than they do about their careers. This is how Major Davis at the Drill Instructors School summarizes the

Marine Corps way of doing business: "Concentrate on doing a single task as simply as you can, execute it flawlessly, take care of your people, and go home." That doesn't leave a lot of room for the "doctrine" that the Army so loves to write and cite. But those four steps offer an efficient way to run any organization.

Culture is important in all the U.S. military services, but nowhere so much as in the Marines. It is, after all, all they really have. And it is what they pass on at boot camp. When 3086 came out of the woods after "Warrior Week," they really didn't know a lot about how to fight a war. But they knew a lot about how to be Marines.

From the outside, the U.S. military may look like a monolithic establishment. Indeed, its critics, and many in the media, still tend to treat it that way. But knocking around inside the American military—at the Pentagon, on Army exercises, on Air Force transports, aboard Navy ships, and on deployments to Somalia, Haiti, and Bosnia—it is striking how much it feels like a group of tribes, sometimes allied to face a greater enemy, but frequently at war with one another. An old Pentagon joke hints at the different perspectives of the services: Each service is told to "secure" a building. The Marine Corps wants to destroy it, the Army wants to establish a defensive perimeter, the Navy wants to paint it, and the Air Force wants to lease it for five years.

Probably the most insightful analysis of U.S. military cultures is *The Masks of War,* a reflective, sometimes playful book by Rand Corporation analyst Carl Builder. Oddly, he didn't include the Marines in the book. But he remedied that omission in a 1994 lecture at the Army War College. In that analysis, he described the Marines as consistently standing apart from the Army, Navy, and Air Force. He saw the three larger services as obsessed with self-measurement: the Navy with the number of its ships, the Army with the number of its troops, the Air Force with the performance capabilities and number of its aircraft. The Marines, by contrast, were not so much concerned with size as with their culture—that is, the preservation of an independent identity and the capability of being self-sufficient, "taking more pride in who they are than what they own." Of course, this makes the Marines less threatened by the post-Cold War cuts in the defense budget—but more worried by social changes, including those relating to gays and women, imposed on the services.

Builder also discerned deep distinctions *within* each of three larger services. In the Navy he saw an "exquisite sense of rationalized pecking order" of at least eight clear levels: At the top, carrier-based aviators, carrying within it a subhierarchy of fighter pilots, attack pilots, and antisubmarine pilots; then submariners, with attack sub types over the "boomers," or nuclear missile boats; finally, surface ships, with surface combatants at the top, followed by amphibious warfare ships (that carry and support Marines), and, dwelling at the bottom, mine warfare. In the Army, Builder perceived extensive distinctions between infantry, armor, artillery, and support services, with "clubs, tiers, and exclusive inner circles" within each branch. One reason the Army has had a harder time than the Marines in adjusting to the post-Cold War era, he suggests, is that it was focused for half a century on slugging it out with the Red Army in Central Europe, a fight that would have required the combined efforts of tanks, big guns, and foot soldiers. The shift away from that focus has upset the balance in the Army's identity, he argues. In the Air Force, Builder saw "two tiers with great separation: pilots and everyone else," with a "rowdy rivalry among pilots"—the notorious competition between the bomber boys and the fighter mafia.

In Builder's view, the Marines again are different, because they are the least stratified. "To be a Marine is enough," he concludes. That sufficiency in identity is reinforced by the Marine uniform, which is devoid not only of the Boy Scout-like badges that festoon today's Army uniform, but lacks even a name tag and the basic unit patches such as "First Division." Indeed, Force Recon types like 3086's Sergeant Carey are resented by some in the Corps just for the small scuba and parachute emblems they wear, signifying to suspicious eyes the badge of an elite within the elite. To hold out one's group as better than the Marines is tantamount to heresy.

Builder also saw within the Marines a kind of "steadfastness," and focus on the mission: What gets it done is good, what gets in the way is bad. The phrase "Every Marine a rifleman," so heavily emphasized by Al Gray, is more than just a common denominator, it is an ethos encapsulated in a phrase, a way of looking at life and behaving. Some 26 percent of new Marine officers in 1996 were drawn from the enlisted ranks—compared to just 9 percent in the Army. It is almost always easier to do the job for a boss who has been there.

In management terms, the emphasis on the rifleman directs loyalty from the top down: The person carrying the rifle, and the name of the organization, is at the bottom of the totem pole. The rifleman is the lowest of the low in the military—the dogface, the grunt, "the poor bloody infantry" where casualties occur. "The infantry, by definition, takes the brunt of fighting," observes the military analyst James F. Dunnigan. "During this century, the odds of serving in the infantry during combat and escaping injury have been less than one in three." Historically, the infantry has been the refuse of armies. "During World War II the average infantry division got as riflemen those the rest of the armed services . . . did not want," Arthur Hadley, an Army tanker who later became a journalist, wrote in *The Straw Giant*. "The infantry that stormed ashore on D-Day were an inch shorter than the average soldier in the Army," with large numbers "classified as below average in intelligence."

In a memoir of his time in the frozen trenches of the Korean War, retired Lieutenant General Trainor explored what it really means to be a "rifleman." A rifle platoon, he wrote,

is a flesh and blood organization that is in the most dangerous of businesses. There are lots of people and things behind it that make up a war machine. But there is nothing in front of a rifle platoon but the enemy and possible death. Its members must care for one another. Its leaders must cherish the men in every fireteam and squad. For a rifleman, a leader's misjudgment, ignorance, or inexperience can be fatal—no second chances. No rerunning the exercise until you get it right. When the word "Go" is given there is no turning back from the consequences.

The cultural focus on the man who is trying to fight and survive on the front lines is one reason why, in late 1950, the Marines on the west side of Chosin Reservoir did so much better than the Army units fighting to the east of the reservoir. It is a lesson taught to every new Marine, including the recruits of 3086. The two groups of retreating American forces were isolated from each other but fought in similar circumstances, taking truck convoys through frozen terrain down narrow mountain roads. The Marines managed to bring out "all their wounded and almost all their vehicles and artillery," while the Army lost all its artillery and vehicles, wrote Faris Kirkland, a Bryn Mawr historian and former Army artillery officer, in his fascinating analysis of the disaster. Of 3,288 soldiers in the Army force, only 385 survived the ordeal in condition to fight.

Why did the Marines perform so much better than the Army? Professor Kirkland traces the difference back to the differing personnel polices of the two services. The Army was commanded by former staff officers lacking combat command experience, while Marine policy was to assign combat commands only to officers who had commanded in combat at the same or next lower level, Professor Kirkland found. Most of the initial commanders of Army divisions in Korea were World War II staff officers who hadn't held combat commands during that war. Of the eighteen colonels initially leading Army infantry regiments in Korea, fifteen were similarly lacking in experience. The result: "Marine commanders at Chosin demonstrated knowledge of tasks, obstacles, and the means to overcome them. Army commanders showed dash, bravery, and hope; but little understanding of such matters as communications, reconnaissance, fire support, and logistics."

The rifleman is also anonymous: not a famous individual, not even mattering as an individual, but as a member of a group. In the Marines, it is the group that matters—remember the lack of identifiable faces in the Iwo Jima photograph. It is difficult to imagine a Marine general acting as the Army's Douglas MacArthur did in World War II, referring in dispatches to "MacArthur's army"; mentioning only one soldier, Douglas MacArthur, in the majority of his early World War II communiques; and issuing the famous vow, "I shall return." The Marines beg to differ: As Staff Sergeant Rowland bluntly put it on his first day with 3086, "Nobody's an individual."

More broadly, that orientation on the embattled man on the front lines, combined with the small size of the Corps, seems to have encouraged both a sense of brotherhood and a culture of candor within the Corps that the other services lack. To be sure, there are liars, knaves, and cheats within the Corps, as there are anywhere—and the Corps' liars can be whoppers, as Lt. Col. Oliver North demonstrated. But it is consistently surprising how honest Marines in the field can be, and how willing their superiors are to let them be that way. One of the things that James Webb says he learned in combat in Vietnam was that, "it was part of my obligation as a leader to question."

Unlike their counterparts in the Army, Marines don't seem nearly so often to be chewed out by their commanders for speaking their minds, even to reporters. That's partly because the Marines are long accustomed to "embedding" reporters with units—issuing the journalist a flak jacket and helmet and inviting him to stay with the unit as long as he likes. This is something the Army has only recently begun to try, after years of botched efforts to assign to every reporter an "escort" to monitor all interviews. The leaders of the Marines have come to expect warts-and-all coverage, while the Army still agonizes over each negative tidbit even in stories that generally are flattering. Army officers know that they take their career into their hands every time they speak to a reporter, a major reason that the average Marine lance corporal is more confident being interviewed than is the average Army captain. In Somalia, Cpl. Armando Cordova, leader of the first squad of the first platoon of Alpha Company of the 1st Battalion of the 7th Marines, was ruthless in describing his unhappiness with his platoon leader. "He's a Gomer," the corporal said. "Get us all killed someday." Nor did he expect the U.S. mission to Somalia to have a lasting effect, mainly because he didn't think much of the UN forces that would take over the mission. "As soon as we leave, these people will be in the same boat." Nonetheless, he liked being on the mission, because he was getting to do what he had trained to do.

This candor bubbles up at all ranks. At the Marines' Combat Development Center at Quantico, Virginia, Harvard's Professor Rosen was impressed to see a colonel say to a two-star general, "No, sir, I disagree." (Of course, he was visiting Col. Gary Anderson, whom James Webb proudly calls "a Webb-trained Marine.")

Nor does this candor blossom only in private. *The Marine Corps Gazette* consistently carries the most hard-hitting, name-naming self-criticism of any U.S. military publication. In a typical article in October 1995, a Marine colonel denounced a basic Marine planning manual, *Command and Staff Action,* as "a prescription for failure." In another issue, Lt. Col. Stephen Lauer, then operations officer for the 26th Marine Expeditionary Unit, denounced Al Gray's pet theory of maneuver warfare as a "dogma" loaded with wishful thinking that "requires us to teach war as we wish it were—battle without violence, hatred, enmity, or bloodshed." Lt. Adam Arnett won a prize for his essay that began by observing that for all the talk of every Marine being a rifleman, "I look around and see young Marines who could not lead a patrol out of the head." A few months later, the *Gazette* carried a series of articles skeptically reviewing Marine helicopter operations in the Gulf War. "There were obviously many problems encountered during Task Force X-Ray's helicopter-borne operations," wrote Maj. Mark Stys, a CH-53 pilot. "Some were unavoidable; most were brought on by ourselves." The helicopter-borne assault into Kuwait, he concluded, "failed on many levels." In a companion piece, Maj. Christopher Conlin, who served as rifle company commander in the assault, criticized the Corps for believing its own "media hype" about the ability to operate at night. He concluded by wryly quoting Clint Eastwood's line from *Magnum Force:* "A man's got to know his limitations."

The *Gazette*'s willingness to be critical even extends to letting junior officers go after serving commanders by name in print. Ask an Army captain or major what would happen to his career if he were so open about criticizing his own service's leadership, and watch his face go ashen. One striking example of the Army's intellectual cowardice: Professor Kirkland's incisive analysis of how personnel policies hurt the Army at Chosin Reservoir, he said in an interview, was offered to and rejected for publication by *Parameters,* the journal of the Army War College. For months in late 1995 and early 1996, by contrast, the *Gazette* carried pointed commentary about the Marines' rescue of Air Force Capt. Scott O'Grady after he was shot down over Bosnia. There was no question that the rescue had been a success. But Marines were upset by the decision of the Marine commander, then-Col. Martin Berndt, to accompany the rescue force. "The souls of our officers and SNCOs (staff non-commissioned officers) have been shaken, and they cannot understand why," wrote Lt. Col. Kurt Stinemetz. "The decision is antithetical to everything they have ever learned." A similar letter was signed by "The Captains of 1st Battalion, 3rd Marines." Capt. Michael Martin charged that Colonel Berndt "did a disservice" to his unit. Lt. William Womack Jr. charged that the colonel—who by this time actually had been promoted to brigadier general—had imprudently succumbed to "the desire to be in on the only game."

Even as they encourage candor, the Marines are notably more formal and hierarchical than the other services. They are by far the most tradition-bound part of the U.S. military, constantly invoking their past. "The Marine Corps feeds on its history," says Webb. "What other service celebrates its birthday as the biggest day of the year? That gives them a sense of continuity—and a very deep anchor."

Indeed, by Week Ten, the recruits of Platoon 3086 are steeped in the lore of the Corps. More than one-quarter of the recruits' red-covered textbook on *General Military Subjects* is actually devoted to the very specific subject of Marine Corps history. They learn, for example, that at Chosin Reservoir, the Marines withdrew with "all of their own men and all of their own equipment," while the U.S. Army "in such a haste to retreat, had deserted some of their men and equipment. The Marines would pick up the Army stragglers and equipment, bringing them along to the sea." Platoon 3086's barracks were decorated by Staff Sergeant Rowland with signs invoking other aspects of Marine Corps history, such as their innovations in developing close air support and in amphibious landings. They learned that as Marines they could address one another as "devildog," a reference to the term German troops applied to the Marine brigade fighting in France in World War I. At its graduation, 3086 will hear a roll call of the battles of the past, and then be inducted into that band of brothers. This all combines to give a powerful sense of obligation: Don't let down those who went before you, the new Marines are reminded as they prepare to leave Parris Island. It is an emphasis that sets the Marines apart not only from the other U.S. military services, but also from a society that is, as the social commentator James Fallows once wrote, "an intentionally 'ahistoric' culture." The Marines are just the opposite: In a typical moment, Martin Berndt, by now a brigadier general, when speaking at Annapolis about the O'Grady rescue, begins by saluting those in his audience who fought at Peleliu, Okinawa, and Chosin Reservoir.

But the driving core of Marine culture, even more than a sense of the past, is its sense of future vulnerability. Every Marine is taught that the very existence of the Marines is always in danger.

"Our paranoia is famous," says Major Davis of the Drill Instructors School, in a typical Marine comment. "Nine presidents have tried to put us out of business." (And, in another typical bit of Corps culture, the photograph on his office wall shows him standing with—who else?—Al Gray.) The current commandant's father once counted at least fifteen attempts to abolish the Corps. "The United States does not *need* a Marine Corps," he concluded, "the United States *wants* a Marine Corps." The commandant himself began an article in *Proceedings* by approvingly citing a book by Intel Corporation's Andy Groves titled *Only the Paranoid Survive.*

It is a lesson taught to today's recruits in almost exactly the same words. Col. Douglas Hendricks, commander of the Recruit Training Regiment, holds a meeting with a group of randomly selected recruits from each graduating company. It is called the "laundry list seminar" because his office, to ensure that recruits aren't prepped to meet the brass, simply sends over random numbers, and recruits whose laundry bags have those numbers come to his meeting room, decorated with even more framed clippings about the Ribbon Creek incident.

"You know why America has a Marine Corps?" he asks the six recruits—two black, two white, one thickly accented Chinese-American, one Hispanic. "Because she *wants* one." He holds up a finger. "Never forget that. Because if she changes her mind, if she thinks we're no longer able to deliver, then we're out of here— and we should be, as should be any organization that has lost its usefulness to the larger society." Ensuring the survival of the institution, he says, keeps the Corps focused. "That's why Marines are so adaptable—we're constantly looking for that edge."

He listens to their accounts of boot camp life, what they'd change, and what they expect life in the Marines to be like. "It's your Marine Corps now," he says. "We're all responsible."

"Anyone here hear of Aristotle?" he asks. The recruits look at one another as if to say, No Sergeant Aristotle in my unit. The colonel explains: "He was a smart guy who lived a long time ago. He said we are what we repeatedly do. Excellence, then, isn't an act, it is a habit."

This abiding sense of vulnerability, and the consequent requirement to excel to ensure the survival of the institution, is *the* central fact of Marine culture. So, rather than sweep faults and weaknesses under the rug, the Marines tend to zero in on them as possible threats to the institution. In the "leadership exam" given to students at the Drill Instructors School, for example, five of the fifty questions are about the Ribbon Creek incident.

Because of that sense of being endangered, the Corps long has sought to justify its existence to the American public. This has made it far more publicity conscious than the other services. Paramount Pictures' *Wake Island,* made with Marine assistance, was the first film to portray World War II combat action. In 1943, Marines from the 4th Division staged a landing assault at San Clemente, California, for Twentieth Century-Fox's *Guadalcanal Diary.* Indeed, the ever-helpful Marines even helped Hollywood stage part of the recreation of the Army's D-Day landing for *The Longest Day.* In 1950, President Harry Truman furiously charged that the Marines operated "a propaganda machine that is almost equal to Stalin's." He eventually was obliged to apologize.

A World War II ditty by a Marine officer, gleefully reprinted in the Marine Corps Combat Correspondents' anthology of their writings about the Pacific war, went:

> *The Marines, the Marines, those blasted Gyrenes,*
> *Those sea-going bellhops, those brass-button queens,*
> *Oh, they pat their own backs, write stories in reams,*
> *All in praise of themselves—the U.S. Marines!*
>
> *The Marines, the Marines, those publicity fiends,*
> *They built all the forests, turned on all the streams,*

Discontent with the earth, they say Heaven's scenes
Are guarded by—you guess—the U.S. Marines!

In *The Short-Timers,* the painful little Vietnam War novel by
Gustav Hasford on which *Full Metal Jacket* is based, a Marine
captain unabashedly links the Marine knack for publicity to its
fighting prowess. "The lesser services like to joke about how
every Marine platoon goes into battle accompanied by a platoon
of Marine Corps photographers," he says. "That's affirmative.
Marines fight harder because Marines have bigger legends to
live up to."

Today's Marines maintain that aggressive posture. In 1996,
the Corps virtually ran away with the hit movie *Independence Day,*
in which the Air Force is nowhere in sight, while the hero is a
black Marine aviator and the chairman of the Joint Chiefs is also
a Marine.

Envious Army public affairs officers sometimes joke that it
takes three Marines to screw in a lightbulb—one to do it and
two to issue the press release. But that joke misses the lesson the
Corps conveys to all its officers and to most of its enlisted personnel, that every single one of them must promote the institution. Even second lieutenants at the Basic School are imbued
with the importance of public relations: A reporter walking
around the campus at Quantico is greeted consistently with lines
such as, "Glad to have you here to tell the Marine story."

That attitude paid off during the Gulf War. The plan of the U.S.
military offensive made the Marines a kind of sideshow. The
main effort was the U.S. Army's "Hail Mary" swing into the
Republican Guard, while the Marines were relegated on land to
carrying out a supporting move, and at sea to feint as if intending
to carry out an amphibious landing on the beaches of Kuwait. Yet
they again managed to dominate news coverage. Despite their sec-
ondary roles, "the Marines garnered most of the publicity," concluded journalist John Fialka in *Hotel Warriors,* a study of press

coverage of the Gulf War. Years later, speaking to a class at the Marine Command and Staff College, a top Marine general said, in almost so many words, Gentlemen, if you go by the number of headlines, *we* won the Gulf War.

Another odd but important element to the Corps' culture is its emphasis on frugality. The Marines pride themselves on making do, using hand-me-downs, and surviving on only 6 percent of the Pentagon budget. One reason the military training is better at Fort Benning than at Parris Island is that the gear is better: Snazzy laser receptors, combined with live fire, teach Army troops to stay low far better than a drill instructor's words can do. The Marine culture of frugality is brought home to anyone traveling on a Marine aircraft who is offered a Diet Coke—and then asked for fifty cents payment. Outside speakers at a meeting at the Marines' Amphibious Warfare School are invited to lunch—and then served a chunk of a Subway sandwich made up of baloney, American cheese, and pickles. Marine infrastructure—barracks, officer housing, day care centers—tends to be the worst in the U.S. military, giving many Marine facilities an anachronistic feel, with old sinks and cracked tiles in the bathrooms, like an unrenovated pre-World War II high school. Al Gray, when once asked about improving the "quality of life" of his Marines and their families, famously responded that the best quality of life he knew was actually having a life, so he would put his money into troop training.

The culture that the Marines most resemble, oddly enough, is that of Japan. The Marines are almost a Japanese version of America—frugal, relatively harmonious, extremely hierarchical, and almost always placing the group over the individual. "In normal situations, Japanese in principle accept the needs of the group as much as possible," writes the commentator Ryushi Iwata, "while on the other hand, they hide and repress their own needs."

Both the Marines and Japanese society operate in a kind of

physical and even psychological isolation from the larger world. And central to both cultures is the sense of being locked in a struggle for existence. This hovering threat hones the warrior culture in both the Marines and Japan. In his fascinating inquiry, *Why Has Japan "Succeeded"?: Western Technology and the Japanese Ethos,* the economist Michio Morishima observes that after the Meiji restoration, "the obligation of national defense fell to the population as a whole, and all Japanese people were considered as potential soldiers." One can almost hear the phrase, "Every Japanese a rifleman." In a more modern expression of that sentiment, Shintaro Ishihara in his diatribe *The Japan That Can Say No* gave expression in a commercial context to the Marine approach. Japan understands, he argues, what America has forgotten: "Everyone in a company contributes, from top to bottom."

Once the peon is acknowledged as the most important member of the organization, loyalty and responsibility flow downward. In Japanese corporations, notes Prof. Thomas Rohlen, a Stanford expert on Japanese education and Japanese corporate cultures, the low-level worker generally is valued, not treated as a commodity to be discarded when not needed. "Distinctions of rank are important, but what is more important is that everyone comes from the lowest ranks," he says in an interview. And what everyone focuses on, he adds, is the external threat: "Japanese organizations don't get caught up internally in their own successes, in the way that many American businesses have. I worked with GM and Ford in the late seventies, and it was hell getting them to focus on the Japanese auto industry."

This point is especially important today for the U.S. military, which for the first time in its history is unquestionably the world's best. That dominant position makes it all too easy to believe that other militaries, down to the ragtag Third-World sniper, have little to teach the American soldier. The Marines seem less prone to this complacency, partly because they cultivate a sense of vulnerability that makes them more willing to entertain internal and external criticism, as seen in the *Marine*

Corps Gazette. In Japanese corporations, noted Professor Rohlen, that system of candid self-review is called "continuous learning": "It's concerned not so much with fixing blame as with identifying problems."

The Marines aren't becoming Japanese. But they are American samurai, in the way they think of themselves and in the way they relate to their nation. Like the Japanese, the U.S. military in general, and the Marines in particular, when looking at America see a society weakened by selfishness, indiscipline, and fragmentation.

This view of America is flawed not for what it sees but for what it doesn't see. The Japanese are continually surprised by America's resilience because they don't see the strengths of America—its diversity, flexibility, openness, and inventiveness. James Fallows once made an observation about the Japanese that can also be applied to the U.S. military: They underestimate the United States, he wrote, "because so many things that can mean vitality in America—immigration, rapid political change—look like chaos to them." Despite its emphasis on values, the American military may be undervaluing America.

But there is value in the Marine perspective on America. The Marine view is most accurate in assessing what the United States offers the kind of people who make up today's recruits. These are kids from the bottom half of society. The military offers them a chance to escape from their limited futures, a chance to move into a kind of world like Japan, which, as Fallows put it, has the best bottom half in the world, where the lower socioeconomic portion of the population is successfully held to high standards. "America probably is the best top quarter or top third," Fallows says in a conversation. "Japan probably has the best bottom half in the world, . . . in terms of income, housing, transportation, communications, the basic level of education, the respect you get in daily life."

For the recruits of Platoon 3086, and for thousands of youths like them, the U.S. military today has become a "haven in a heartless world." The phrase originally was used by cultural critic Christopher Lasch to describe the modern family, but for many young Americans, the military is a haven from abusive families, or from the absence of family. In its separateness from the larger society, the Marine Corps especially among the services offers sanctuary from a chaotic nation where honor, courage, and commitment are values often misunderstood, frequently ignored, and sometimes mocked. It is an institution that, at its best, urges them to make a habit of excellence, as Colonel Hendricks did when he invoked Aristotle to the group of recruits.

But a sustaining strength can also be a limiting weakness. The powerful culture that distinguishes and sustains the Corps also sometimes makes the Corps narrow—that is, the least inclined to operate hand-in-hand with the other U.S. military services. Of all the services, the Corps seems the most "anti-joint." This defiant stance is a prime sin in a defense establishment where, in the wake of post-Grenada reforms, "jointness" has been next to godliness. "Jointness has become a virtual religion," the *Gazette* once quietly complained.

On the face of it, the Corps' hesitancy in operating with the other services is counterintuitive. It is, after all, the only service that routinely combines land, sea, and air operations, and so has a better understanding of the environment in which the other services do their jobs. However, the Marines operate on the sea and in the air with just one purpose in mind, that of supporting the all-important rifleman on the ground. This isn't the way the Air Force, Navy, or even the Army looks at life. What's more, the Marine culture, the Marine way of doing things, runs so deep that it sometimes irks other services in unexpected ways. In both the Korean and Vietnam wars, notes Arthur Hadley, the Corps was "extremely reluctant" to share its aircraft with other services, so much so that at one point General Westmoreland threatened to resign over the issue. More recently, two odd examples came out of the Somalia operation. First, Army women, accustomed to sleeping in the areas where their units sleep, usually behind a blanket or poncho draped over a rope, were upset when the Marine commander overseeing the operation got wind of those arrangements and ordered them to move to sexually segregated sleeping areas. Air Force personnel stationed in Kenya for the operation were similarly put out when Marine commanders again unthinkingly imposed their own rules and deprived them of the per diem payments they had been receiving. Col. Charles Dunlap, an Air Force colonel who criticized the move, concluded that, "the Marine Corps may not sufficiently appreciate the cultures of its sister services to allow it to function as the lead service in another major joint operation." As the Parris Island saying goes, there is a right way, a wrong way—and the Marine way. Trying to get the Marines to operate in another service's way would be like trying to have Platoon 3086 operate while speaking only French.

More importantly, the Marine culture also sometimes seems too narrow for some of its own people—the 27,000 Marines who are black. In 1994, for example, the Center for Naval Analyses, a Defense Department-supported think tank, trying to determine why minorities did relatively poorly in joining and rising in the Marine officer corps, pointed to the culture as a problem. "All of the black former Marines present (at a symposium) spoke about the narrowness of Marine Corps culture," the CNA reported. They went on to speak of "the need for blacks to conform to this culture to succeed in the Marine Corps. A particular style of dress was expected: khakis, polo shirts, and deck shoes. Those wearing jeans or silk shirts off duty were subject to ridicule or chastisement from senior officers." One of the black former Marines, retired Brig. Gen. George H. Walls Jr., "mentioned his discomfort at often being the only black in the officers' club who wasn't serving food." They also complained that the juke-boxes in the clubs, the report said, are "typically limited to country and western music." A 1996 report by the North Carolina NAACP echoed that complaint. NAACP inquiries with black

Marines at Camp Lejeune, which is in eastern North Carolina, also found complaints that blacks sometimes are treated differently. "When three or four black Marines hang together, they are described as a gang," said one. Added another: "There are no black activities on base—e.g., concerts are country." When racial slurs are used and reported, the reports aren't believed, said another complainant: "They may say this is the Corps, and it can't happen here." (In the same vein, the Marines do worst in Defense Department surveys of sexual harassment, with some 64 percent of Marine women polled in the mid-1990s reporting harassment, compared to a military-wide average of 55 percent.)

There is no question that the Corps lags the Army in finding and promoting black officers. There are barely a thousand black officers in the Marines—less than 6 percent of its officer corps. And there certainly are racists in the Marines. Yet the complaints of black Marines about the Corps generally seem to point more to insensitivity, and perhaps an ignorance of how to alter the Corps' culture to make blacks more comfortable, than they do to a deep-seated racism.

And the Corps seems to be changing, partly because of its powerful commitment to the brotherhood of all Marines, and partly because black and white Marines find after a few years in the Corps that they have more in common with one another than they do with members of their races outside the service. At a dinner at the Basic School, where young lieutenants are made, 2nd Lt. Travis Oselmo, a black Brooklynite, told the story of how he prepared to become an officer. A Marine reservist, he was working as a security guard at a Gap clothing store when his attention to detail and crisp responses caught the attention of his roving supervisor. "You a Marine?" asked the supervisor, who turned out to be a retired Marine gunnery sergeant. Oselmo explained that he was pursuing a college degree so he could become an officer. "You're doing the right thing," said the supervisor, who also was black. He then volunteered to help get Oselmo ready for the rigors of the Basic School, helping him after work with drill and physical training.

The lesson of all this, said Lieutenant Oselmo, is that, "It really is a brotherhood."

On the morning of May 13th, the Saturday at the end of Week Ten, Platoon 3086 brings its training to a close. The event is the platoon's "Final Drill Evaluation," a kind of half-inspection, half-ceremony held out on the Third Battalion's parade deck, where 3086 has spent so much time drilling toward the mess hall.

"Final Drill" is the opposite of the "Pick-up," the bit of shock theater that began 3086's life in the Third Battalion. That was sheer chaos; this is pure order. The platoon was surrounded by shouting drill instructors. This morning it is surrounded again, but now the drill instructors are absolutely quiet, except for the occasional brief order, followed by the simultaneous movement of fifty-five rifles. The platoon moves as one, its footsteps ringing on the asphalt like a giant boot smacking down. The only other sounds come from songbirds chirping in the bright Carolina morning.

The inspecting sergeants silently jot notes on the clipboards, moving alongside as Staff Sergeant Rowland expertly "drives the bus" around the parade deck. At his order of "To the rear!" the platoon simultaneously swivels 180 degrees. In slow, low minor tones, Staff Sergeant Rowland sings out "Leeeeeft/ right!" making it sound like an Appalachian lament, perhaps a personal farewell to this platoon.

The one lapse in the crackerjack precision comes at the order of "inspection arms." Rifles are raised; fifty-five empty chambers are inspected. But only fifty-four rifles come back down. Buijs absentmindedly lingers on the movement, gazing skyward for a moment into the chamber of his M-16. His hesitation hurts the platoon's grade, and it comes in second in the series.

CHAPTER SIX

GRADUATION

O n the day before graduation, Platoon 3086, looking Marine-like in fresh "high and tight" haircuts, shaved on the sides, with a little hairbrush-size rectangle of hair on top, moves out as one into the warm, hazy morning for its final 4.3 mile "motivation run" around Parris Island. "You *own* this island," Gunnery Sergeant Camacho shouts at them. The sound of rifle fire pops through the woods. 1st Sergeant Tucker, also joining them for the run, adds, "You're the best on the island, understand? You're the senior company on the island."

They shout as they run:

> *Feels good*
> *Like it should*
> *Feels fine*
> *Double time!*

At 9:00 A.M., the platoons of Kilo Company assemble to receive awards for the best drill and PT tests. Watching the ceremony, Captain Chessani, the company commander, worries about what will happen to the recruits on boot leave. "Something I've seen as a platoon commander out in the Fleet is that the Marines who get in trouble are the ones who hang out with civilians," he says. He worries that some recruits will fail to cut their ties to the old friends.

Gunnery Sergeant Camacho is especially worried by Earnest Winston Jr. He predicts the Washingtonian will flop as a Marine, beginning by going back to drugs while on leave. "He'll go UA (unauthorized absence) once in the Fleet, and then it will become a pattern."

Winston privately harbors the same doubts. He offers a clear analysis of the dilemma he will face on leave. "This recruit knows he'll be accepted" back in his neighborhood, he says, "but this recruit has to find out which way he'll go. He now has two families."

On the one hand, "The Marine Corps is a band of brothers." On the other, he adds, "This recruit loved what he was doing being a criminal. This recruit was perfect at it—armed robbery, drug distribution, distribution of firearms, drive-by shootings."

Daniel Keane has more confidence in Winston. With his Wall Street father and psychologist mother, and a childhood in the leafy suburb of Summit, New Jersey, Keane is in some ways as different from Winston as is possible. Yet the two recruits have similar personalities. They each have an essential reserve; each keeps his own counsel. And they sense in each other a basic reliability. Keane concludes that Winston is "the kind of person who doesn't give a shit what people say about him, who doesn't always look good in the rear, but of the whole platoon, he's one of the guys I'd want in the next foxhole."

In the quiet of the barracks, with the DIs leaving them alone, several recruits prepare to leave the island for the first time in months. Three near the quarterdeck say they feel transformed. Oddly, two of these three will be out of the Corps within a year. Christopher Anderson, his face no longer round, but drawn with either fatigue or pain, says, "Civilian life is nasty and undisciplined." Unlike Winston, he insists that he won't run with his old drug-dealing friends when he gets back to Adelphi, Maryland. "A lot of my friends are selling to help get through U. Maryland and Howard. I've worked too hard for that. I'd rather not have those friends, and have my Marine Corps buddies."

Daniel Sabella Jr. says he feels the same way: "I don't believe I'm going to be with the same people when I get home. I don't like the way they act." Sabella has told the other recruits that his mother is a Marine gunnery sergeant, that his father is a sergeant major, and that his brother until recently was a drill instructor. Like Anderson, he won't last long in the Corps.

Doing his final paperwork at his "scribe" table at the edge of the quarterdeck, Charles Lees says, "I'm not the person I used to be." He is right. Unlike the others, his life has been transformed. Though a reservist, he has become far more "Marine" than the other two, having lost his fat and gained a new confidence.

The platoon assembles for graduation rehearsal on the edge of Parris Island's main parade deck, an asphalt expanse the size of a suburban shopping mall parking lot. Helping the platoon begin to decompress by showing them a human face, Staff Sergeant Rowland idly asks, "Stephenson, what's the first thing you're going to eat when you get home?"

"Suzy, sir!" shouts Marcus Stephenson, a nineteen-year-old from Coventry, Rhode Island, who usually is quiet.

Staff Sergeant Rowland does a double-take, bowing his campaign hat forward in an effort to hide his laughter. "What?" he sputters.

Stephenson diplomatically withdraws the crack. "Uh, *sushi*, sir."

Sergeant Carey joins the conversation. "If it tastes like sushi, I wouldn't go near it."

But aside from that crack, Sergeant Carey plays the heavy hat until the last moment. Recruit James Andersen, in a forgetful moment, tells Sergeant Carey that a confusion about his graduation photographs has been resolved. "You see, I did order two," the happy recruit says. Sergeant Carey has this individualist become a human Ping-Pong ball: Carey and another DI stand on the quarterdeck as Andersen crawls back and forth between them. When he reaches Carey's shoes, the DIs holds up his hands as if flicking a paddle and says, "Pop." The recruit turns to crawl in the other direction. Staff Sergeant Rowland comes out of the DI house, looks down at the recruit, and asks, "What are you doing?" Andersen looks up: "Sir, this recruit is playing Ping-Pong, sir."

Preparing the recruits for the emblem ceremony, Sergeant Zwayer advises them to dress like Marines. "Whatever you want to take on recruit liberty—money, military ID—put it in your sock," he says. But Sergeant Carey roars in like a fast-moving cold front, insisting one more time on the importance of paying attention to detail. "You don't put collar stays in your charlie shirt!" he bellows as he enforces another all-important bit of Marine Corps trivia.

Joshua Parise, the Pittsburgh artist, drops his emblem on the red-painted cement of the barracks floor. Sergeant Carey shakes his head. "I'm tired of baby-sitting you!" he shouts. Without being told, Parise drops to the floor and begins doing push-ups in his dress uniform.

"Whether you like it or not, you have a purpose in life now," Sergeant Carey shouts to the assembled platoon. "You're representing the 3rd Battalion. Ears, '86: Listen, you need to be productive under stress! You need not to spaz out! You need to SNAP and POP."

Andrew Lee shouts back: "The count on deck is fifty-five rough, tough, can't-get-enough United States Marine Corps recruits! Sir!"

Staff Sergeant Rowland concludes that his work is done. "They are morally and ethically sane, basically trained Marines," he pronounces.

He includes in that Buijs, if just barely. As the emblem ceremony—a prelude to graduation—approaches, Recruit Buijs concedes that his views have shifted a bit from his steadfast pacifism. "It depends on the circumstances. If there's good reason, then killing is justified," he says. Then he marches outside and pins on the Corps' eagle, globe, and anchor. He isn't the natural-born killer of the movies, but in his own roundabout way he has become more dedicated to the Marines than many other members of the platoon.

Fueled by Staff Sergeant Rowland's supercharged *hup-hup-hup* triple-time cadence, the platoon marches across Parris Island to see their families for the first time in eleven weeks. A crowd of two hundred waiting outside the Parris Island visitors' center greets the platoon with applause as it steams into view.

But their families don't quite recognize these Marines. Elizabeth Lees walks right past her brother, who has shed seventy-six pounds since enlisting. "My God, you're so *thin*," she exclaims, patting his flat stomach. The mother of Recruit Buijs and the parents of Patrick Bayton, James Andersen, and several other recruits also fail to identify their sons at first sight. Many recruits have five or six relations on hand, and Nathan Manczka has eight down from Edinboro, Pennsylvania, including the mother who didn't recognize his voice when he called home. The platoon is now granted "recruit liberty"—which means they can spend six hours with their families, but still aren't allowed to leave the island.

Staff Sergeant Rowland quietly watches the crowd, making sure that the recruits who have no families coming to visit aren't left alone, and either are included with the families of buddies or are hooked up with one another.

The families break away to walk the island. As the afternoon wears on, the quick shock of physical recognition gives way to a deeper understanding that their sons and brothers also have been transformed internally. The parents of Mickeal Perkins, the recruit who so enjoyed the night combat movement course, don't recognize him until he walks up and actually lays a hand on his mother's shoulder. "Tell you what, it's made a big change in him," his father, Hurley Perkins, says with some awe. "He carries himself a whole lot better. He's matured a lot."

"And his manners!" exclaims his mother. "He never used to hold doors open for me."

Staff Sergeant Rowland strolls alone back to the empty squad bay and makes a few final notes on the Recruit Evaluation Cards. Most members of 3086 get a farewell pat on the back. Nathaniel Behrendt, the classic man in the middle, receives a simple, "An average recruit." Staff Sergeant Rowland's feeling that he never really connected with Earnest Winston is reflected in his ambivalent comment on that recruit's card: "An average to below average recruit from the city who still has a touch of it in him. Understands how things work in the Marine Corps." One of his few comments that will be proven wrong by subsequent events is his notation on Daniel Sabella: "Was a quitter when he first arrived, however he has definitely overcome that." Even Buijs gets a respectful sendoff: "An average recruit who showed a lot of immaturity due to his age. Has shown major improvements and will do fine as a Marine." But the dour Anderson sticks in the drill instructor's craw. "A minimal performer," he concludes.

The evening brings "Family Night" in a small brick auditorium near the water. Early May is bringing summer to South Carolina. Captain Chessani walks to the front of the hot, humid room and tells the assembled parents he is about to introduce them to "the people responsible for the changes in your son— the drill instructors of Company K." The Marines are good at putting on shows, and this is one more act in the eleven-week-long piece of performance art that is Parris Island. The drill instructors solemnly march into the room. They execute sharp lefts at their platoon guidons. Staff Sergeant Rowland, wearing his grim work face, stands at parade rest, hands at the small of his back, elbows out. Sergeants Carey and Zwayer assume identical stances just behind each of his elbows. The eyes of each man are almost invisible, shaded under the inclined brims of their olive-green felt campaign hats. 1st Sergeant Tucker invites the parents to step up: "Feel free to ask them anything you like about your son's training, or anything about training."

A grateful line forms in front of Staff Sergeant Rowland. Parents purchase cold cans of Miller Lite at a small cash bar at the back of the room and bring them to him. A stack of fourteen cans forms next to his polished black shoes, American working-class tokens of gratitude: Buy that man a beer. "I'm impressed. I'm very impressed," Earnest Winston Sr., a used-car salesman who is separated from his wife, tells Staff Sergeant Rowland about his son. "I think he's gained quite a bit of maturity."

There are exceptions. The parents of Andrew Lee, the guide and honor graduate of 3086, are standoffish. They hesitate, watching Staff Sergeant Rowland from a few paces away before deciding to get in line to talk to him. Nancy Lee, the Boston school counselor, says she was "devastated" by her son's enlistment and still considers herself "antimilitary." "He signed up without telling us," she recalls. She notes that her son has "struggled" in the past with dyslexia, but doesn't seem particularly impressed with his top-flight success in boot camp. Throughout the graduation period, Lee's face will remain tight with tension. Not only do his parents appear unappreciative of his accomplishment here, his drill instructors are placing enormous pressure on him to abandon his plan to be a reservist and "go active." They dislike the fact that their top graduate isn't a "real" Marine.

Similarly, Staff Sergeant Rowland is taken aback by the edgy tone of his conversation with Eric Didier's mother. "She had a real sharp attitude," he says later in puzzlement. "It was like I was the bad guy." (Explains Didier, "My mother, she's the protective type, so she didn't like the idea of me going to war.")

The next morning dawns hot and steamy. Platoon 3086 arrived at the end of winter. They will leave at the beginning of summer. The drill instructors assemble the recruits of 3086 for the final time. The near-graduates are dressed in khaki shirts and blue dress pants—almost exactly like their drill instructors. The platoon waits on the edge of the graduation parade deck. As if worried that eleven weeks hasn't been long enough to complete the job, Staff Sgt. Rowland and Sergeant Carey try to cram in a final few thoughts for the recruits to take with them when they leave the island for the first time as Marines.

"Today's the day you become a Marine, understand that?" asks Sergeant Carey. "Now you're going to follow them."

"Now, what are you going to do afterwards?" asks Staff Sergeant Rowland.

One giddy recruit shouts, "Kiss the man?"

The senior drill instructor grins and laughingly snarls, "Now, don't go kissing me!"

He turns serious. "Everything you learn here, carry it with you. These are your roots."

Sergeant Carey adds: "Never quit, never die, understand? It doesn't matter what you do, just do it the best. You've got to test yourself *when?*"

"Every day, sir!" shouts back 3086.

Then Staff Sergeant Rowland leads his platoon onto the main parade deck. A crowd of more than a thousand watches from the metal stands along the southern side of the parade ground. Until the late 1970s, graduating from Parris Island was a low-key, even haphazard, affair: the drill instructor marched out a platoon, the battalion commander congratulated it, the best marksman was recognized, and the new Marines were sent on their way. In the seventies, the Corps decided that one way to improve discipline, and especially "unauthorized absence" rates, was to enroll the families of Marines into "the Marine family." So today graduation is a two-day extravaganza, from the emblem ceremony to recruit liberty and family night to the final elaborate graduation ceremony of marching, awards, speeches, and the introduction of every drill instructor. In recent years, graduations have always been held on Fridays. One result is that on most Thursday nights it is nearly impossible to find an empty hotel room in nearby Beaufort.

The band in front of 3086 plays a fanfare. A narrator begins speaking over a loudspeaker, sounding very much like a baseball stadium announcer giving the starting lineups. The difference is that the roster here is the U.S. Marine Corps, and the lineup is their great battles.

"Marines have served aboard Parris Island since 1891," the voice echoes across the asphalt. "And more than one million Marines have trained here. They departed Parris Island for combat and conflicts throughout the world, including places and names that are immediately associated with Marine courage and dedication. Names such as:

Guadalcanal
Tarawa
Iwo Jima
Chosin Reservoir
Inchon
Khe Sanh
Hue City
Lebanon
Grenada
Panama
And Kuwait City."

The narrator then turns the crowd's attention to the recruits striding crisply across the deck. "Marching before you this morning are four hundred twenty-one success stories, each of them a testament to the physical courage, determination, and unyielding commitment to excellence behind the title 'United States Marine.' They now join the proud ranks of over one million Marines who have graduated from Parris Island.

"From this day on, they will be known as Marines."

It is high ceremony, induction into the church militant of the U.S. military. Gunnery Sergeant Camacho and his fellow series gunnies announce that their platoons are all present and accounted for. Each noncommissioned officer present wears a sword. Then a chaplain wearing the summer whites of a Navy lieutenant reads a prayer written by the religious lay leaders of the graduating recruits. "Gracious heavenly Father," he intones.

"Dear God, you have stood beside us and guided us these last months. We thank you for the courage to attempt recruit training, but more for the confidence and determination to complete it." The next part of the prayer echoes the speech that Staff Sergeant Rowland and the other senior drill instructors gave to their platoons during the "Pick-up," the day the recruits met their DIs. "There were times when we wanted to give up, but you never gave up on us."

God is the most senior drill instructor of all. "Dear Father," the chaplain continues, "when we stepped on those yellow footprints, you were with us. When we were weak, you made us strong. When we were sick, you healed us. When down, you bolstered our spirits. Make us truly faithful to our Corps, our country, and to you, our God. Amen."

Col. Humberto "Rod" Rodriguez of the Recruit Training Regiment, a Zeus-like character to the drill instructors, remote but occasionally descending to walk among men, succeeds the chaplain at the cement lectern. "These new Marines in front of you have met the challenge," he says with a slight Spanish accent that sharpens his vowels. "And like those who have gone before them, they have earned the right and privilege to be called United States Marines. Their training has been mentally and physically demanding. We who train them, and they who receive it, would have it no other way."

The colonel then formally asks the crowd to excuse him as he turns his back to them in order to face the recruits on the parade deck.

"Good morning, Marines," he says. That is it: They have made it, at 9:45 on the morning of May 19, 1995. This is the high point in the lives of many members of 3086. Indeed, for some, life will go downhill from this point, as they begin to stumble and as the Corps fails to live up to their expectations.

The platoons roar back in one voice: "Good morning, sir."

"I am privileged to be the first to formally address you as

United States Marines," the colonel says. "Marines you are, and Marines you will always be.

"As you look around and see how your ranks have thinned, you realize that not everyone who tried succeeded. You did. You are, by every measure, a United States Marine."

That reward made, the colonel quickly reminds them of what that entails. "All Marines in every instance are expected to employ and live by the principle of responsibility. It means being personally responsible and accountable for one's actions, particularly in relation with other Marines. Ultimately it is the acceptance of such responsibility that bonds all Marines throughout the world all their lives.

"It means living by standards that others will seek to emulate. It means an uncompromising tenacity in guarding the mores and reputation of the world's finest military organization. It means unerring application of the highest standards of personal conduct on the battlefield, in garrison, and on liberty. It means doing *nothing* to tarnish that proud heritage.

"In a few minutes, you will be dismissed for the final time on Parris Island. Just prior to that, the band will play 'The Marine Hymn.' You have heard it many times before. This time, it will be for you.

"Take with you our motto: 'Semper Fidelis'—Always Faithful. I charge all of you to always be faithful to your God, your family, our country, and our Corps. I wish you the very best of luck." Colonel Rodriguez turns to face the crowd. "Ladies and gentlemen, I would like to present to you four hundred and twenty-one of the very best Marines America can produce."

The top recruit and best shooter in each platoon are recognized. In addition to Andrew Lee, three other members of 3086 have won meritorious promotion to private first class, instead of graduating as mere privates. One is Lonnie Christian, who scored highest on physical testing. The second is Nathan Weber, who met Staff Sergeant Rowland's standard of being so good that he never attracted attention, except when he took the rap for the doughnuts during mess and maintenance week. The third is Randy Barrows, whose brother's provocative letters seem to have paid off. He has done an immense amount of extra exercise, and come through all right, with a new self-confidence that threatens to grow into cockiness. In his last weeks on the island, Barrows even developed a rasping way of saying "Yes, suh." It sounds suspiciously like an mocking imitation of Sergeant Humphrey, the demon of the first inspection and of night combat movement class. But because Barrows has done so well, and because graduation was nearing, the DIs let it pass.

Andrew Lee is so tense as he marches that his arms barely move. Gunnery Sergeant Camacho whispers to him: "You got to swing your arms, son."

A huge horsefly lands on Sergeant Carey's bare forearm. He notices it but doesn't move. It takes a painful bite, leaving a red welt that will last a week.

All former Marines in the audience are asked to rise for recognition. Across the crowded stands, old and middle-aged men proudly rise and stand at attention. It is hard to recognize them as Marines under their big bellies and gray hair—but most of their eyes are glistening. The audience applauds for them.

At 10:28 A.M., Staff Sergeant Rowland faces his platoon. "Platoon three thousand eighty-six," he bellows. "Dis-misse-d!" The platoon responds, "Aye, sir," takes a step backward—and ceases to exist.

As Colonel Rodriguez promised, the ceremony ends with the playing of "the Marine Hymn." And as he also said, they are now and will always be Marines. "Everything changed in one second," remembers Charles Lees. "It was suddenly: 'Now you're one of us—you're worthy.' " He walks up to Staff Sergeant Frasier, the senior for Platoon 3085, and says, "Take it easy, sir." The sergeant responds in kind. Just a day earlier, such an exchange was the stuff of insubordinate fantasy.

Private Winston, always observant, shakes Sergeant Carey's hand and says, "That was the biggest horsefly I've ever seen."

Private Prish seeks out Sergeant Zwayer, his tormentor for the last eleven weeks. He stares at the DI, then sticks out his hand and shakes Zwayer's vigorously. "He put me through a lot of pain," Prish says later. "He thrashed me three times a day. I'll always remember him. I think he's a great guy. 'Cause I started giving up, and he never gave up on me. I'll remember him to the end of my life."

Private Parise, who a few weeks earlier had angrily confronted Winston, is pleased to be given a graduation photo by another black recruit, Gary Moore Jr., who because of the alphabet had bunked next to Parise. On the back, Private Moore has written a farewell message: "You were my good friend from the first time I met you here. You didn't look at color or background, and just treated me like a brother from the start. Take care, and stay in contact."

Moore, who barely made it, confesses that, "I do have to say that this worst part of my life was also the best time I ever had in my life."

Leave beckons. Mickeal Perkins plans to go home to North Carolina and "spend time with kin people." Craig Hoover wants to get home to Maryland "to strut around and show people I can do it." Earnest Winston Jr. feels a powerful need to "try to find my self and my place in the 'hood." Daniel Armstrong has more elemental plans: "Get drunk and get laid—not necessarily in that order."

Staff Sergeant Rowland strolls off the parade ground with his wife, heading back to their home just three blocks away. Andrew Lee catches up with them near Boulevard de France. Sweat stains his uniform. There are tears in his eyes. "Sir, this recruit doesn't know what to do when he leaves Parris Island," he says, almost pleading. But Lee, for once, is incorrect: He is no longer a recruit.

The aging drill instructor looks the tough young Marine in

the eye. "Lee, where's your mom and dad?" he asks softly. "Go find them, and go home with them."

They are Marines now—not just for the terms of their enlistments, but forever. The Corps' line is that there is no such thing as an ex-Marine, except for Lee Harvey Oswald. This loyalty sometimes pops up in startling places. In August 1996, for example, when Hussein Farrah Aideed succeeded his father, Gen. Mohammed Farrah Aideed, as leader of Somalia's dominant faction, he took a moment in an interview to look back fondly on his time in Battery B of the 14th Marine Regiment, a reserve artillery unit. "I always wanted to be a Marine," he told the Associated Press in his first interview as faction leader and self-proclaimed "president" of Somalia. "I'm proud of my background and military discipline."

The training sometimes remains when everything else is gone. General Krulak, the commandant, tells of the old Marine who, suffering from Alzheimer's, responded to nothing but the orders of Marine Corps ceremonies.

"The Marine experience is lifelong," confirms the Rev. J. Edwin Pippin, a Marine in the 1950s who is now rector of St. Anne's Parish in Albemarle County, Virginia, just south of Charlottesville. Interestingly, he sees a common thread between serving in the Corps and serving in a church. In both, he says, "There's a camaraderie and male bonding." In the mid-1980s, when he was assigned to a parish in South Carolina, he adds, fourteen of the eighty-three Episcopal priests in the state were former Marines.

Peter Braestrup, a Marine officer in Korea and later a war correspondent for the *New York Times* and the *Washington Post,* argues that the Marines are uniquely adept at maintaining their culture, and points to its alumni as a major reason for this. "Of all the institutions I've been associated with—Harvard, Yale, *Time* magazine, the *New York Times,* the Marine Corps," he says, "the only one that has really clung to its essence has been the Marine Corps.

"The interesting thing," Braestrup continues, "is how does this institution of the Marines survive in this American society? I would make the argument that what makes it happen is the continuity of the tribe—its alumni, its supporters in Congress, its unswerving nature."

The strength of the Marine Corps bond is visible on any American highway. There are only one-sixth as many Marine veterans in the United States as there are Army vets, but Marine decals and stickers are far more common on the roads. One rear window will have the small round red-and-black globe-and-anchor emblem, a pickup bumper will wear the bright yellow-and-red bumper sticker reading "SEMPER FI," and another will tote a sticker saying "A FEW GOOD MEN." Lately, a new one has been appearing: "MY SON IS A MARINE." These emblems resemble the university stickers that Americans uniquely post on their automobile windows. And the Marines, after all, play the role in the American working class that the Ivy League colleges have played for the upper middle class.

But the Marine hold is far deeper than any Ivy League connection. Walk into the living room of Jim Vinyard's house outside Hartsville, South Carolina, and you will be greeted by his dog Brittany. "Brit, would you rather be in the Army or be dead?" asks Vinyard. The dog rolls over on its back and thrusts its four paws in the air.

The bumper sticker on the back of Vinyard's station wagon repeats the phrase: "Once a Marine, always a Marine." The license plate on his other car reads MARINES. (It has helped him sidestep at least one speeding ticket.) Instead of a rec room, his house has a "Marine room," with a doormat that says "Semper Fidelis." One section of the room is a monument to the 4th Marine Division, in which his father served as a tank officer at Iwo Jima. A 7.7-millimeter Japanese rifle his father brought back from that battle hangs above the map his father used there.

Another wall of the room is dedicated to Vinyard's time in Vietnam, where he served about five miles away from where

James Webb had fought a year earlier. "I always wanted to be a Marine. It's the desire to be associated with the best. It's also a patriotic thing—I wanted to fight in my generation's war, and I drew Vietnam." A big topographical map of the Dai Loc area is accompanied by an AK-47 and a Chinese assault rifle. On the pool table is a photo album of his time in Vietnam: "This is the Arizona Valley. . . . This is Football Island. . . . This is the outpost on Hill 210. . . . This is the day we killed those colonels. . . . This is Liberty Bridge."

Vintage Marine recruiting posters fill in the gaps on the walls. "The Marine Corps Builds Men." "We Don't Promise You a Rose Garden." "A Few Good Men."

The oddity is that Vinyard served only three years on active duty in the Marines, and then a few more in the reserves. "I became semidisillusioned in 1975," the low point for the Marines. "There were a lot of guys who wanted to wear the uniform, but weren't really Marines."

On this particular evening in March 1996, Vinyard presides over a meeting of the Palmetto detachment of the Marine Corps League. Some thirty-eight veterans and their wives meet in a warehouselike building behind a shopping mall on the western outskirts of Columbia, South Carolina. They begin the meeting by facing the United States flag, standing at attention, and reciting the Pledge of Allegiance. Then, still facing the flag, they sing the first stanza of "The Marine Corps Hymn," ending with the phrase, "We are proud to claim the ti-i-tle of United States Marines." Then they address a prayer to "The Supreme Commandant"—God as the top Marine of them all.

The Marines are about remembering. Paul Quattlebaum, who now works for BellSouth as a technician, has brought photos from Vietnam, where he served with Charlie Company, 1st Battalion of the 7th Marines. He graduated from Parris Island just as James Webb was leaving Annapolis. "I was out there in the Arizona Valley, and west of Da Nang," he says. He shows a photograph of Charles "Audie" Caldwell grinning. "He was killed by a sniper as we were going into a treeline." Then there is Lewis Dittmer. "It was the middle of the night. He said, 'Koala Bear, do you have any C rations?' I said, 'No'—I hadn't brought any because it was a really hurry-up operation. So he stretched and he was cut in half by machine gun fire. I'll never forget his eyes then." He points at another picture, of two Marines in the Arizona Valley, one with an M-16, the other with an M-79 grenade launcher. "This is Dave Robertson. He got shot real bad in the legs. I never saw him again."

Quattlebaum looks up from the photo album. "When they tell you to get up, in the Marines you don't have to worry if the guys on your left and right is gonna get up." He has already given his family written instructions on how he wants his funeral conducted. First they will sing "The Old Rugged Cross." Next, "Amazing Grace." Then "Onward Christian Soldiers." Finally, "perhaps most importantly," he writes, "The Marine Corps Hymn." His tombstone will read: LANCE CPL. PAUL EDWIN QUATTLEBAUM.

Also at the meeting is Art Caselli, who was in the Marines for just three years and in the Army for seventeen—but is here at a Marine Corps League meeting wearing a Marine Corps League cap. "Semper fi," he says. Then there is Larry Clark, who was wounded in Vietnam. He tells of one of his "Marine tickets," an encounter with a sheriff near Augusta, Georgia, who pulled him over when he was doing close to eighty. The sheriff eyed the Marine emblem and the Viet vet sticker. "What unit were you with in Vietnam?" the lawman asked.

"Echo 2/5," Clark replied.

"I was with Echo 2/7," the sheriff said. "Have a nice day." And he drove away.

Another old Marine attending tonight's session is retired Col. George Ayers, who served in both Vietnam and the Gulf War, and who is now a social worker. "I owe the Marine Corps more than I could ever repay," he comments.

That sense of indebtedness to the Corps is common among its veterans. In Akron, Ohio, Ernie Passeos, owner of Liberty Harley-Davidson, one of the largest Harley dealers in the country, credits the Marines with making him a success in business. He joined in 1956 after being expelled from high school. "I truly believe that without the discipline instilled by my drill instructors, Sgt. James Farhat and Sgt. William Mitchell, I would have ended up in a less than desirable situation," he said.

But of the 2.1 million vets of the Marine Corps alive today, none seem more dedicated to the Corps than those from South Boston. In *A Country Such As This,* James Webb, a son of the Confederacy, honors South Boston as "the greatest Marine Corps enclave north of the Mason-Dixon line." In another novel, *A Sense of Honor,* Webb has one of his heroes come from that embattled corner of Boston. "South Boston flocked to the Corps with the eagerness that Scarsdale reserves for Harvard," Webb wrote in that book, artfully compressing a decade of resentment into fourteen simple words.

Physically, the scale and feel of South Boston is slightly medieval—a huddle of three- and four-story buildings surrounded on three sides by water, with the fourth walled off from downtown Boston by a ship channel and Interstate 93. Boston is one of the few American cities that continually fights a two-front war, deeply divided along lines of both race and class. So South Boston's overwhelmingly white 38,000 residents remain girded for battle not only with black Bostonians but also with Boston's elites—the rich folk in Brookline and up on the North Shore, the intellectual snobs over at Harvard and MIT, the smart-asses down at the *Boston Globe.* "We take care of our own," could be South Boston's motto. It is a warfighting cry, probably not apt for civil society.

But then society hasn't always been civil to South Boston. Think back to what the world looked like to a Southie at the end of the 1970s. First there was the Vietnam War, begun by that crowd from Harvard that went to Washington with Kennedy. It consumed twenty-five men from this neighborhood. Just as that war was grinding to a close, a judge in a courtroom in Boston ordered that forced busing begin here. On September 12, 1974, the busses began rolling into South Boston; eight months later, the last Marine helicopter lifted off the U.S. embassy in Saigon as the city fell. In the eyes of Southies, the Vietnam War and bussing were of a piece: In each case, they heard liberal elites saying, "Let's you and him fight"—first the yellow man, then the black man.

It is no accident that the drive to build a Vietnam Memorial, the first in the country, began in South Boston in the wake of the busing riots. Nor is it an accident that Andrew Lee, Platoon 3086's honor graduate, when sitting at home in his family's house across the street from that memorial and trying to explain South Boston to a visitor, pulls a book called *Southie Won't Go* from the shelves of his parents' library. That memoir, with its title oddly echoing the Vietnam War protesters' chant of "Hell no, we won't go," is by Ione Malloy, a English teacher at South Boston High School during the busing troubles.

It is typical of the Marines, with their in-your-face love of confrontation, that their recruiter now assigned to South Boston is Sgt. Alfonso McNeil, who despite his name is a black Marine from New York. Asked what it is like being a black man working in Southie, he notes that he was told he could turn the job down without any repercussions, but instead accepted it. "It was a leadership challenge," he says as he drives along Southie's West Broadway, resplendent in his stiffly creased khaki shirt, necktie, and dress blue pants with a scarlet "blood stripe" down the outside seams. He is wearing his decorations, including one for service in the Gulf War. The Marines use him to send a message to Southie: Join the Corps, and you might very well take orders from someone this color. The only drawback he has found to working here, he says, is that Marine veterans are constantly trying to pull him into bars for beers. Does he ever come down here without wearing his uniform? No, he smiles.

James Webb had been interested in South Boston ever since he heard some of the Marines in his platoon in Vietnam, clearly broad-accented Bostonians, calling each other "Southie." He thought *he* was the Southerner. "I said, 'What is this 'Southie?' "

So when Tommy Lyons telephoned Webb in 1981 to ask him to

be the guest of honor at the dedication of the South Boston Vietnam Veterans Memorial, Webb was interested. Lyons had joined the Marines with six friends in June 1967 after graduating from South Boston High. Three of them died in Vietnam. In 1978, he and his surviving friends began talking about putting up a Vietnam Memorial, when it was clear that no one else would.

Lyons offered to pay for Webb's transportation and lodging. Webb said he'd stay with a Marine buddy, and didn't want any money. But he did have a favor to ask: "I want to come up a day early and have you show me around South Boston."

Then came the dedication. "They put out the word," Webb remembers. " 'We're having a parade for Vietnam veterans. If you're one, fall in behind the piper.' " The Kevin Barry Irish Bagpipes and Drums played, with about 250 veterans marching behind. The inscription on the memorial was phrased as a message from the grave: IF YOU FORGET MY DEATH, THEN I DIED IN VAIN.

"Because of the memorial, people starting looking (at their military service) with honor and respect," Tommy Lyons recalls. "That's all we wanted."

The event was so successful that they repeated it again the next year, and then again, until it became an annual ceremony. On the fifth anniversary, Lyons suggested that they round up some friends a few months later on November 10th to celebrate the Marine Corps' birthday. The date also carried a private meaning for Lyons. "For me, this is a double-edged sword, because Johnny and Joe died November ninth and tenth," he says, referring to two of the names on the memorial, John Henry Cole and Joseph Desmond. On those days, he found, "I think about where they'd be now, what their families would be like."

Word got out, and thirty-eight former Marines from around Boston showed up at the lunch at an Italian restaurant in the North End. The next year, sixty-eight appeared. So was born "The Semper Fi Society." In 1995, the luncheon, moved to Anthony's Pier 4, drew 1,400. It has grown from a few Vietnam vets to what Lyons calls a "history of the Marine Corps," pulling in people like Eddie

"No Toes" Toland, "who lost his toes at Frozen Chosin." But it has always remained a lunch: "If guys had dinner, they'd have all the time in the world to drink, and it would go on forever."

One cold afternoon in Boston, Lyons gathers four other members of the Semper Fi Society for lunch. Over clam chowder, they talk about what the Marines mean to them. Ed Quinn, a retired FBI agent, notes that every November 10th, "The Marine Corps Hymn" is played on a harmonica over the office intercom in the Boston office of the FBI. In 1974, he remembers, some forty FBI agents in New York, all of them former Marines, got together for a Marine Corps dinner. Now opened to other law enforcement personnel, the dinner now draws more than 700, he says. Having served in the Marines and the FBI, he says, "I feel like I've been part of two of the three most exclusive fraternities—and the third is the priesthood."

"It certainly affected my career," adds Bob Howe, chairman of Atlantic Data Services Inc., which writes software for banks. "You use the shortest lines of communication. You don't have a lot of staff. You put a lot of weight on loyalty, esprit de corps. I judge people as a team—and the team takes care of itself. The downside is, you get a little crazy coming out of that environment. You tend to be a risk-taker." You also learn about remembrance and honor: Howe fondly tells of the time when, driving up Interstate 95 through Quantico, Virginia, he took his wife to lunch at the officers' club at the Marine base there. He had never been in the club before, but explained that he was a Marine veteran of Vietnam. When he got up to leave, he found that someone had picked up the tab anonymously. Clearly, it was the gesture, not the few dollars, that was important to this company chairman.

Then it is the turn of Tom White, who like many of his colleagues in Boston has been a firefighter ever since he left the Marines. "The fire department is a semimilitary organization," he says. "Out of twelve hundred Boston firefighters, about nine hundred are Marines."

But the most compelling tale of the continuing influence of the Corps comes from John Nolen, a Marine veteran of Beirut who is now operations director for the New England Shelter for Homeless Veterans. "It's applied every day of my life," he says. A visitor to the center, in downtown Boston, is met at the front door not by a receptionist, but by a "command post." Behind it is a mural of the Iwo Jima flag-raising. In front of it on this February day is a movable-letter sign that on this day commemorates "James J. Stewart. South Boston. 2 15 68." Upstairs, on the wall of the director's office, hangs an autographed portrait of Al Gray—posted just slightly higher than the adjacent photograph of P. X. Kelley.

But this isn't just another collection of Marine Corps memorabilia. In fact, it is a little outpost of Parris Island smack in downtown Boston. About half the 250 men who sleep there on an average night are Vietnam veterans. Look around the long, bare rooms, the just-cleaned beds, and the swept floors, and one place comes to mind: a barracks at boot camp.

The resemblance is intentional, explains Nolen. "A guy comes through the door, maybe twenty or twenty-five years of substance abuse, and says, 'Fix me.' We rely on the one common denominator they all have—recruit training, which may be the last time a lot of them felt pride in themselves." As at Parris Island, there are strict rules and regulations. To stay here, you must be clean and sober, and you must be actively looking for work. "In a nutshell," says Nolen, summarizing the familiar formula, "you have to go through a lot of pain, you have to strip yourself down and start all over again."

CHAPTER SEVEN

BACK IN THE WORLD

They know they have changed, but they don't realize how much. Staff Sergeant Rowland does. Watching them walk to their parents' cars after graduating, he quietly predicts, "They're going to be in shock for a couple of days."

Pvt. Craig Hoover is jolted by the Amtrak ride home to Kensington, Maryland. Unlike many of his comrades, Hoover hadn't been as quick to condemn civilian society. For the yin of discipline, he argued during "Warrior Week," there has to be a yang of indiscipline. Then he gets on the train with his father. "It was horrible. The train was filled with smoke, people were drinking, and their kids were running around aimlessly," he says a few days later. "You felt like smacking around some people."

Hoover also finds the train ride a sad contrast to the relative racial harmony of Parris Island. "It felt kind of segregated by race and class—a poor white car, a poor black car, a middle-class white car, a middle-class black car." Even McDonald's, which had become a fantasy-like symbol to the recruits as they ate military rations in the piney woods, proves to be an odd letdown. "You look around and notice that a lot of the civilians are overweight, and a little sloppy," says Private Hoover.

Also riding on the Amtrak, Private First Class Weber goes to the diner. "You want beans with that?" the waiter asks.

"Yes, SIR!" Weber bellows back. Startled heads turn to look at him. "I didn't realize I was sounding off," he chuckles later.

Like many members of 3086, Pvt. Frank DeMarco undergoes disorientation followed by repugnance. "Driving off the island was weird. You're released. It felt unbelievable to get off. Everything looked different. We saw trees you wouldn't see on the island. It was great." Then his family stopped at South of the Border, a giant tawdry gas station and tourist attraction on Interstate 95, on the northern edge of South Carolina, advertised by hundreds of billboards along the lines of "Pedro's Weather Report: Chili today, hot tamale." "I didn't care for it. It was very low," says Private DeMarco, a stocky, ever-smiling fireplug who plans on going into motor transport work—truck driving—in the Marines.

The recruits find that they feel distant from their old friends and repelled by crowds. Pvt. Jonathan Prish, the former white supremacist, goes to a bar back in Mobile, Alabama. "We played pool and drank," he reports. "It seemed like everyone there was losers. All they want to do is get smashed. They're self-destructive. They're not trying. They're just goofing around."

In the Washington suburb of Potomac, Maryland, Eric Didier feels the same way. "I think I matured a bit on Parris Island, 'cause I look at what my friends are doing, and it seems dumber to me than it did before. They're not getting anything accomplished.

"There are some friends I've stayed away from," he confesses. "They're not going anywhere, and I don't want to be around them. We don't have any common ground." Though they are in their early twenties, he says, "they're not doing anything, living at home, not working, not studying."

In Pittsburgh, Pvt. Patrick Bayton goes to a Saturday night party and also winds up calling two old friends "losers." But, he says, "They respected me for it. They knew I was right." Over a beer he says, "Everything feels different. I can't stand half my friends no more." They are still doing what he used to do: living

at the corner, "drinking the forties"—that is, big forty-ounce
bottles of Mickey's, St. Ives, and other malt liquors. "That's all we
used to do," he has realized. Finding that is all they still want to
do, he begins avoiding them after a few days. "I just can't sit with
my friends and drink and watch them messing up their lives. My
friend John, I can't stand to see him."

He is far more comfortable spending time with his new peer
group, the four other members of 3086 from the Pittsburgh
area. As they sit in an upscale bar and grill overlooking the
Monongahela River, Bayton dismisses civilians. "Some of them are
okay, but they need motivation," he concludes. Mark Beggs
agrees: "They lack self-respect."

The new Marines soon realize they are part of a nationwide
brotherhood. Nathan Weber is speeding down a residential street
in West Chester, Pennsylvania, doing forty miles per hour in a
twenty-five mph zone, when a police car pulls him over. He produces his military ID, "'cause I'd heard stories that it helps." It does.
"He just smiled and said, 'Slow down and have a nice day.'"

Later, Weber's girlfriend is in a minor car accident. Weber, who
is in uniform, goes to help, directing traffic around the scene while
a cop talks to the driver who hit his girlfriend's car. A carload of
Marines also in uniform stops and asks him, "Marine, you need
help?"

They revel in their separateness and marvel at the respect they
receive from civilians. "I've noticed that civilians get out of your
way. And they call you 'sir,'" says James Andersen. What's more,
they are intrigued by some of the negative reactions they receive.
Donald Campas relates an incident that occurred one night at
South Park, when he was showing off his uniform, standing at
parade rest, feet apart, hands together behind his back, and
hanging out with friends. A passing driver, "a kind of pathetic
thirty-year-old who hung out with a younger crowd," yelled out,
"Oh, you're in the Marines, huh? They just teach you how to kill,
that's all you know." Campas continues: "I said, 'I get paid to
defend trash like you.' He just drove away." Campas grins.

In Boston, Pvt. Charles Lees, trying to keep the weight off his huge frame, extends his usual eight-mile run to ten. The new route takes him through Harvard Square. There, a knot of teenagers, most likely suburbanites pretending they're not, shout at the reservist in his distinctive yellow Marine T-shirt and green Marine shorts. One kid says that Lees should be ashamed of himself. "I wanted to hit him, but I knew that wouldn't be good for the Corps. I started to walk away. But it really bothered me." So Lees walks back to the loudest kid, puts his hands on his hips, and quietly says, "Look, I'm willing to die to defend your right to say that. Just don't say it to me." Then he jogs off.

But even the genial Lees is surprised at how aggressive he can be. Showing off his Marine uniform to old friends at Holy Cross, they go out for a beer. He gazes at a woman in the bar, not noticing that she has a man with her. Her male friend looks at Lees in a challenging way. Lees accepts instantly. "What are you looking at, freak, you want to go outside right now?" he snarls. The man backs off. In retrospect, Lees is amazed at his own behavior: "I opened my mouth and Sergeant Zwayer came out."

Later that day, Lees, not feeling entirely comfortable with the college crowd yet not ready to go home to his family, stops at the Marine Corps League's bar in Worcester, Massachusetts. "I said, 'I'm not a member, but can I come in?'" A knot of older men at the bar sees him. "Buy that devildog a beer," says one. They are Korean War vets. For two hours they ply him with free drinks and stories about fighting their way out of Chosin Reservoir.

At McDonald's, in parks, at bars, and in stores, almost every member of 3086 seems to experience a moment of private loathing for public America. For Private DeMarco it occurs at a street fair in Bayonne, New Jersey. "It was crowded. Trash everywhere. People were drinking, getting into fights. People with obnoxious attitudes, no politeness whatsoever." But, says the smiling private, "I didn't let it get to me. I just said, 'This is the way civilian life is: nasty.'" When he experiences civilian rudeness, he lets it pass. "You don't want to get down to their level.

"I don't know what it is" about civilian life, he continues, sitting at his mother's dining room table in Scotch Plains, New Jersey, wearing a blue THIRD BATTALION T-shirt. "Everybody is at each other's necks. If you're driving, and you're not going fast enough, someone's on your tail. There's no politeness." But, he adds, he did encounter one small and unexpected moment of friendliness. Driving on Route 22 through the nearby town of Union in his mother's Chevrolet, which sports five Marine Corps stickers, all new, he passes another car with its own Marine sticker. "He saw my stickers and waved," the private recalls. "It was very nice—kind of a relief."

DeMarco's buddy John Hall, a fellow graduate of Bayonne High School, also feels transformed. On the plane ride home from Charleston, he dons his headphones and leans back to relax. "I closed my eyes, and I saw Drill Instructor Sergeant Carey yelling at me." (This vivid internalization is a common experience for members of 3086. Private Bayton, for example, reports that, "I was shopping yesterday for civilian clothes, and I found myself thinking, *Would Drill Instructor Sergeant Carey like this?* Then I was at a party and I find myself drinking a beer and Irish pennanting my new baseball cap," he says, borrowing Sergeant Carey's term for removing loose threads on clothing.) Arriving at Newark Airport, Hall gives his girlfriend, Jill—by then, eight months pregnant—a stiff hug. "That's all?" she asks. He grins: "Save that trash for later. I'm in uniform. Let's get out of here."

Jill is also stunned to see Private Hall, who used to keep his bedroom a "pigsty," hop out of bed by 7:00 A.M. every morning and begin "squaring away" the room. "*Everything* has to be shipshape, that's what bothers me," she complains.

Private Hall also finds himself avoiding many old friends. "I was talking to Jeff, and after awhile I just said, 'All right, let me go,'" he confesses. He thinks the Marines—or at least the military—is the answer to what ails them, and so tries to talk his brother and then two old friends into joining. "Mikey," who weighs close to 300 pounds, tells Hall that he is too fat for the

military. "I said, 'You're got to stop looking down on yourself,' "
Hall recalls.

Over coffee in his mother's second-story walk-up on Bayonne's
Twenty-fourth Street, in a gritty Ukranian-American neighborhood of two-family houses and soot-colored churches, Hall half-
jokingly calls civilians "a bunch of freaks."

His mother looks at him wide-eyed. "Do you really feel like
that?" she asks.

He considers for a moment, and then says, "Yeah, I do." The
bells of St. Joseph's church ring outside.

Not everyone in 3086 thinks civilians are freaks. Down in
southern Jersey, the easy-going, even-keeled Edward Linsky says
simply, "They don't know any better." He still hangs out on
leave at his old haunt, Stef and Ed's Bar. "I don't believe all civilians are nasty. I was a civilian before I joined the Marines."

Interestingly, the member of 3086 who is perhaps most
estranged from his surroundings is probably Daniel Keane, the
one from the most privileged background. Keane seems dis-
turbed, almost in pain, as he sits in the living room of his parents'
house in a leafy Merrill Lynch-ish neighborhood in Summit, New
Jersey. A baby grand piano sits near the window, which, true to
the town's name, enjoys a sweeping view of the valley below. The
maid leaves for the day as his mother, who teaches psychology at
the nearby College of St. Elizabeth, walks in and makes a pro-
nouncement to a visitor: "I had reservations about Daniel's joining the Marines at first, but now I think every eighteen-year-old
in America should do this for three months. It's made a real difference in him."

Keane is set to leave for training at the Marine School of
Infantry, near Camp Lejeune, in just a few days—and he can't
wait. He was even at odds with his family when he first got home
from Parris Island. "I didn't know how to act. They said, 'What
do you want to do?' I'd say, 'I don't know.' I didn't know how to
carry on a conversation." The family's dog, a baby pug, strolls
into the room and asks to be picked up.

But his friends were even worse. "Going out at night, hanging out, the atmosphere—it's the same as it was, but it's different to me. It doesn't seem so interesting." Keane, now eighteen, dropped out of Morris County Community College before enlisting. "All my friends are home from college now, drinking, acting stupid and loud. I'm just sitting there watching." For him, he says, being a beer-swilling frat boy "would be almost tougher than boot camp." He is acutely conscious of his new status in life. "If a policeman comes over to a group I'm with, and he knows I'm a Marine, maybe from my haircut or answers, he'll say, 'Why are you letting this happen?' "

He struggles to articulate his profound new sense of alienation from his old life. "It's so hard to put into words," he continues. "I went to Six Flags Great Adventure yesterday. I've got nothing against fat people, but these were young people, overweight, smoking and eating when they could be working out."

The big, soft-spoken Marine looks at his old friends in the same harsh light. "There's been a couple of times when I've been disappointed in my friends." Most painfully, there were the two who refused to postpone smoking marijuana for a few minutes, until he was away from them. "They were getting ready to smoke their weed. I said, 'Could you just hang on for a minute, can't you wait 'til you get to the party instead of smoking in the car?' They said, 'Then we'd have to give it out' "—and lit up in front of their Marine friend. "I was pretty disappointed in them doing that. It made me want to be at SOI"—that is, infantry school.

Like many members of 3086, Keane feels like he has joined a new cult or religion that his old friends don't know about. "People don't understand, and I'm not going to waste my breath trying to explain, when the only thing that really impresses them is how much beer you can chug down in thirty seconds."

In southeast Washington, D.C., at the other end of the American socioeconomic scale, Earnest Winston Jr. sits in his mother's living room under a framed "Wake-Up Call" by Minister Louis

Farrakhan. Like the other black members of 3086, he isn't experiencing the profound shock that the white recruits are undergoing. These black kids have always been suspicious of the mainstream of American society; boot camp has just added another layer to that alienation. Most of all, he says, Parris Island simply wasn't the transformative experience that it was for the white kids. "Boot camp really wasn't that intense for me. Here, you've got to watch your back. I've got to get back in the habit of walking the side cuts and alleys," because on the main streets there are too many drive-by shootings.

"It's like I never left," he says of his old neighborhood. As for his being a Marine, his friends "kind of look up to it—they're proud." He won't attempt to recruit them, though: "With their records, they can't get in." Winston doesn't blame them for what they've done, just for their doing it incompetently: despite eleven weeks of lectures about honor and integrity, he still believes that, "a crime is only a crime if you get caught." And he still doesn't regret the drive-by shootings he committed himself. "It's almost like a ritual, something that's gotta be done."

Like Keane, Winston is surrounded by old friends using drugs. "Marijuana, PCP—my former drugs." But, he says, when he is with them, "I'm not even tempted anymore. I wouldn't do anything to jeopardize my Marine Corps career. If I need to get a little high, I'll get a little bottle of Tanqueray. Smoking (marijuana) would be disrespectful of what I learned at Parris Island."

The one characteristic that Winston does seem to share with the rest of 3086 is the internalization of Sergeant Carey. His face hints at a half smile, or at least looks less grim than he usually does. "It's funny," he says. "I thought about him yesterday when my guys were out there smoking (marijuana). I think he would have said, 'What are you doing, Winston?' He was the Truth. He could make it out here, even though he's white. He's what makes the Marines. He helped me become a Marine. I appreciated him and respected him more than any other person on that island."

But Christopher Anderson isn't buying that. Unlike Winston and most of the rest of 3086, he never developed an awe of Sergeant Carey. "I respect him for his knowledge and ability, but as a person, that's a different story."

Though living in far better circumstances than Winston, in a garden apartment complex not far from the University of Maryland, Anderson is far more bitter about American society. "If I could live my life over, it would be in Africa," he says glumly. That may be one reason his career in the Corps will prove to be far shorter.

Sitting on the patio of the apartment in the humid darkness of a warm early summer night, Anderson is a stew of anger and resentment. He always thought America sucked, and now he sees even more things about it that he dislikes. He has dropped all his old drug-dealing friends, he says. "I didn't just dis them. I explain to them, 'I've been to hell and back for eleven weeks. I lose it all if you've got that trash.' They understand." He doesn't much like civilians in general: "They're all 'me, me, me.' People at the 7-Eleven arguing over stupid stuff." Nor does he have much good to say about his white comrades in 3086. "Bayton, he didn't know how to put his uniform on right. Marching, he'd dittybop, bouncing up and down, like he was back on the block. Linsky, he was the type of guy who would toy with you. Mendez, he was the only person in the platoon I wanted to strangle. He'd always smile. He was always the last to finish eating, and we'd have to pay for him" with extra exercise.

So how does Private Anderson feel about being a member of the armed forces that protect this society he despises? "Defending my country? Well, it's not really my country. I may live in America, but the United States is so screwed up."

He sees no contradiction in the fact that he is wearing the dress blue pants and tan shirt of a private in the United States Marine Corps. "The Corps is less screwed up" than society, he argues. "It's more disciplined, and everybody is under the UCMJ." So he is, after all, glad that he enlisted: "I wanted the title. I've always wanted to be the best."

He add one final thought, which in retrospect reads like a foreshadowing of his future troubles: "I don't see change in myself, tell the truth. But it did teach me to hold my tongue."

Depot Sgt. Maj. Harold Moore, the top sergeant on Parris Island, where sergeants are king, has long worried about sending newly minted Marines back out into society. "It's difficult to go back into a society of 'What's in it for me?' when a Marine has been taught the opposite for so long," he says. "It's a large adjustment to make." Society's troubles nowadays are widening this gap, Sergeant Major Moore argues. "When I came up" in Sandersville, Georgia, "I think there was more teaching of patriotism. We prayed in school. In the Marines, we still put an emphasis on patriotism, on being unselfish, on trying to serve society.

"When I look at society today, I see a group of young people without direction because of the lack of teaching of some of those things. We see that when we get them in recruit training. The recruits are smarter today—they run rings around what we were able to do, on average. Their problems are moral problems—lying, cheating, and stealing, and the very fact of being committed. We find that to get young people to dedicate themselves to a cause is difficult sometimes."

Because of the nature of American society today, the reentry shock of leaving recruit training appears to be greater now than it was in the past. Asked to explain this difference, retired Marine Lt. Gen. Bernard Trainor noted that, "When I got out of boot camp in 1946, society was different. It was more disciplined, and most Americans trusted the government. Most males had some military experience. It was an entirely different society, one that thought more about its responsibilities than its rights."

CHAPTER EIGHT

IN THE MARINES

Ask an American soldier to identify himself, and he probably will say he is "in the Army." By contrast, a Marine—especially if he is one of the better ones—is likely to say, "I'm a Marine." The small linguistic difference is significant: The first is a matter of membership or occupation; the second speaks to identity. One belongs to the Army (or, sometimes, to a branch of the Army—infantry, artillery, armor, Special Forces, and so on). But one is a Marine—and to be a Marine is sufficient. Army officers wear "U.S." on their "Class A" uniform lapels. Marine officers wear the globe, anchor, and eagle emblem of their service. And while Army officers wear nametags on their uniforms, Marine officers don't. That's partly because it is enough to simply be recongized as a Marine. To be in the Corps is to be in a state of mind that dictates one's relationship to the rest of the world.

The story of the experiences of the members of Platoon 3086 in the actual Marine Corps is the story of the testing of their new identities as Marines. Most will struggle at times to maintain their new selves, and most will succeed. But some falter and fall away from the Corps—especially those who maintained ties to home, to their old lives. Over 3086's first year in the Marines, six of the platoon's fifty-five graduates will be discharged. Another two will desert. These eight had made it through boot camp and been certified as Marines, yet somehow couldn't hold on.

Hearing about the discharges, Lt. Col. Michael Becker, 3086's old boot camp battalion commander, says the eight unfortunates who didn't make it through are "casualties in our war"—the Marines' battle with contemporary American values. About one-third of all Marines fail to complete their first term of enlistment in the Corps. "When we take young people off the streets of America, we're in a war to transform them from their old values, or no values, into Marine values," the colonel concludes.

The testing of their identities begins soon after "boot leave," when the new Marines report for three weeks of Marine Combat Training near Camp Lejeune, on the North Carolina coast. If Parris Island was the place of birth for these new Marines, then Marine Combat Training is their adolescent phase—awkward, baffling, difficult, and generally unsatisfactory. The biggest difference is that at Lejeune, the new Marines lack the mother hen DIs who watched their every move and constantly corrected their posture, both physical and mental. In place of Rowland, Carey, and Zwayer are mostly second-rate sergeants who make it clear they don't give a rat's ass whether these new Marines succeed or not. The members of 3086 soon become like teenage boys discovering just how lame their fathers can be.

"MCT sucked," Joshua Parise reports. "It was a joke. You get out of boot camp all motivated, and then you don't do anything." The only significant moment he remembers is inadvertently stabbing himself in the thigh while trying to clip off a cartridge belt with a knife. Most of all, he is shocked by the low standards of the NCOs. "One of them would come in drunk," Parise said. "He was an idiot. And then there was this freak corporal who cut up live turtles in the swamp. Frogs, too. Sick little monkey."

Listening to Parise, Jumal Flow nods in agreement. He learned more about combat out in the piney woods of Parris Island than he did at MCT, he says. "At Parris Island, Sergeant Carey, he used to look like you could cut yourself on his cammies. He shined. At Marine Combat Training, our NCOs were overweight, and they looked like they slept in their cammies."

"They just put you out in the swamps, kind of goof around," says Marcel Laplante, one of the quieter members of 3086. Paul Bourassa, the ex-accountant, recalls that his unit had to march an extra five hours in the woods one night because some of the instructors had been drinking during the exercise, but left behind their garbage bag of empty beer bottles, and so had to walk the entire unit back to get the bag in the middle of the night.

Parris Island was theory—a showplace of what the Corps would like to be. There the recruits of 3086 were constantly told things like, "A Marine never lies." Lejeune is practice. Here the members of 3086 are a bit surprised to see that, in fact, some Marines do lie, cheat, steal, and whore around on the weekends in the strip bars just across the highway from the camp. On weekend leave from MCT, Jonathan Crigger and some 3086 buddies check into a hotel near Lejeune. He meets a woman who tells him she works at the motel. They drink, then sleep together. He then takes her out to a nearby dance club. Back at the room, two buddies also staying there tell him to get out, then both get into bed and have sex with her. He still puzzles over the night months later. "She was a nice girl from a small town but she turned into a whore," he says.

Charles Lees is astonished one night in the barracks to see a Marine pull a knife on another Marine. A staff sergeant escorts the offender from the room, but takes no subsequent formal action. "It kind of amazed me, after hearing all this talk about honor, courage, and commitment," Lees says.

Gregory Tenhet, who in boot camp received the salacious letters from his sweetheart, also goes through a difficult time. His girlfriend puts down her foot: her or the Marines. They break up while he is at artillery school at Fort Sill, Oklahoma, provoking Tenhet into a theatrical "suicide" attempt reminiscent of Trujillio's at Parris Island. After drinking with his buddies, a depressed Tenhet goes into the latrine barracks with a disposable razor. He stares at the razor and at his wrist for fifteen minutes, until a lance corporal sees him and pulls him out. Tenhet recovers yet still contemplates desertion. Then he reports to the 10th Marines at Lejeune. 3086's Robert Warren, also at Lejeune, takes him home one weekend to Murfreesboro, North Carolina. Tenhet meets Warren's eighteen-year-old sister, a senior in high school, and soon is dating her every weekend. They make plans to marry.

Worst off are those who try to straddle their old and new lives. Little Frank DeMarco and John Hall, 3086's two buddies from Bayonne, head out the camp gates every Friday night and drive 600 miles back to New Jersey, turning around on Sunday afternoon to make the ten-hour dash back to Lejeune. When Hall's girlfriend has their baby, their departures from the Corps become a matter of time.

DeMarco begins to sour on the Corps in MCT. Truck driving school was even worse. "It was shocking," says Hall, who attends it with his buddy. "You go from seeing guys like Sergeant Carey snap and pop, look good in their uniform—and then you go into the regular Marines and my platoon sergeant was all belly, and the company gunny was a mutt—didn't shave, his hair was long."

One lance corporal in particular gets on Hall's nerves. While marching he berates Hall for failing to show adequate respect to a higher rank. Hall pulls him aside. "If you ever talk to me like that again, I'll drop you," Hall whispers. The lance corporal begins screaming again, so Hall, a big man, unloads a punch that dislocates the corporal's jaw. Hall is docked two month's pay, which exacerbates his financial troubles. He falls behind on payments for his Jeep—all-important to making those 1,200-mile round trips every weekend. When he does get home, his girlfriend asks why, if he is such a big Marine, he can't support his own baby.

In July, during one drive home from truck driving school, DeMarco says he is thinking of leaving the Corps. "The more he went back home, the more he missed it," says Hall, who is still his best friend. "So he tried for a 'psych eval,' trying to get out." When DeMarco is assigned to a unit in the Fleet, continues Hall, "he did the crying game, and they gave him a psych discharge." Back home, he began to sleep all day and drink at night, Hall says. "I think he's changed for the worse."

For his part, DeMarco says he is still glad he went to boot camp. His '95 Saturn bears a Marine Corps globe-and-anchor sticker. But he wouldn't recommend the Corps to his friends. "If you don't have to join, don't," he says. "It's not what it's cracked up to be."

Hall soon follows his friend. He is told two months later that he is going to be posted to Hawaii. It sound like paradise to someone who grew up in the smoggy, small streets of Bayonne. He begins to make plans to marry his girlfriend and take his new family with him. Then his actual orders arrive: He is to go to Okinawa, which for enlisted Marines is an "unaccompanied tour." The Corps won't pay for families to travel and be housed there. Hall goes UA. After two months, he is declared a deserter. But he stays in touch with his platoon sergeant, calling about once a week, trying to figure how to put back together his life as a Marine. At night, Staff Sergeant Rowland and Sergeant Carey loom up in his guilty dreams. "You got to go back," the DIs tell him.

So eventually he reports back. His mother takes over his Jeep payments, but is unable to meet them, and is forced to file for protection from creditors under the personal bankruptcy law. The Jeep is grabbed by a repossession man one night. Hall has troubles securing medical benefits for his baby. He receives an "other than honorable discharge" and heads back to Bayonne.

Now he collects unemployment benefits, works on the side at a buddy's pizza parlor, and fantasizes about moving to Florida and starting over again. But as he speaks, his voice somehow conveys his knowledge that he won't ever go, that he is stuck in Bayonne—and that he somehow blew the one big chance he may have had for a different life. "I feel like I did all this work, and I'm back where I started," he says. "To be honest with you, it sucks."

He is haunted still by Sergeant Carey's teachings. "I always remember something he said: 'I don't just train Marines, I train winners.' I keep on thinking of that. All I wanted to do was become a drill instructor. Not become a commandant, or a big officer. A drill instructor. That is what I wanted to do in the Marine Corps, and it lingers in my head."

Scott Glica, the pizza parlor worker from near Buffalo, New York, who got off to a bad start in boot camp, begins equally badly at Marine Combat Training. At the end of MCT he is told he must stand guard duty for five weeks before attending a technical school. Instead he walks off base and catches a bus home. He eventually returns, but gets into trouble for drinking. On a tip from a sergeant, he requests a psychiatric evaluation and is given what he calls a "personality disorder" discharge. He now plans to become a prison guard in Arizona.

Christopher Anderson's knee condition continues to worsen. He is medically discharged in the summer of 1996, more bitter than ever. He soon falls back into his old identity of blaming the world. He now simply has more targets, most particularly Sergeant Carey, for pushing him to run when his knee hurt. "He fucked me," he says. Anderson's modus operandi is to blame everybody but himself. He could have dropped out of Platoon 3086, but he doesn't see it that way. "I'm only twenty-three, and excuse me, but I'm fucked for the rest of my life." He says he is taking lessons to drive trucks and buses, "because I'm looking for a job that won't keep me on my feet"; later in the same conversation he mentions that he is studying for a barber's license.

Craig Hoover, the community college dropout from Kensington, Maryland, never experienced an identity crisis at Parris Island. He probably was the member of 3086 least altered by boot camp, which never really reached him. But this also meant that he had no new identity to take with him into the Marines. "Everything washed right over me," he shrugs over stir-fried noodles at the diner where he had worked before enlisting in the Marines on a whim. "It just kind of happened, like I wasn't even there. It was just running through a process."

At Marine Combat Training, his fellow Marines sensed this lack of commitment. He is involved one night in a small incident that provokes endless rumors about him in the 3086 network. As Hoover tells it, he was on guard duty one summer weekend and snuck into a dark air-conditioned room behind the guard-post to sleep. The next morning, he is awakened by Winston pounding on the door for an early morning formation. "I ran out. I didn't know there was another Marine in there. He ran out behind me pulling up his pants." Winston, he says, initiated the gossip that "we'd been doing some weird bisexual act." Suddenly, 3086ers begin to recall that, "Yeah, Hoover used to look at me kind of funny in the communal shower." In their homophobia there may be a kernel of understanding that Hoover is in fact different: His identity is not that of a Marine.

Hoover's response is, essentially, "So what?" In the Marine reserves, Hoover's officers try to cajole and threaten him into getting with the program. Finally, when Hoover simply states that he is quitting, his battalion commander asks the essential question: How does Hoover feel about reneging on his commitment to God and country? "I told him that if you don't mean it, it's really just words.

"And I left. I've been happy ever since," he adds, as if this were the ultimate justification.

Today Hoover works for the Montgomery County Parks Department. During the winter he is a rink guard at a skating rink. "It's real laid back. You really don't do much." He says that approvingly. During the summer he drives a miniature train through the woods and fields of Wheaton Regional Park. He likes the pace: "They don't ask much of you." But he dislikes the atmosphere and especially the patrons: "These lesser-endowed people, Silver Spring people, minorities, get all irate over the wait and over paying a dollar a ride." On the side, he runs an Internet-based business called "The Toy Scout," locating toys such as *Star Wars* figurines for collectors.

Overall, Hoover has concluded that it is foolish to serve in the Marines, because there is no profit in it for the individual. "Being in the military, a lot of the time, doesn't pay off," he says. In fact, he adds, "all the military is is a system of slavery. They tell you where to be, how to be, how to cut your hair, and if you don't do it right, they punish you." In his view, that system is immoral. Sitting in the diner booth with his blue baseball cap on backward, he rubs the stubble on his chin. "You should be able to do what you want to do."

He walks back to his blue Chevrolet pickup in the diner's parking lot. On the bumper is a circular Marine Corps sticker. "Yeah," he explains. "I'm proud I made it through boot camp. I'm glad I went there. I enjoyed it. But people who don't fit in the Marine Corps shouldn't be there."

Tracking down other dischargees and deserters unexpectedly opens a door onto the disconnectedness of American life. There are mothers who say they don't know how to contact their sons, and brothers who lack telephone numbers for brothers living just a few miles away. But there is little surprise in whom the deserters prove to be. Sitting in a South Boston pub under a painting of the South Boston Vietnam Memorial, Andrew Lee guesses instantly when asked which member of 3086 deserted first. "Sabella," he replies without pausing. "He was a scumbag from day one. He lies about everything."

At boot camp, Sabella had insisted that he missed nothing about civilian life, where he had driven a towtruck on the highways of eastern Pennsylvania. "Marine Corps life is a hundred percent better," he had reported. "I feel like I belong to something now." But he was insecure in that feeling. Sensing that he could never really earn a Marine Corps identity, he built a false one, lying to fellow recruits that both his parents were senior sergeants in the Corps.

Sabella's troubles begin at the end of boot leave, during which he gets married to the girl who said he shouldn't come home to her unless he came back as a Marine. Now she wants him to leave the Marines. Bored at the School of Infantry, he begins doing just that, heading home without leave three times, and then, after staying at home in Bethlehem, Pennsylvania, for a few weeks each time, eventually reporting back to Camp Lejeune. The fourth time he goes home and decides he isn't going back at all. Now a deserter, Sabella, and his wife, take off for Florida. "There were too many people looking for them," reports one of his wife's relatives. "He's just one problem after another." He finds work as an automobile mechanic in Daytona Beach.

The Marines officially declare Sabella a deserter. One late winter morning he is awakened by a knock on his door. A buddy who deserted with him and was later caught when stopped for speeding has turned him in. The two policemen at the door ask him if he is Daniel Sabella. "No," he lies, "that's my nephew."

Asked for identification, he claims he is on vacation and has none with him. The police ask him to step outside and handcuff him. He is shipped to the brig at Camp Lejeune and held in that jail-like atmosphere for nearly three months, until he is court-martialed in March 1996. The Marine Corps dismisses him with a bad-conduct discharge and a loss of pay for the time he was in the brig. He heads back to Florida to the pregnant wife he left behind. She gives birth in October, but, he says, the child died in December. Soon afterward they head home to Bethlehem, where he goes back to work driving a towtruck.

For all that, Sabella says he is grateful to the Marines. "It changed me," he says. "I was wild, aggressive, out of control. Now I have a job, I'm married, I'm one of the head people at my job."

Another member of 3086, an unremarkable man in the middle who never attracted much attention while on Parris Island, also deserts from Camp Lejeune and disappears somewhere into the South. Chad Shelton reports that this Marine went home without leave to deal with family problems and then, on his return, had some other difficulties. Soon thereafter, Shelton says, this Marine left for good.

The common thread between Wells, Sabella, and the third Marine is that all three had wives or children or both—which underscores the wisdom of the Marines' aborted 1993 initiative to ban marriages among first-term Marines. Young Marines marry at a much higher rate than do civilians of the same age. And that causes enormous problems for the Marines who manage them, and who worry about their housing. It is much cheaper to keep a single soldier in the barracks than it is to house him and his wife and children, and also pay for their medical care, and perhaps build schools and day care centers for the children. 1st Sgt. Reginald Lewis, the senior sergeant of Alpha Company, 1st Battalion of the 7th Marines, commented during that unit's deployment to Somalia that he spent about half his work time dealing with spousal problems—"like teaching them that you have to cook, even if it's just microwaving some broccoli, that you can't call Domino's every night." Nor, he added, when the husband is away for a six-month tour aboard a ship or overseas, should the wife become too friendly with the Domino's man. The Marines may attempt again in a few years to impose the first-term marriage ban. They are likely to succeed the next time, if only because the enormous savings in time and money that could be realized will become more enticing as the defense budget gets tighter.

Not all members of 3086 have a turbulent time becoming full-fledged Marines. Some simply revel in their new selves. Andrew Lee knows he is a Marine, and nothing can take that away from him. He charges through MCT and into infantry training without breaking stride. He is selected as one of the top two graduates of his platoon and is promoted to lance corporal, placing him two ranks above many 3086ers, a powerful performance in the rank-conscious Corps.

Nathan Weber fatalistically figures that whatever happens, it is what he signed up to do. "It rained constantly in the field, and I learned how to live with misery." His wet feet turn a pale green. Two toenails fall out. He reports to the medical corpsman, who asks him if he can still walk while carrying a rifle. Weber can, so he stays with the unit. "I felt this was what war would be like," Weber says approvingly.

Continuing his turnaround of the last few weeks of boot camp, Buijs solidifies his new identity as a Marine. He learns how to repair the radio jammers on EA-6B electronic warfare aircraft. He drives across America by himself, discovering, perhaps, that he is just as American as anybody else on the road. He gets a tattoo on his wrist. He writes to Jonathan Prish, the former white supremacist with whom he shares a taste for alternative rock music, to tell him about the design.

Buijs comes to love the Corps: "The camaraderie is awesome. People take care of you like you're their brother." He sometimes thinks he would like to go through boot camp again, and do it right this time. Along those lines, he applies for admission to the U.S. Naval Academy. But even if he goes to Annapolis, he says, he intends to return to the Marines after graduation. He may go further in the Corps than any other member of 3086. Having added drive and ambition to his existing intelligence and strength of personality, he now possesses a powerful mix of traits. He is just the sort of eccentric that the Marine Corps, unlike the U.S. Army, traditionally has indulged among some of its officers.

The middle group of 3086 settles into the reality of Marine life. They learn to live with the ambiguities and compromises of adulthood. No, their sergeants frequently don't live up to the standards set by their drill instructors. But most find what they were looking for in the Marines: genuine brotherhood. This is the foundation on which their identities now stand.

Private First Class Andersen, one of the Pittsburgh Marines, sips a Coke in the McDonald's on the Marine base at Quantico, forty-five minutes south of Washington, D.C. "In boot camp, you had drill instructors screaming in your face every time you screwed up," he says. "Here, it's more like a job." His NCOs especially "fall short of Careyism," Andersen says, coining a term easily grasped by anyone who knows Sergeant Carey. "The intensity isn't there. They're more like supervisors." But, he says, the sense of brotherhood "really is there. The people you meet look out for you."

Earnest Winston stays himself—but also somehow, just barely, stays a Marine. Gunnery Sergeant Camacho was correct in predicting that Winston would have a turbulent time in the Marines. The Washingtonian scuffles all the way through his first year in the Corps. At MCT he gets into what he dismisses as "small fights." At aviation school in Millington, Tennessee, he gets into bigger trouble. One night he and a friend, a white Marine, are on the town in nearby Memphis. A policeman tries to stop them. The friend runs. When the police catch the friend, they beat him, Winston says, for three reasons: because he is with a black man, because he ran, and because he has two marijuana joints on him. Winston testifies later that they called his friend a "nigger-lover." The friend says in a subsequent statement to Navy investigators that Winston is involved in selling marijuana—a charge Winston denies. Walking into a mess hall, Winston is picked up for interrogation by military police. He is restricted to barracks for weeks until cleared.

When the "legal hold" is lifted, Winston is posted to the Marine Corps Air Station at Iwakuni, Japan, where he specializes in the recovery of aircraft making emergency landings. He is pleasantly surprised by life in Japan. "It's beautiful," he says. "The people, they're nice. There's not as much violence as there is in the States. Drugs aren't tolerated. Not a lot of people on my block get to go to places like these."

But the scraps continue. Winston doesn't go out of his way to mess with people, but he won't shy away from insults. One night at the enlisted club, a drunk gets in his face, "disrespectful and vulgar, spitting, saying he needed to talk to me." Winston pushes him away. "You need to back off here," I said. "He came swinging at me." So Winston went at him with a flurry of slashing hits. In a few moments he breaks the other Marine's jaw and nose and inflicts cuts requiring twenty-two stitches.

"In a way, it's a fine institution," Winston says of the Corps. "But it's got its bad parts. It's got a bad problem with racism." After being called "Sambo" by a sergeant, Winston says, he brought charges and saw the man reduced in rank to corporal. "Some NCOs lack leadership ability," he adds. "They got a bad alcohol problem over here."

Still, Winston believes he owes his life to the Corps. "If I wouldn't have joined, I'd be in a grave or jail somewhere." He is a Marine.

The greatest single predictor of satisfaction in the Corps for the members of 3086 is simple distance from home. Generally, the farther away from their hometowns these new Marines are posted, the more they like the Corps. Parris Island draws recruits from the eastern United States, so the seven 3086ers who wind up at Camp Lejeune and stay the course are all able to get home on weekends. Daniel Keane, who had been impatient to go to infantry school, counts the years until his enlistment is up and he can go back to college. "When I first got here, I was excited. But then you see how they operate, and it's really just a job." He also finds the standards fall far short of what he expected. "I came in thinking nobody would do nothing wrong here. I was so fucked up." He grins at his own naiveté. "You come here and reality sets in." His reality only worsened. The heavy work of carrying a mortar wears on him. In the summer of '96, a bone spur just below his knee begins to affect that joint. That fall he takes advantage of the opportunity to punch out of the Corps early on a medical discharge.

Another Lejeune Marine is Chad Shelton, the young recruit who nearly slugged Sergeant Carey during his first week on Parris Island after the DI's spittle spewed across his face. He eventually dropped out of 3086, but maintains his allegiance to the platoon. "I love him to death," he says of Sergeant Carey. "If I saw Carey, I'd run to him." And he would tell him that this Marine Corps isn't what he expected. "We got a lot of Marines using drugs," he says with dismay. "It's an easy way for them to get out." In his unit, the 1st Battalion of the 8th Marines, he says, one guy grows marijuana in his locker.

Three thousand miles to the west, another handful of 3086ers wind up at the sprawling Marine base at Camp Pendleton, just north of San Diego. It is no accident that these Marines are far happier than are their old comrades back east. The Pendleton Marines boast about their units, even about the quality of their sergeants. Parise, the Pittsburgh artist, says, "I work with some really great NCOs." Jumal Flow finds that even working in a mess hall keeps him engaged in the pursuit of excellence: "We have thirteen people on our watch, and we make sure each other is locked on and squared away. The work gets done—but our NCOs don't just want it done, they want it done as best it can be done in the available time." He says that his mess hall unit runs at least six miles every other day, more than he did back at Parris Island with 3086.

And on the weekends, the Pendleton 3086ers find their identity as Marines reinforced. Life is an adventure. They go out with members of their units, and have wild times on the beaches and in the exotic alleys of Tijuana, Mexico, less than an hour south on the interstate. "I go to Mexico almost every weekend," says

Parise. He pulls out his wallet to display a photograph of himself with Tamara, a sultry-looking long-haired woman who works at a club in "TJ." On quieter nights, Marcel Laplante walks down from his barracks to the Pacific Ocean and sits on the beach. Being a military reservation, off limits to civilians, it is probably the least-crowded, most tranquil stretch of shoreline in the San Diego-to-Los Angeles megalopolis.

Nathan Weber is even more remotely based. Out at the isolated Marine post at Twenty-nine Palms, beyond the Joshua Tree National Monument in the high California desert, he contentedly works as a tank mechanic for the 7th Marines, frequently putting in twelve to fourteen hours a day. He isn't bothered by the miles of bare rocks, the dust storms, the persistent thirty-five mile-per-hour wind, or the tiny town dominated by the Corps and the desert. Out on the highway, the barbershop is called "Combat Barber" and one bar is named "The Gung Ho Inn."

"It's a base surrounded by nothing," Weber says over a sandwich. Black engine grease outlines each crease in his knuckles. "The more you isolate yourself, the better you do in the Corps. I hardly even call home a lot. We do good work." In his isolation, he sometimes forgets that there even are alternatives to the Marine Corps way of life. "Living on base, you kind of take it for granted. Then you go off base and see a kid not holding a door open for a lady, and you can't comprehend it."

Weber speaks for many in 3086 when he summarizes his journey into the Corps. "In the Marines, you get an identity," he says. "People who never had a family, they belong to something— maybe for the first time in their lives." And in finding a new self, he also has found something larger than himself: "You know you're part of a brotherhood that will never die."

A few miles away, further out in the desert, Landon Meyer and Paul Bourassa take a break from a big military exercise to sit in a dusty communications tent. A bare lightbulb sways in the gritty wind that manages to find its way through the flaps and into the tent. Meyer, who had dropped out of 3086 with pneumonia, eventually graduating from boot camp with another platoon, says he isn't sure he would have an identity if he hadn't joined. "I'd be spending my paycheck on every drug I could find—coke, weed, speed." Cobra attack helicopters clatter about 100 feet overhead. Then an F/A-18 fighter jet roars down and catches its tailhook on the expeditionary metal landing strip across a dusty road.

Listening to Meyer, Paul Bourassa says he has more mixed feelings. "To be honest, there are days when I say, 'What the fuck am I doing? I'm twenty-seven years old, and I make six hundred dollars a month.' I don't want to eat dog food when I'm sixty-five, you know?" Nonetheless, he still thinks enlisting was the right move. "I needed to get away. And the Corps lifestyle, I enjoy. It is an adventure. It pretty much is a band of brothers."

A sergeant sitting in the tent listens to Bourassa's account. "You went to U. Mass?" the sergeant says. "You should go to OCS"—officer candidate school. Bourassa replies that he has been thinking about that. In 1997 Bourassa ships to the Basic School to become a second lieutenant.

Nathaniel Behrendt is stationed in Washington, relatively close to his hometown in central Pennsylvania, but he has achieved great psychological distance. He is now part of the Marine security program codenamed "Yankee White," guarding the presidential retreat at Camp David, Maryland. One of Staff Sergeant Rowland's anonymous men in the middle, consistently graded "average" in his recruit evaluation card, Behrendt apparently was exactly what the military psychologists look for in selecting personnel for the presidential security detail. "Yes sir, I am glad I joined," grins Lance Corporal Behrendt. "I feel like I'm part of something, like we're head and shoulders above the rest. Standing in my dress blues, I get a tingling feeling in my back."

And then, of course, there is the time Behrendt is speeding down I-95 to Quantico, gets pulled over—and the Virginia state trooper is, of course, a former Marine. "It really is a brother-hood," Behrendt smiles.

Perhaps happiest of all are Jonathan Prish and Jonathan Crigger, who both wind up working as Marine security guards at a U.S. military installation near the American embassy in London. Sitting in an Oxford Street pub called "The Marlborough Head," they sheepishly grin that they are knee-deep in women and beer. This isn't what they had expected when they joined the Marines. "I always figured Marines were mud and war," Lance Corporal Crigger says over his Budweiser. "Here it's guard duty and parties."

"It's real fun," seconds Lance Corporal Prish. "There's a lot of places to skateboard here." He looks like a cop in his big suit, purposely loose in order to accommodate the bulletproof vest he wears underneath when on duty. Prish is notable for the calm bearing he has achieved. He is relaxed but focused. He holds himself well. He learned at Parris Island that he is a man who must try harder than other men—and he does.

Soldiers always have complaints, but Prish's and Crigger's are unusual. They are most irked by the IRA's bombing campaign, which sometimes interferes with the morning rush hour, making it difficult to get to their posts—especially when they awaken in strange beds, as they do frequently. "I was in Earl's Court, coming back from this South African girl's house one morning," says Crigger. "The elevator (in the underground) stopped 'cause of a bomb threat." Some mornings they are compelled to take expensive cab rides to get from girlfriends' beds to work on time. This isn't a common complaint among Marines in the Fleet.

Their second biggest complaint is British women. "They're not that good in bed, kind of dull," reports Prish. But they have found alternatives. "You can go to a club in the shittiest part of town and there will still be beautiful women there," says Prish. "I met a Swedish chick last week, went over to her house, played 'Truth or Dare,' and screwed her," he reports matter-of-factly.

Also, the food sometimes puts them off, even though they steer close to American tastes. "It's a weird country over here," Crigger says over his Budweiser. "The McDonald's is different—

I think the grease is different." Prish, sitting next to him in the pub, smokes a Marlboro and sips a Coke.

Prish says he is "happy as hell" he joined the Marines—not only because he has landed in a cushy post in London, but also because of the troubles encountered by his old friends in Mobile. Since he left for boot camp, one has been jailed for assault and another for armed robbery.

So now Prish is getting his racist tattoos, like the ring of inter-locking seven's, covered up. "I've left all that behind," he says of his white supremacism. "You go out and see the world, you see there's cool people in all colors." He is particularly indebted to a Vietnamese-American corporal named Tran who helped him out when he first arrived in London and was hazed by other mem-bers of the company. "He's out in the Fleet now, and he's written me twice." Those letters mean a lot to him.

Finally, there is Charles Lees. His new identity as a Marine is solid—but as a reservist, he spends most of his life in a non-Marine world. He works for TTG Inc., a management software company in Woburn, Massachusetts, and reports to the reserves one weekend a month and for two weeks in the summer. "I kick myself sometimes for not going active duty," he says. There are days when he finds himself missing boot camp—and even a bit lost. "I loved that camaraderie down there, that feeling of being a Marine. Sometimes I wish I was back there."

A bright red Marine Corps flag hangs in his bedroom in the apartment near Boston he shares with three Holy Cross buddies. "Even when I'm having a bad day, I can still look at myself and say, 'Well, at least I'm a Marine.' " He also has experienced "the Marine ticket." Speeding home on Route 128 from a reserve duty weekend, he was pulled over by a Massachusetts state trooper. Seeing the Marine decals, the trooper simply smiled and said, "Slow it down, devildog."

On November 10, 1996, the Marine Corps' birthday, Lees is

in New York City. Not having an invitation to that city's Marine Corps ball, he observes the occasion by going out to the military cemetery on the border between Brooklyn and Queens and visiting the grave of Dan Daly, one of two Marines awarded two Medals of Honor. Lees is pleased to see that others have left a Marine Corps emblem and a sergeant major's stripes.

Lees thinks the Marines have the answer to the troubles of American society. "Parris Island was in some ways easier than I thought it would be. The abuse I thought would be there wasn't. And you'd see them teach kids who barely made it through high school that they weren't stupid, that they could do things if they had the right can-do attitude.

"It was," he concludes, "all the basic things that you should learn growing up, but for some reason society deemphasizes."

Sergeant Carey also has an identity problem. He is so much a Marine that others sometimes think they detect a "more Marine than thou" attitude. Throughout 1996, they have their revenge: For the entire year, Sergeant Carey is kept in agonizing suspense as to whether he would be allowed to remain in the Corps, or would be forced out because he hadn't been promoted to staff sergeant, under the military's up-or-out system.

After seeing 3086 march across the graduation field and out of his life, Sergeant Carey does two more cycles as a heavy hat and then is promoted to Senior Drill Instructor. This last is a job he performs well. But it doesn't come naturally. He was born to be a heavy hat—the disciplinarian. "As a heavy, I looked at them as a Marine Corps unit. I didn't really think about them as individuals. They were faceless." The promotion to senior forces him to acquire a new perspective. "I had to treat them as individuals. I almost lost my competitive edge, getting caught up in aspects of their lives." If given a chance, he says, "Absolutely, I would be a hundred-percent heavy. That is me."

In January 1996, Sergeant Carey ships out to Okinawa to rejoin his beloved Force Recon. The day before he leaves, he cites

Platoon 3086 as his favorite from his time on Parris Island. "I was closer to that platoon than I have been with others. Everything came together. I peaked out at my best. The recruits peaked. The drill instructors got along well.

"3086 was slower, 'winter in the pool hall,' but they had more of the intangibles," he says over a beer in the kitchen of his parents' ornately decorated Victorian gingerbread house on the south shore of Long Island. ("Intangibles" is one of Sergeant Carey's favorite accolades—it refers to matters of the spirit, rather than to "little boxes that can be checked off, that officers like," he explains, casually dismissing the credentialism that dominates the thinking of his yuppie contemporaries.) "They weren't as intellectual, and maybe they were weaker than most. But they had more to lose, something to prove." On Okinawa, Sergeant Carey runs into Beggs, the tough little pugilist, who in mid-'96 is the first member of 3086 to make full corporal—a genuine NCO just a year out of boot camp, an impressive performance in the peacetime Marines. He learns that Beggs's little brother has enlisted and been assigned to Kilo Company of the Third Battalion, 3086's old company.

One evening in the summer of '96, William Wells is sitting in a bar in Okinawa when someone taps him on the shoulder. He turns and sees Sergeant Carey. His first impulse is to run. His second is to jump to attention. His third, which he follows, is to buy his old DI a beer. Sergeant Carey spends much of 1996 aboard the U.S.S. *Germantown* as it steams around Southeast Asia on a mission to train the militaries of Malaysia, Thailand, Indonesia, and the Philippines. "It was fun," he says. "It was basically jumping, diving, and shooting." At the end of the trip he takes a week's leave on the beaches of Bali. He spends most of it sitting on Kuta Beach being unimpressed by visiting Australians stoned on the local hallucinogenic mushrooms, which are even served in the grilled "jaffles"—hot Aussie pocket sandwiches—sold by vendors on the beach.

Sergeant Carey returns to the States in the fall to attend

Marine Scout/Sniper School in Quantico. He is like a duck in water, sneaking through woods, lying motionless for hours, and remaining undetected by experts looking for him as he lies in a field just yards away from them—even after getting off a shot. Predictably, he is the honor graduate of his sniper class.

But while he is at Sniper School, he is also notified that he has been passed over for staff sergeant. This appears to spell the end of his career in the Marines.

Sergeant Carey's endangered career finally catches a break: He winds up under the command of Col. Gary Anderson, a gravel-voiced, bandy-legged officer with a gimlet eye for bullshit, a Carey-like love of the Marines, and, well-hidden under his grunt demeanor, the inquiring mind of a genuine intellectual. Listening to the crusty colonel talk about his ambition of opening a bait shop, one would-n't know from that after the Berlin Wall fell in 1989, he spent months meditating on the role the U.S. would play as the world's sole military superpower—and then produced a jewel of an essay comparing the American situation to the Roman Empire, the Byzantine Empire, and the nineteenth-century British Empire. (He noted, among other things, that the distance from the center to the edge of the empires was similar: It took Roman troops sixty days to march from Rome to the closest point on the periphery, the German frontier at Cologne—while it takes the U.S.-based strategic reserve the same amount of time to deploy to the Middle East with enough sustainment to be credible. He concluded that the U.S. should imitate the middle Roman Empire and use a small, forward-deployed military.) Colonel Anderson was the officer who once had so impressed Harvard's Professor Rosen by disagreeing in public with a general.

Best of all for Sergeant Carey, Colonel Anderson, who was trained decades ago by a young captain named James Webb, is an officer who looks out for his men. Early in 1997, he assigns Sergeant Carey a key role in an exercise using Recon troops as long-range spotters for precision-guided artillery and missile fire. Carey runs the Recon units that act as "sensors." Then, in a small war exercise, Colonel Anderson has Sergeant Carey play the role of a faction leader. "I find sergeants and below make good players when simulating non-state actors, as they aren't wedded to conventional doctrine," the colonel explains. In both exercises, Carey shines. Colonel Anderson comes away confident that he will be able to promote Sergeant Carey by midsummer—and keep him in the Corps.

It is a near-run thing. In February, 1997, Sergeant Carey's paycheck stops coming, although he doesn't notice the cutoff for several weeks, because his pay is deposited automatically and he only withdraws the small amounts required by his spartan lifestyle. Finally in May, near the very end of his string, word arrives: He has been approved for promotion to staff sergeant. He can remain a Marine. A few weeks later, he is assigned a key role in a Force-Recon platoon attached to a Marine Expeditionary Unit: He is named the "breacher"—that is, the first man through the door in any rescue of hostages.

Staff Sergeant Rowland, troubled by an old ear injury, stops working as a drill instructor and becomes operations NCO for the 3rd Battalion, a desk job. An ear operation in the spring of '96 is successful, and a few months later he transfers to the 10th Marines, an artillery unit at Camp Lejeune. "It's the gun club for me," he says. He has served in the unit once before, just before leaving the Marines to work back in Arkansas. Back in the 10th Marines, he is now serving alongside three members of 3086: Tenhet, Donald Campas, and Edward Linsky.

Staff Sergeant Rowland remembers Platoon 3086 fondly. "It's got a special place in my heart. We were a three-hat team"— that is, a group of only three drill instructors, as opposed to four and even five for some. On top of that, it was Rowland's first cycle as a senior, "and everyone was waiting for us to crash and burn. We didn't. We had good communications."

Back at Lejeune, Staff Sergeant Rowland finds that, like his old recruits, he must make a difficult adjustment to the real Marines.

"A lot of them are sluggish and slow, kind of rusty," he is surprised to find. "Simple drill movements, they have a hard time doing it." He makes his platoon of communicators shape up. "They don't like it. I tell 'em: I'm not there to make friends."

Sergeant Carey's friend Sergeant Humphrey, the demon of inspection, comes to an unhappy end in his tour on Parris Island. He is relieved of duty by Lieutenant Colonel Becker. "The platoon was at the rifle range," explains the lieutenant colonel. "A recruit went UA"—that is, unauthorized absence, the modern jargon for AWOL. The recruit strolled out of the rifle range barracks at about two o'clock in the morning. He made it out the front gate and was found near Shell Point, a few miles from the boot camp. Yet his absence wasn't discovered until 6:00 A.M., when the platoon was on the rifle range and an instructor noticed that there was one more rifle than there were recruits. Humphrey wasn't on duty that night, but he is held responsible. "He was the senior drill instructor," says Lieutenant Colonel Becker. "He obviously didn't train his drill instructors and his security watch." In mid-1996, Humphrey, back in the Fleet, runs into Earnest Winston in Japan and encourages him to stay in the Corps.

Since 3086 graduated, sweeping changes have also come to Parris Island and the entire system of Marine recruit training. In the following year, the officers overseeing Parris Island and those overseeing the entire Corps engaged in far-reaching discussions about how to revise boot camp. They all agreed that the Corps needed to mount a stronger defense against a disintegrating society. "In the past, we could assume that society would give someone some values," says Maj. Stephen Davis, director of the Drill Instructors School. "We can't assume that today. So today the question is, How do we ensure someone's spiritual and moral fitness to be in the Corps?"

Kicking around ideas about how to instill values, a panel of officers at Parris Island essentially suggested a series of ethical tests—perhaps giving recruits too much change when they visit the PX, and seeing who returned the money. Or maybe issuing too many rounds at the rifle range, and seeing who tried to use the extra bullets to raise his shooting scores. Similarly, they proposed giving recruits permission to take liberty when they are pressed for time to prepare for an inspection, and then see whether they go to the movies or demonstrate responsibility and do the necessary preparation work. They also suggested giving recruits more leeway toward the end of boot camp and judging how they handled it—rather than simply cutting them loose.

At meetings in late spring of 1996, Commandant Krulak swept aside those suggestions. He was thinking in grander terms. He told the brainstorming officers that he wanted boot camp to culminate with "a defining moment." Asked to explain that, he said in an interview that he wanted "something so tough, so powerful, that unless you join together, you can't accomplish the defining moment. Your team will not make it unless you pull together."

Ultimately, the commandant ordered the recruit training command to create a final phase of boot camp far tougher than the Warrior Week that Platoon 3086 experienced. The new phase, called "The Crucible," involves sleep deprivation, punishing marches, and live-fire exercises. It is designed to be "the defining moment" in a young person's life, a three-day process that begins with the recruits being roused from their bunks at 2:00 A.M. Over the next fifty-four hours they are allowed a total of eight hours of sleep. They begin with a night march to a series of "reaction course problems," such as a water obstacle that can be crossed only if a squad works together. Next comes a "casualty evacuation," in which recruits carry a member of their team through one mile of woods and swamp. In keeping with the Marine Corps' emphasis on its history, this portion is called "Lance Corporal Noon's Casualty Evacuation," in memory of a Marine who received the Medal of Honor posthumously for carrying four wounded comrades to safety in Vietnam before being killed as he carried a fifth. The first evening of "The Crucible" brings a "night resupply" mission, in which team members must carry water, ammunition, and food through an obstacle-laden course in the woods while their buddies cover them. The obstacles require novel approaches. At the "blown bridge," for example, recruits must use three boards to get three ammo boxes and a squad of Marines across the pilings. "This will train recruits and their drill instructors for twenty-first century warfare," said Lieutenant Colonel Becker, who began working on "The Crucible" while 3086 was on the island. "That's feeding starving children on one block on Mogadishu, standing between two factions on the next block, and being in a firefight on the third." Then come team pugil fights, a live-fire exercise, and more night movements. Finally, after a 3:00 A.M. reveille, the recruits march nine miles in combat gear and arrive back at their battalion parade deck, where their DIs pin the Marine emblem on them and recognize them for the first time as members of the Corps. Then, for the last several days of boot camp, they are treated as Marines.

The new system sends a double-barreled message to recruits. First, they must work together. Second, they must think. "We tried to design everything so nobody can get through by themselves," explains Lieutenant Colonel Becker. "It's the team that gets through."

Eventually, the changes will extend into training at the School of Infantry, which so many members of 3086 found a letdown. There they will be grouped according to their future units. For example, the three or four Marines designated to report after training to the first platoon of Bravo Company of the 1st Battalion of the 3rd Marines will begin learning and living together while still in school. The next change may be the most significant of all: Midway through infantry school, a squad leader from their future platoon will come down and begin working with them. Not only will this increase unit cohesion, the commandant predicts, it also will address the problem of the slack sergeants in the Fleet, another big disappointment for 3086. "It will put pressure on the NCO to get his act together," General Krulak says in an interview. "This thing could really have a major impact on the Corps."

Hearing about these changes, a veteran U.S. Army trainer says, not critically, that they remind him of the methods used by the German Army in World War II to achieve unmatched unit cohesion and combat effectiveness. He cites Martin van Creveld's *Fighting Power,* which describes the German training system as an arrangement that

> gave the regiments a strong incentive to look after their own replacements' training, made it possible to employ as instructors the very officers and NCOs who would later command the men in battle, and created opportunities for experienced personnel to be temporarily taken out of the line. After a period of training in the field replacement battalion, the replacements would reach the front already knowing both each other and their commanders and forming part of a well-integrated team.

That system, concludes van Creveld, was a major factor in enabling German army units in World War II to consistently inflict casualties at rates about 50 percent higher than those they suffered—an extraordinary military achievement. By contrast, he says, the contemporaneous American system of moving about anonymous individual replacements supervised by transient officers, culminating in almost no effort to integrate new soldiers into line units, was, "perhaps more than any other single factor . . . responsible for the weaknesses displayed by the U.S. Army during World War II."

Of course, the Marines' newer, tougher training might well kill a recruit or two, an event that every drill instructor is taught could seriously damage the Corps. But Commandant Krulak emphatically disagrees about the effect a training incident might have. "That's not what kills the Marine Corps," he says, raising his voice. "What kills the Marine Corps is Marines who do not act like Marines—Marines who lie, cheat, and steal, who rape little girls on Okinawa. That's what kills the Marine Corps."

The commandant also tells the recruit training command that he wants boot camp to spend more time explaining to recruits how Marines serve the U.S. Constitution. "We don't want our Corps to be separated from the people we serve." And yet the changes the commandant is making in boot camp—however much they are needed—can only make Marine boot camp even more of an oddity in American society, a place that is sometimes brutal, but where standards are enforced, where unquestioning teamwork is the rule rather than the exception, and where no excuses are accepted. As a rite of passage, there are few if any other places like it left in American society, with the frontier long closed and the part of the economy that runs on muscle power dwindling to insignificance. One startling sign of the exceptional place of boot camp is that in the spring of 1996, the Walt Disney Company began running tours of Parris Island, busing vacationers in from nearby Hilton Head. Disney, which makes its millions partly by being highly attuned to the cultural appetites of Americans, recognizes that there is something so unusual going on at Parris Island that tourists will pay to see it. The tour begins just as does Platoon 3086's passage, with the new arrivals standing on the yellow footprints outside the Recruit Receiving Building. One day in the spring of 1996, Staff Sergeant Rowland is walking across the main parade deck when he runs into a Marine public affairs officer accompanying one of the first Disney tours. The officer, a woman, asks Staff Sergeant Rowland if he could do something for her. Normally self-effacing, Staff Sergeant Rowland is in an unusually rambunctious mood. "Ma'am, I can do *anything*," he bellows. And so, as requested, he puts on his DI rasp and tells the tourists how to stand at attention—arms straight, fingers curled, heels at a forty-five-degree angle. The experience "weirds him out," he reports.

Thomas E. Ricks

Disney's interest, and the very fact that a tour can be conducted of boot camp, may not be entirely healthy for the
Marines. Within the Corps there is some worry about the type of
person they are recruiting—not that he is too tough, but that he
isn't tough enough. "We're almost getting to the point where
we're believing our own bullshit," worries the DI School's Major
Davis. He thinks the Corps may lose something by insisting on
taking only high school graduates with relatively trouble-free
backgrounds. "There's a lot to be said for taking the tough kids.
You need to provide forty thousand graduates a year with great
characters who don't abuse alcohol or women, who aren't
racists—yet are able to turn on the fury of a trained killer when
the Marine Corps calls on them. Do you want all-star high
school athletes who went to Sunday school? Maybe you want a
percentage. But what happens with them on the battlefield?
What happens to the others when you lose five? I don't know."

One of those tough kids is Armando Cordova, the feisty corporal in Somalia with the can-do, gung-ho attitude. In 1996, he
isn't permitted to reenlist, and so is forced out of the Corps after
ten years' service, including in the Gulf War. His troubles begin
when he gets home from Somalia. He is promoted to sergeant
and moved out of his rifle company to become an instructor at
Camp Pendleton's School of Infantry. He finds the officious
atmosphere there stifling. "If you're not a kiss-ass, you're fucked,"
he says. "It's not like the grunts, where it works on merit.

"It's time to get out," he says one hot California morning just
before he leaves the Corps. "The Marine Corps is changing too
much. There's too much thinking about careers, and not enough
about just doing your job."

He believes that once again the "warrior" types are being
pushed aside by the peacetime Marines, who look better on the
parade ground than the battleground. His solution? "They should
just keep us under glass, keep our record books, and call us in case
of war."

* * *

Of course, no one joins the Marines in order to sit in the rainy swamps of coastal North Carolina. People may be enticed into the Army or Air Force by the prospect of vocational training and GI Bill educational benefits, but they enlist in the Marines to measure, better, or change themselves—and to have an adventure. The Marines are at their best when actually out on a mission, and it is on a mission that they must be judged.

Take Haiti, first in the summer in 1994. Every one of the eight hundred Marines aboard the U.S.S. *Inchon* off the Haitian coast has learned in boot camp about the exploits of Smedley Butler, Dan Daly, and Herman "Hard Head" Hanneken, who all earned Medals of Honor in Haiti when the Marines fought there from 1915 to 1934. Now they are following those heroes back to the waters off Haiti in a deployment typical of the post-Cold War world. Sailing aboard their amphibious assault ship, loaded with helicopters up top and artillery pieces, trucks, ammunition, and troops down below, they had been among the last wave of U.S. troops to leave Somalia in March 1994. Then they steamed to the coast of Bosnia. Finally, in midsummer, their tour of foreign-policy hotspots takes them to the coast of Haiti, an emergency rescue team available if the situation further sours and the Clinton administration wants them to evacuate American citizens.

"We've got a lot of little fires to put out in the world," says Sgt. Maj. James Rogers, a twenty-five-year veteran of the Corps, as he sips ice water in the sergeant majors' mess. "If you look at the history books, it's nothing new. We sit on ships close to hot spots and, if the president deems it necessary, we go in."

Several decks above the sergeant majors' mess, Staff Sergeant Vernon Clark briefs his platoon from India Company of the 3rd Battalion of the 6th Marines on what they might expect in Haiti, and how to use force. Sergeant Clark hasn't heard of the *Small Wars Manual,* but like many Marines he has absorbed its lessons subliminally, through the Corps' culture. At a time when the

Army is still steeped in the Weinberger/Powell doctrine of having the U.S. military act only when it possesses overwhelming, decisive force, Staff Sergeant Clark is lecturing his troops on the necessity of using "minimal force." "One of the things you want to accomplish is to get the locals behind you," he tells his platoon as it crowds in the shade of a CH-53 Sea Stallion helicopter parked on the flight deck of the *Inchon*. If fired on by someone hiding in a mob, says Sergeant Clark, he will wait for specialist Marine snipers to respond. "You don't want to hose twenty people to get one guy," he explains.

Standing on the flight deck and watching the platoon exercise, Lieutenant Adolfo Rodriguez, commander of the battalion "STA" platoon—for "Surveillance and Target Acquisition" — comments, "We're an expeditionary force. We always have been. We were never a force for a ground war in Europe."

Down in the officers' mess, Lt. Col. David Young, the battalion commander, says, "It's the kind of thing we do well. And all these guys here have a pretty good level of confidence from Mogadishu." He spoons some tuna fish salad out of his steel canteen cup. "They were shot at every day. Some of its aura has gone away. They know it's dirty, hard work, with a lot of monotony—searching people, searching vehicles." He has brought a copy of the *Small Wars Manual* with him.

The Marines bring an ease to deployments like Somalia and Haiti that comes from two factors: they are used to doing it—"packing their trash and going into the field," as one general puts it—and they are elite troops. The Army's elite units, such as its paratroopers, are as good in some ways, such as being aggressive but disciplined in a manner that allows them to adjust quickly to changing rules of engagement. But often they seem edgier, a bit tightly wrapped. Only Army Special Forces, which at times acts like a service unto itself, really seems to feel like the Marines. Platoon 3086's Sergeant Carey, who has spent an enormous amount of time exercising with special operators from other services, has come to the same conclusion, saying that the only part of the Army he would want to be in is Special Forces. Indeed, there is a steady trickle of Marines like him, who want to stay in reconnaissance work, and so go into Army Special Forces.

One of the clichés of post-Cold War militaries is that "peace-keeping isn't a soldier's job, but only a soldier can do it." In carrying out the distinctively aggressive American style of peacekeeping in Somalia, Haiti, and Bosnia, the Marines—and, to be fair, the best units in the Army, such as Airborne troops and Special Forces—have demonstrated a new corollary to that saying: The tough American style of peace enforcement isn't a soldier's job, either, but only very good soldiers can do it well.

Two months after the *Inchon* floats off Haiti, another amphibious assault ship, the U.S.S. *Wasp,* sails to the same area as the U.S. prepares to invade the Caribbean nation. Ultimately, the Marines go in unopposed. But in the days before, the invasion is expected to be a hostile move, opposed to some degree by the Haitian military and police. It provides a terrific opportunity to see how the Marine training is applied—that is, how Marines just a few months out of boot camp prepare themselves to go over the beach.

Typical of the Marines, who have learned to be open in order to justify their existence to the American taxpayer, the force brings along a platoon of reporters—and then briefs them fully on their operations, bringing in Col. T. S. "Lightning" Jones and his operations and intelligence officers to lay out the plan. Capt. Sean Griffin, the intelligence man, briefs reporters on his concerns about the Haitian army, and provides what he knows of its strength in the area and its local commander.

After they finish, the *Wasp*'s captain, U.S. Navy Capt. Robert Chaplin, comes over the ship's loudspeaker. "We will be putting the Marines ashore tonight in Cap Haitien. This will not be practice. This will be the real thing." The speakers then play "Anchors Aweigh" and "The Marine Corps Hymn." On the hangar deck, a Marine reconnaissance unit begins packing white signal illumination grenades, 5.56 millimeter tracer clips, CS tear gas grenades, and red smoke grenades. They are very focused, with little of the horseplay and catcalls that units in the field usually display.

Staff Sgt. Timothy Brown, platoon sergeant for the first platoon of Echo Company of the 2nd Battalion of the 2nd Marines, gathers his unit around him near an old gray, oil-streaked CH-53 transport helicopter. "Uphold the traditions of the Corps," he lectures. "I don't want them to fear you. I just want them to know not to try anything. Last of all, there is no dignity in killing people. That's not what we want to do. I don't want you to kill these people. Most of all, I don't want you to get killed."

He reads off the preinvasion schedule to the squatting unit:

"1600, chow, rest period.

"1800, final gear check.

"2130, hangar deck. We draw ammo. Then chow. And we'll go in whenever needed."

A few minutes later, the captain again comes over the loudspeaker. "We have just received the execute order," he says. "Let's get all of our thoughts in order, and may God be with us all." The ship's mood turns deadly serious, with many Marines sitting down to write letters to home, always conscious of the remote possibility that they could be their last.

Then everything changes. When the *Wasp* is just twenty-five miles off the coast of Cap Haitien, while Army Airborne troops actually are in the air on their way to jump into Port-au-Prince, and as Marines are coming out of the ship's preinvasion Mass, President Clinton announces that the military rulers of Haiti have agreed to step down. Marines in battle gear—flak jackets, face camouflage, carrying automatic rifles—stare in disbelief at the loudspeakers as the captain makes the announcement. Down in the troop bays, Marines from the 2nd Battalion's Echo and Fox companies grumble: "Annoyed," says one. "Sold out," says another. "We were all cammied up and everything." Adds a third: "We need a Republican back in office." Instead of launching an invasion, the troops will spend that night sleeping and watching Eddie Murphy smirk in *Beverly Hills Cop* on the ship's internal television system.

Tuesday morning brings a Marine operation that looks just like an invasion, except that there is no shooting. It is "small wars" in action. At 4:20 A.M. Navy SEALs go in to secure the beaches. Amphibious assault vehicles begin sliding out of the U.S.S. *Nashville,* part of the *Wasp's* battle group, and circle in the water until a dozen are ready. Then they chug single file three miles toward Cap Haitien as two Cobra attack helicopters lift off the bow of the *Wasp,* followed by a wave of six CH-46s helicopters and two CH-53s carrying troops and gear. The troop helicopters touch down along the runway of the city's airport as the Cobras, bristling with high-explosive rockets and 20-mm cannons, fly "rotary CAS"—that is, a racetrack pattern in the air in order to provide close air support, if needed.

Touching down on the runway that juts from the slums and swamps on the edge of town, the Marines running off the helicopters are greeted by Haitian kids waving U.S. flags. The Marines throw themselves to the ground in the grass along the runway, facing outward, to establish a security perimeter for the troops following them. In the shade of a wing of an old wrecked two-engine propeller aircraft shoved off the runway, a two-Marine scout-sniper team sets up, one with binoculars, the other with a sniper's M-40 rifle, with a camouflaged barrel and a specialized Unertl scope. "Nothing's conventional warfare anymore," shrugs Cpl. Joseph Cooper. "We're in these people's neighborhood, and we've got to be nice."

As the Marines move into the old colonial town's decaying downtown of mud streets and two-story gingerbread houses, the local police try to demonstrate to the newcomers that they are in control of the populace. They do this by wading into the watching crowds and whacking people with lead-lined whips. The executive officer of the battalion's Golf Company orders the police to desist, and the crowd cheers. "These people live in fear of their government," concludes Lance Cpl. Michael Williams, a Golf rifleman.

Watching all this from behind a louvred window on the top floor of a two-story yellow office building with a red metal roof on the city's main wharf is Cpl. Steve Krueger, the battalion's best sniper. His platoon has pushed together three desks to support an observation post with sweeping views of the city. With the camouflaged barrel of his long rifle hanging inches from the window, the soft-spoken twenty-three-year-old Marine and his partner, Cpl. Chris Holodny, methodically survey the crumbling tropical city, swinging left to right from south to north, sensitive to the slightest change that might indicate a potential threat to the Marines from Golf Company patrolling beneath them.

As he watches the city, Corporal Krueger, who wanted to be a Marine ever since he watched John Wayne movies with his grandfather in Palm Beach, Florida, describes what makes a good military sniper. It is also a good description of himself: "Very self-reliant, a lot of self-confidence, but easygoing. A lot of common sense, too."

Peering through a twenty-power scope that allows him to probe into windows and alleys, Corporal Holodny narrates what he sees, noting the unusual into a minicassette tape recorder next to the scope. He follows a six-station visual tour of the city, sweeping from a Catholic school on a hill one kilometer to the southwest, continuing to a rooftop that has become a Marine outpost, then to a crowd on the street near battalion headquarters, and on to the College Christ Roi. Corporal Krueger keeps a parallel record in a green cloth-bound notebook. He also prepares a range-finding chart by drawing half circles on a topographical map of the city, enabling him to estimate with precision the distance of potential targets.

"Is that the Curious Clan?" asks Corporal Holodny, seeing the reappearance of a family that has spent much of the day on the balcony of a house, intently watching the American troops pouring ashore.

"Yeah," responds Corporal Krueger, peering through his rifle's Unertl scope. "The lady is doing the wash."

"And there's the guy in the ballcap," says Corporal Holodny.

They continue along those mundane lines for four hours at a spell. "You sit here looking all day at the city, you notice pretty quickly anything out of the norm," says Corporal Holodny.

Late on the first day of the invasion, Marine scout-snipers posted on a hillock overlooking the slums in the southern end of town notice a blue pickup truck carrying six Haitian policemen toting automatic weapons. The truck is never stopped or confronted by the Marines—but every move it makes across the city is tracked by hidden snipers, scout helicopters overhead, and Marines at checkpoints. If the police make trouble, their truck can be stopped by Corporal Krueger's other rifle, a .50 caliber Barrett—an ominous-looking six-foot-long rifle with a blast deflector at the tip of its barrel that resembles the head of a copperhead snake. One five-inch-long explosive-tipped Raufoos round from the Barrett would wreck the truck's engine. Clearance to fire would be easy to obtain, making ambiguous rules of engagement less of a problem for snipers, because they can instantly communicate with senior commanders.

The snipers' surveillance skills are particularly helpful in the "small wars" environment, says Lt. Sean Tarver, the battalion's intelligence officer. "The development of intelligence in a peacekeeping or low-intensity conflict situation, like Somalia or Northern Ireland, takes a long time," he says, sitting in battalion headquarters, which really is just a few folding chairs in a waterfront warehouse piled high with aromatic sacks of dried orange peel. "You have to look for patterns, and put it on a map." Rifle platoons patrolling the city are frequently excited by the insignificant, he says. But a scout-sniper, taking the long view in both time and space, will note in his notebook, for example, that a particular car has pulled up to a crowd. "Thirty minutes later, violence erupts," the lieutenant says. "Eventually, the picture will emerge. These guys will notice the vehicle that moves in that pattern."

Lt. Col. Steve Hartley, the commander of Marine ground forces in northern Haiti, has assigned two-man scout-sniper teams to accompany rifle companies on hills to the south and west of the town. Combined with Corporal Krueger's position on the downtown wharf, the three locations give the Marines clear shots into a broad triangle of territory. Using snipers rather than rifle companies to respond to threats permits the Marines to minimize casualties on all sides—an important consideration in an operation being carried out under the glare of a live-via-satellite global media.

Corporal Krueger's platoon begins to piece together a picture of Haitian life from a detached perspective, not unlike that of the laid-up photographer played by Jimmy Stewart in Alfred Hitchcock's *Rear Window,* who peers into the lives of his neighbors through his telephoto lens. In their first two days, the snipers grow deeply suspicious of the Haitian police, whom they had seen still asserting their continuing authority by beating locals. "We don't want guys going out through our lines, harassing people and then coming back into our lines like we're protecting them," says Sgt. Haven Smith, a sniper veteran of Somalia.

Indeed, a few days later, the battalion confronts the Cap Haitien police in a short, sharp firefight that leaves several Haitian police dead. Reportedly, a Haitian police officer at the police barracks points the barrel of his weapon at a patrolling platoon. The platoon then opens fire. That exchange sends a quieting message—the Americans are serious, and are willing to open fire—that is heard across Haiti. Probably more than any other American military action in this operation, that firefight of a few minutes ensures that the American occupation, and restoration of the elected president of Haiti, will remain unopposed. The Cap Haitien confrontation was a move right out of the *Small Wars Manual:* "Troops engaged in small war operations must be thoroughly indoctrinated with a determination to close with the enemy at the earliest possible moment."

CHAPTER NINE

ON AMERICAN SOIL

Some Marines say they can see the day when the Corps will be required to execute Haiti-like missions, or worse, within the borders of the United States. "The next real war we fight is likely to be on American soil," three writers argue in a 1994 essay in the *Marine Corps Gazette,* capturing in a sentence Marine estrangement from American society.

The idea of a gap between the military and American society is hardly new. For much of the nation's history, notes Harvard political scientist Samuel Huntington in *The Soldier and the State,* the classic study of the role of the military in the American system, the armed services had "the outlook of an estranged minority." A decade ago, in *The Straw Giant,* journalist Arthur Hadley called this strained civil-military relationship "The Great Divorce." Hadley defined this as "the less-than-amicable separation of the military from the financial, business, political, and intellectual elites of this country, particularly from the last two."

But because of changes both in society and in the military, that "divorce" or "gap" appears to be more severe now than it frequently was in the past. There are two overarching reasons for this. First, after twenty years without conscription, the ignorance of American elites about the military has deepened. Second, with the end of the Cold War, the U.S. has entered into historically unexplored territory. If the Cold War is indeed considered to be a kind of war, then for the first time in American history, the nation is maintaining a large military establishment during peacetime, with 1.4 million people on active duty and millions more serving in reserve and supporting civilian roles in the Defense Department and the defense industry.

Several trends already underway in society and in the post-Cold War military threaten to widen this gap in the coming years, further isolating and "de-civilianizing" the military. The bookend to Huntington's study is the other great academic examination of the American military, Morris Janowitz's sociological *The Professional Soldier.* Writing in 1974, Professor Janowitz confidently concluded that there wouldn't be "a return to earlier forms of a highly self-contained and socially distinct military force; the requirements of technology, of education, and of political support make that impossible." But with the end first of the draft and then of the Cold War, the conditions that shaped the military observed by Professor Janowitz no longer apply. It now appears likely that the U.S. military over the next twenty years will revert to a kind of garrison status, largely self-contained and increasingly distinct as a separate society and subculture.

Seen in this light, the Clinton administration's frictions with the military—over gays in the military, the supposed "dissing" of a uniformed general by a White House aide who supposedly said at the White House gate that she doesn't speak to the military, military resentment over the administration's ham-fisted handling of the later phases of the Somalia mission, and military resistance to U.S. interventions in Haiti and Bosnia—are not the unique product of the personal histories of one president and his advisers, but rather a preamble to future problems. As Harvard political scientist Michael Desch concluded in a preliminary assessment of post-Cold War politico-military decisionmaking in the U.S., it now appears that "civilians are now less able to get the military to do what they want them to do compared with previous periods in recent U.S. history." Having a semi-autonomous military—especially a large one—is worrisome in a democracy.

To understand why this gap appears to be widening, it is necessary to look at three broad areas of movement. They are, first, changes in the military; second, changes in society; and, finally, changes in the international security environment.

"Today," notes retired Admiral Stanley Arthur, who commanded U.S. naval forces during the Gulf War, "the armed forces are no longer representative of the people they serve. More and more, enlisted as well as officers are beginning to feel that they are special, better than the society they serve. This is not healthy in an armed forces serving democracy."

By far the most important change in the military is the termination of the draft in 1973. Twenty-four years later, the consequences for the military of this shift are still unfolding. Today, all 1.4 million people on active duty are volunteers, a fact that carries vast implications for how the military operates and how it relates to society. In contrast to the post-World War II demobilization, for example, the current post-Cold War drawdown is being met with fear and loathing by many in the military, because all volunteered to be there, and indeed are fighting to stay in.

Partly as a result of the end of conscription, the last fifteen years especially have seen a marked professionalization of the military, even in the enlisted ranks. Today the average enlisted soldier has more than seven years of service, a far cry from the two-years-and-out mentality of a draftee military. While far better trained as soldiers and more stable as a society, this professional military also is vastly more expensive, because it brings with it a "tail" of families and all the social infrastructure they entail, from health care to substance abuse counseling to on-base higher education. John Luddy, a Republican Senate aide, estimates that the Defense Department's family-related costs now run to more than $25 billion a year.

Especially on newer bases, such as the Army's Fort Drum, in

upstate New York, the quality of the base's infrastructure far out-strips the resources available to enlisted personnel in the world outside the base gates. One typical soldier, Spec. Marc Walker, a member of a medical support unit, lives a life that puts his civil-ian peers to shame. At age twenty-two, he and his wife, also a sol-dier, have a purple Camaro and a black Isuzu Trooper parked in the driveway of their two-bedroom pastel blue apartment in Fort Drum's Remington Village. They pay no rent, and no bills for their electric heat, gas stove, and water. Inside, their home has a powerful stereo with Bose speakers, a twenty-seven-inch tele-vision, two leather couches, and a nursery that awaits the birth of their first child. With its trimmed lawns, lack of litter, and safe parks, Remington Village is the nicest place in which Marc Walker, a native of southside Chicago, has ever lived. Compared to his old world, said Spec. Walker, "It's almost make-believe."

It isn't clear that this strong social safety net will be sustained in the coming years and, if it isn't, what the implications will be for the effectiveness of the all-volunteer force and for civil-military relations. In the fiscal year 1995, for example, the Defense Department paid out some $260 million to subsidize its network of day care centers. If it were a for-profit organization, its chain of facilities would make the Defense Department the nation's sec-ond-largest private day care operator.

Given today's conflicts and force structure, good day care cen-ters make sense in that they do more to enhance military readi-ness by supporting deployed personnel than would, say, an additional B-2 bomber. Yet with a defense budget "train wreck" looming around the turn of the century, with weapons-purchas-ing plans far outstripping the planned budget, the military's vast social infrastructure is likely to come under severe attack by Congress. The military, and especially the Army, which is the most vulnerable of the services on force structure issues, face a dilemma in addressing those cuts. The Army's powerful social safety net appears necessary to supporting a professional service with a high "operating tempo." But to find the funds to maintain that net, the Army likely would be required to cut tens of thousands of troops, which senior officers maintain would endanger its ability to carry out the missions it is being given nowadays in Haiti, Bosnia, and elsewhere. Either course—curtailing support for personnel, or curtailing the personnel themselves—likely will engender resentment in the military.

The postdraft professionalization of the military also has wrought cultural changes. The officer corps today acts and feels differently than it did during the Cold War, argues Richard Kohn, a former chief of Air Force history who now teaches at the University of North Carolina at Chapel Hill. "I sense an ethos that is different," he says. "They talk about themselves as 'we,' separate from society. They see themselves as different, morally and culturally. It isn't the military of the fifties and sixties, which was a large semimobilized citizen military establishment, with a lot of younger officers who were there temporarily, and a base of enlisted draftees." What's more, as Samuel Huntington observed in *Soldier and the State,* the American people have never much liked professional militaries, theirs or anybody else's. Reviewing American history, from the Hessian mercenaries of the American Revolution to the German militarism of World War I, he observes that, in the American view, "the professionals have always been on the other side."

In addition, two related post-Cold War trends are further isolating the military: base closing and privatization. The base closing process is returning the military to its pre-World War II political and geographical remoteness, when most military posts were in the South and West. The base closing process so far has hit especially hard in the Far West and the Northeast—areas that have the twin characteristics of being more liberal and more expensive than the rest of the nation. An odd side effect of this retreat south of the 40th parallel is that the majority of big Army bases in the continental U.S. now are named after Confederate officers: Fort Bragg in North Carolina, Fort Benning in Georgia, Fort Rucker in Alabama, Fort Polk in Louisiana, and Fort Hood in Texas. (In addition, there are minor installations like Fort Gordon in Georgia and Fort Lee and Fort A. P. Hill in Virginia.) It would be interesting to inquire if black members of the Army feel any unease about honoring this Confederate heritage, or believe it should be balanced by naming, say, a facility in the area of Norfolk, Virginia, dedicated to teaching insurgency or "escape and evasion" techniques after Nat Turner, who led the South's only sustained slave rebellion in southern Virginia in 1831 and then evaded capture for six weeks.

The military is also "privatizing" some logistics and much of its huge depot structure, which has the effect of getting many military officers out of the job of performing or supervising "civilian-type" work. One of Professor Janowitz's key conclusions was that the military inextricably was becoming "civilianized" by new technological tasks. Privatization may be reversing that trend. In Somalia, Haiti, and Bosnia, for example, a company called Brown & Root has performed a host of functions once done or at least supervised by the uniformed military, from staffing mess halls to purifying water to preparing for shipment home the bodies of soldiers killed in firefights.

Meanwhile, broader changes are occurring in American military culture, the most notable being the relative politicization of the officer corps. There has, of course, always been a conservative streak inherent in U.S. military culture, just as there has always been an element of antiauthoritarianism inherent in American journalism. But today's officers appear to be both *more* conservative than their predecessors, and more politically active.

The evidence is skimpy, and the definitions of "conservative" are unstated but almost certainly shifting. But the data that is available indicates that a massive reversal is underway in how the American military thinks about and participates in politics. In a 1954 survey, Professor Janowitz found the military to be heavily conservative, but found that this inclination tended to take a non-partisan form. Military honor, he wrote, required the professional soldier to avoid "open party preferences." He also found the military becoming more representative of society, with a long-term upward trend in the number of officers "willing to deviate from the traditional conservative identification." And he detected a correlation between rank and intensity of conservative attitudes.

Today *all* these findings appear to have reversed. The military increasingly appears to lean toward partisan conservatism. It also seems to be becoming less politically representative of society, with a long-term downward trend in the number of officers willing to identify themselves as liberals. Open identification with the Republican party is becoming the norm—even, suggests former Army Maj. Dana Isaacoff, part of the implicit definition of being a member of the officer corps. And the few remaining liberals in uniform tend to be colonels and generals, perhaps because they began their careers in the draft-era military. By contrast, the junior officer corps, aside from its female and minority members, appears overwhelmingly to be hard-right Republican, largely comfortable with the views of Rush Limbaugh. Oddly, this trend has been exacerbated by the controversy over gays in the military, which has resulted in some universities banning ROTC from their campuses: Air Force Col. Charles Dunlap, a thoughtful commentator on the estrangement of the U.S. military from the society it protects, notes with dismay that some officers welcome the expulsion of ROTC units because it reduces the number of officers educated in liberal environments.

A variety of recent formal and informal surveys point toward the conclusion that the military is moving toward a new kind of open and active political conservatism. At Annapolis, midshipmen, who in 1974 were similar in their politics to their peers at civilian colleges, are now twice as conservative as the general population of students, according to an unpublished internal Navy survey. "The shift to the right has been rather remarkable, even while there has been an infusion of rather more liberal women and minorities," concluded one person involved in conducting the survey.

Similarly, Major Isaacoff, who taught at West Point in the early 1990s, routinely surveyed her students on their politics, assessing about sixty students during each of six semesters. In a typical section, she reported, seventeen would identify themselves as Republicans, while none would label themselves Democratic or Independent. She concluded that to today's cadets at West Point, being a Republican is becoming part of the definition of being a military officer. "Students overwhelmingly identified themselves as conservatives," she reported in a 1996 talk at the Massachusetts Institute of Technology. Here the definition of conservatism is important, for this doesn't appear to be an identification with the compromising, solution-oriented politics of, say, Sen. Bob Dole. "There is a tendency among the cadets to adopt the mainstream conservative attitudes, and push them to extremes," said Major Isaacoff. "The Democratic-controlled Congress was Public Enemy Number One. Number Two was the liberal media. . . . They firmly believed in the existence of the Welfare Queen." In another, more formal survey, conducted by political scientist Volker Franke in October 1995, two-thirds of West Point cadets identified themselves as conservative.

These tendencies toward right-wing attitudes aren't limited to malleable students at the military academies. A 1995 survey of Marine officers at Quantico found similar views. The Marines aren't the most representative example, but rather—because they are the most tradition-bound and unabashedly culturally conservative of the services—the most dramatic. They should be viewed not as an indicator of where the U.S. military is today, but instead of where it is heading. The Corps was less altered by the Cold War than any of the other services. With the end of the Cold War, the other services are becoming more like the Marines as they too become smaller, insular, and expeditionary.

In the Quantico survey 50 percent of the new officers studying at the Basic School identified themselves as conservatives. In
a parallel survey of midcareer officers at the Command and Staff
College, 69 percent identified themselves as conservatives. In a
striking indication of alienation from the larger society, an overwhelming proportion of the Basic School lieutenants—some 81
percent—said that the military's values are closer to the values
of the founding fathers than are the values of society. At the
Command and Staff College, where students generally have at
least ten to fifteen years of military experience, the proportion of
those agreeing with that statement was 64 percent. A majority
of officers also agreed that a gap exists between the military and
society, and stated that they expected it to increase with the passage of time. Fewer than half believed it desirable to have people
with different political views within their organizations.

"I believe these results indicate the potential for a serious
problem in civil-military relations for the United States," concludes Army Maj. Robert A. Newton, who conducted the survey
and analyzed the responses in a study titled "The Politicization
of the Officer Corps of the United States." "In particular, I
believe these results indicate a growing alienation of the officer
corps from society. Instead of viewing themselves as the repre-
sentatives of society, the participating officers believe they are a
unique element within society."

Not only do today's officers appear to be more conservative
than in the past, they also appear to be more active in politics,
both in their identification and their voting behavior. This change
is all the more striking because, while conservatism has long
been present in the American military, political involvement is
something of an anomaly. After the Civil War, reported Professor
Huntington in *The Soldier and the State,* "not one officer in five
hundred, it was estimated, ever cast a ballot." In *Once an Eagle,*
one of the more illuminating novels about the twentieth century
U.S. Army, Anton Myrer has his young hero tell a congressman,

"When I serve my country as a soldier, I'm not going to serve her as a Democrat or as a Republican, I'm going to serve her as an American." In a similar novel, *A Country Such as This,* James Webb has his hero, a naval aviator, grasp his brother by the shoulder and emphatically state, "I ain't any Republican. I ain't a Democrat, either. I'm a Navy man, that's all. I go anywhere in the world they tell me to go, any time they tell me to, to fight anybody they want me to fight." As Huntington emphatically concluded, "the participation of military officers in politics undermines their professionalism, curtailing their professional competence, dividing the profession against itself, and substituting extraneous values for professional values."

Nowadays that defining characteristic of U.S. military professionalism also appears to be reversing direction, which is troubling both for the military and the nation it serves. After historically shying away from voting, military personnel for the last decade have been voting in greater percentages than that of the general population, according to a study by Army Maj. Robert Hahn. In his survey of Marine officers, Major Newton finds that "although a majority of the officers did not believe the military should play an active role in political decisions, a significant minority did believe such activity was appropriate." He concludes that "these results could indicate potential long-term problems for the nation's military."

In this context, it is worth noting that the last two chairmen of the Joint Chiefs of Staff have injected themselves into election-year debates over issues touching on the military. During the 1992 election, Gen. Colin Powell twice spoke out against military intervention in Bosnia, which the Democratic candidate, Bill Clinton, was proposing. In 1996, his more retiring successor, Gen. John Shalikashvili, spoke out, as he put it in his speech, "in the midst of the presidential primary season," against isolationism and antiimmigration rhetoric—two major issues for Republican candidate Pat Buchanan.

Suspicions about politicians are hardly new to U.S. military culture. But they take on new meaning when they emanate from a more politically active military. An odd little book titled *Clint McQuade, USMC: The New Beginning* is unintentionally revealing in this area, far more so than the more sophisticated novels by Myrer and Webb. Reading this novel, privately published by the author, a retired Marine major, feels like taking a spelunking trip through the collective unconscious of the Corps. Indeed, the author, Gene Duncan, states at its outset that much of it "springs from my subconscious, over which I have no control."

The story turns on an intriguing literary device: A retired Marine master gunnery sergeant is reborn with the body of a sixteen-year-old while retaining the knowledge, memories, and experience of his old self. He eventually—of course—joins the Marines. The book is most interesting for what it states as matter of course—essentially that American society is decaying, corrupted, misled by its elected officials, and deserving of resentment by the Marines who protect it. "Americans are selfish people," McQuade explains to his buddies. Later, expanding on that point, he tells them, "I think I have lost all faith in our politicians, so I take the narrow view and confine it to those around me of like mind, minds which dictate unselfishness and honor."

In a postscript to *Clint McQuade,* the author states that his "purpose in writing these books is to give the reader a sense of the heart of the United States Marine Corps." He flatly concludes that he tries to show the Marines to be "special people with special hearts who serve a seemingly ungrateful nation." Major Duncan does in fact care deeply about the Marines. He routinely visits Parris Island on Christmas Day, the loneliest day of the year in boot camp, and delivers pep talks to the recruits. They aren't the usual motivational spiel: "The natural state of man is war. I think that peace is an interval for preparation."

The novel is significant because is effectively represents part of the military talking to itself when it doesn't think it is being overheard. Though obscure to the outside world, Gene Duncan is known within the Marines. His books are sold by the Marine Corps Association, which at its Quantico bookshop has a special "Duncan's Books" area for his works. In a more official endorsement, *General Military Subjects,* the textbook used to train all recruits at Parris Island, begins by quoting Duncan on its inside cover. (The job of a drill instructor, it quotes him as saying, is to undo "eighteen years of cumulative selfishness and 'me-ism.' ") Following the table of contents, the textbook gives Mr. Duncan another full page. The only other person honored with even one full-page "stand-alone" quote in the entire 199-page textbook is former President Bush.

These isolating attitudes, while perhaps most extreme in the Marines, are also found in varying degrees elsewhere in the U.S. military. "There is a deep-seated suspicion in the U.S. military of society. It is part of the Vietnam hangover—'You guys betrayed us once, and you could do it again,' " observes Andrew Bacevich, a retired Army colonel who is executive director of the Foreign Policy Institute at Johns Hopkins University's School of Advanced International Studies. This suspicion, he adds, "isn't going away, it's being transmitted" to a new generation of officers. Indeed, the museum of Marine history at Parris Island teaches that in Vietnam, "American forces, though never defeated in battle, were removed from war by a wavering government and a divided populace." This interpretation of history is gospel throughout the Corps.

Here again, the long-term consequences of the end of conscription are still unfolding. Without a draft, it has been easier for the middle class in general, and liberals in particular, to follow their traditional impulse to turn away from the military. Within the military, the end of the draft also has meant the end of its leavening effect: people from nonmilitary families frequently were conscripted, or spurred by the draft to enroll in ROTC, and found they actually liked military life. General Powell, for example, came from a nonmilitary background and attended the distinctly nonmilitary City University of New York. His successor, General Shalikashvili, was himself a draftee. There were spells in the early 1990s when the majority of the members of the Joint Chiefs came from universities well outside the traditional routes of West Point and Annapolis. But that generation of draft-era officers is now retiring out of the military, and it is a virtual certainty that the chairman of the Joint Chiefs twenty years hence will not be a draftee. All this will make it easier for the military and the liberal professionals of the middle class to look upon each other with contempt.

There is, of course, much in American society today deserving of dismay. But it is another matter to propose that it is the role of the U.S. military—especially an all-volunteer, professional military oriented to a conservative Republicanism—to fix those problems. Yet that is what some are doing. "It is no longer enough for Marines to 'reflect' the society they defend," retired Col. Michael Wyly advises in the *Marine Corps Gazette*. "They must lead it, not politically but culturally. For it is the culture we are defending." This emerging position worries thoughtful observers such as the University of North Carolina's Professor Kohn, who notes that "the purpose of the military is to defend society, not to define it."

It is possible to make too much of this. Some argue that the U.S. military really is just reverting to its pre-World War II, pre-Cold War stance—socially isolated, politically conservative, and geographically located primarily on bases in the South and West. In that context, military contempt for civilian society is nothing new. In *The Professional Soldier,* Professor Janowitz states that, "Military ideology has maintained a disapproval of the lack of order and respect for authority which it feels characterizes civilian society. . . . In the past, most professional soldiers even felt that the moral fiber of American manpower was 'degenerating' and might not be able to withstand the rigors of battle."

That complacent view ignores at least three key differences between the U.S. military today and its pre-Pearl Harbor ancestor. First, today's military is far larger—some six times the size of the 244,000-man active-duty force of 1933. (Over the same period the U.S. population has merely doubled in size.) Second, it appears to be more politically active. Third, it is being used frequently as an instrument of national policy, with large deployments to Somalia, Haiti, and Bosnia occurring in recent years. A fourth possible major difference is the quality of the U.S. military: For the first time in the nation's history, it is generally regarded by military experts as the best in the world. If, as now appears likely, the size of the U.S. military is cut significantly over the next ten years, frustrated officers may express their resentments in more politically open ways than in the past: It may become routine to see high-profile resignations, deeper alliances between political factions in Congress and parts of the services, and even direct denunciations of administration policies by active-duty officers.

Changes in society have helped widen the gap between it and the military. These are more a matter of culture than of politics. Although there are disagreements over the implications of the changes, there is widespread agreement that over the last several decades American society has become more fragmented, more individualistic, and arguably less disciplined, with institutions such as church, family, and school wielding less influence. These changes put it at odds with the classic military values of unity, self-discipline, sacrifice, and placing the interests of the group over those of the individual.

Related to this, and deepening the split, is the fact that while the U.S. military has addressed effectively the two great plagues of American society, drug abuse and racial tension, American society has not. From the military perspective, says Colonel Hendricks, commander of the Recruit Training Regiment at Parris Island, "There has been a separation of cultures."

In addition, the U.S. military is doing a better job in other areas where society is faltering, such as education. With the growth of realistic training at facilities such as the National Training Center, the Joint Readiness Training Center, and the Combat Maneuver

Training Center, the Army especially does well in this area. Younger enlisted soldiers and Marines frequently exude an air of competence that is rare in today's eighteen- and nineteen-year-old civilians. America's high schools, by contrast, don't seem to infuse youth with that sort of confidence. The Marine recruiting station in Boston reports that in 1995, not a single graduate of Dorchester High School was able to pass the military entrance examination, the Armed Services Vocational Aptitude Battery. "The kicker is, it's at the tenth grade level," a simple test of reading, writing, and arithmetic, says Staff Sgt. Michael Marti. At Madison Park, another Boston high school, three graduates passed, out of 150 taking the test. This dismal performance comes in a school system that once was numbered among the nation's best.

"I think the federal government should intervene, do something like pull their accreditation," concludes Sgt. Alfonso McNeil, the black Marine recruiter in South Boston.

Also, the end of the draft has altered the way society looks at the military. Charles Moskos, the Northwestern University military sociologist, traces the American people's supposed intolerance of casualties to the end of the draft: Because the elites aren't putting their own offspring in harm's way, the American people don't trust them to send everyone else's children into battle. That explanation is credible, but more persuasive is the theory put forward by James Burk of Texas A&M that the American people simply won't tolerate casualties in situations where they dislike a policy or don't understand it, as with Somalia.

Yet Professor Moskos is pointing in the right direction: American political and economic elites generally don't understand the military. As military commentator Tom Donnelly has observed, "political power and military expertise are divorced in ways without precedent since the United States became a great and global power." Nor is such understanding deemed important even when someone is involved in making national security policy. Consider, for example, the conspicuous lack of staff members with military experience at the Clinton White House—an administration that has proven to be militarily activist. Even after bungling an inherited mission in Somalia and then using U.S. forces to care for Rwandan refugees, invade Haiti, and enforce a peace agreement in Bosnia, the Clinton administration did not see fit to follow suggestions from Pentagon officials that a person with a military background be appointed to a senior post at the National Security Council.

A comment published in *The Utne Reader*, the *Reader's Digest* of the New Age crowd, captured this upscale disdain for today's military. In an editorial introduction to an article in the spring of 1997, the magazine said that, in light of Tailhook and other recent scandals, "it's hard to imagine why any woman—or any man with a conscience—would want to join the military."

Not to understand the military is dangerous both for the military and the nation. Nowadays civilian policymakers tend to overestimate what the military can do. It isn't clear, for example, just how the Clinton administration expected the appointment of a four-star general, the Army's Barry McCaffrey, to revitalize its counter-drug efforts. Overestimating the military is probably even more dangerous than believing the military is peopled by incompetent buffoons, as the Baby Boomer generation seemed to believe in the 1970s.

This uncertain grasp of military affairs is likely to characterize policymaking for the foreseeable future. Even as late as the Vietnam War, two-thirds of the members of Congress were veterans. Today, almost two-thirds are not. For most, what they know of the military is what they saw on television during the Gulf War. They took two lessons away from that war: That high technology weaponry works, and that the U.S. needs missile defenses. Partly because the Army effectively blacked out media coverage of its Gulf War triumph, its best moment since 1945, the Congress didn't come away from watching the war with much interest in training or personnel issues or ground forces in general. So, despite the expectations of many in the military that the Republicans would be their allies, it should have been no surprise that after the Republicans won Congress in 1994, they pushed missile defenses and B-2 bombers while trying to cut military pensions. Nor are Republicans necessarily better informed about military affairs: One draft of a 1995 GOP bill would have authorized the president to send troops to Bosnia, but forbid him to ever place those troops under any sort of foreign command. The bill moved along until one staffer with military experience asked, What happens if an American command post gets hit by a shell—does this mean the American troops who have lost their commanders are on their own, and cannot be taken under the wing of the officers of, say, an adjoining British or Canadian unit?

Simply explaining defense issues to Congress is becoming more difficult, notes retired General Merrill McPeak, the former Air Force chief of staff, "with fewer and fewer people having any military service up there." Many in the military were taken aback by Senate Majority Leader Trent Lott's crack in the spring of 1997 that the military should "get real" and stop prosecuting cases of adultary, fraternization and insubordination. The Republican leader's comments came in response to the Air Force's attempt to court-martial Lt. Kelly Flinn, the nation's first female B-52 pilot, on just those charges. One angry colonel said in private conversation: "Let me get this right: The Congress makes the laws, and then gets mad at us when we enforce them?" Even more vehemently, a Navy officer said, "I am beginning to lose what little faith I still have in our elected officials." His remark points to the interesting question first posed by Professor Bacevich at John Hopkins: What will a politicized military do when it realizes that the new conservatism is no longer automatically pro-military? Will the military then become de-politicized—or even more deeply alienated?

But the most salient point about Congress and defense nowadays is the relative lack of congressional interest in defense issues. This isn't a matter of ideology. Even before the Republican victory, the Armed Services Committees were declining in prestige. "Most Americans don't care that much about national security and defense issues anymore," notes Senator John McCain, a former Navy pilot and Vietnam POW who now sits on the Senate Armed Services Committee. "When I'm on a talk show and I mention defense, no one calls. We've seen even in the last few years less emphasis on defense in the American people, and that's reflected in Congress."

The third major area widening the gap is changes in the security environment—that is, the end of the Cold War.

With the evaporation of the Soviet Union, a lot of Americans don't understand why the nation needs a large standing military. Arguably, for the first time in its history, with the possible exception of the two decades preceding the Spanish-American War, the U.S. Army must justify its existence to the American people. This has huge implications for how the military relates to the Congress and the American people. It suggests that the Army itself will become more like the Marines—small, expeditionary, and, for the good of the institution, better at explaining itself to the Congress and the media. Even so, the trends of American civil-military relations in previous eras of peace point toward huge budget cuts in the coming years. The Army is likely to absorb a disproportionate share of the resulting cuts, most of them aimed at personnel (rather than the procurement or operations and maintenance accounts).

Even more importantly, with the end of the Cold War, the U.S. military's definition of "the threat" is up for grabs. Everybody used to agree that it was the Soviet Union. Now there is a lot of talk in the military, especially in the Marines, that the new threat is "chaos." General Krulak, the commandant of the Corps, told the *Armed Forces Journal,* for example, that "when we go into the twenty-first century, warfare as you and I know it will occur maybe 10 percent of the time. The other 90 percent is going to be chaos." At the other end of the chain of command, 3086's Sergeant Carey taught the platoon that "today the threat is the low-intensity things, the 911, that you never know what's going to happen—it's Bosnia, Haiti, Somalia. I'd also teach that the threat is the decline of the family, the decline of morals."

As Sergeant Carey's comment indicates, it is very easy when defining the threat as "chaos" to blur the line between foreign and domestic enemies. This haziness may already be occurring on an institutional scale with the Marines, for whom the Los Angeles riots of 1992 were a preamble to the Somalia deployment later that same year. From a military perspective, the operations were similar. In both cases, Marine combat units based in California were sent to intervene in fighting between armed urban factions. "As soon as we got to Mogadishu, we were struck by the similarity to LA," commented one Marine colonel involved in both operations.

Some of the "lessons learned" by the Marines in Los Angeles are worrisome, especially when seen in the context of a strongly conservative, politically active military. Marine Maj. Timothy Reeves argued in a paper written at the Marine Command and Staff College with the evocative title "The U.S. Marine Corps and Domestic Peacekeeping" that because of "the rising potential for civil disobedience within the inner cities" it is "inevitable" that the U.S. military will be employed more often within American borders. The trouble, he continues, is that a variety of U.S. laws inhibit execution of the mission. "These restrictive policies are in direct conflict with the overall tactics of peacekeeping in a phase level IV response, which require forces to detain suspected enemy and search and confiscate weapons."

In Los Angeles, Major Reeves notes, when faced with violating doctrine or violating the law, some Marines chose the latter course, and detained suspects and conducted warrantless searches. Indeed, with characteristic Marine Corps bluntness, the major states that, "in interviews with Marine officers involved in domestic peacekeeping missions and with officers responsible for articulating the Marine Corps' policy on domestic peacekeeping, it became apparent to the author that Marines took whatever action was necessary. At times, these actions required Marines to violate

U.S. law." Similarly, Marine Capt. Guy Miner reported in the *Gazette* that Marine intelligence units were initially worried by the need to collect intelligence on U.S. citizens, which would violate a 1981 Executive Order, but that "this inhibition was quickly overcome as intelligence personnel sought any way possible to support the operation with which the regiment had been tasked."

To enable the Marines to execute these new domestic missions in the same way that they do abroad, Major Reeves calls for major alterations in U.S. law. These proposed changes, incidentally, could carry long-term consequences for U.S. civil-military relations. "Experience from the Los Angeles riots," he warns, "demonstrated the need to grant U.S. Marine forces the legal right to detain vehicles and suspects, conduct arrests, searches, and seizures in order to accomplish the peacekeeping mission." The Los Angeles mission also demonstrated a need for the Marines to coordinate terminology with the police: When police asked some Marines to cover them while they confronted an armed suspect barricaded in his residence, Major Reeves reports, the Marines laid down covering fire, shooting at least thirty rounds into the building before the police were able to stop them.

Major Reeves's thoughts about a domestic role for the Marines shouldn't be dismissed as the isolated noodlings of a midcareer officer on a one-year lark at school. More likely, they represent a strain of thinking within the Marine Corps that remains a minority view but is gaining new adherents. For example, Gene Duncan, the Marine novelist and commentator, predicted in a 1992 article that the United States is moving toward "violent revolution."

More prominently, in a December 1994 article in the *Gazette,* William S. Lind, a military analyst who has been influential on the doctrinal thinking of the Marines, wrote with two Marine reservists that American culture is "collapsing":

> Starting in the mid-1960s, we have thrown away the values, morals, and standards that define traditional Western

culture. In part, this has been driven by cultural radicals, people who hate our Judeo-Christian culture. Dominant in the elite, especially in the universities, the media, and the entertainment industries (now the most powerful force in our culture and a source of endless degradation), the cultural radicals have successfully pushed an agenda of moral relativism, militant secularism, and sexual and social "liberation." This agenda has slowly codified into a new ideology, usually known as "multiculturalism" or "political correctness," that is in essence Marxism translated from economic into social and cultural terms.

There is little remarkable about that paragraph, which reads like fairly standard right-wing American rhetoric of the nineties, not all that different from Pat Robertson or Pat Buchanan on a prolix day. Its significance lies in the conclusion that Mr. Lind and his coauthors draw from their analysis: "The point is not merely that America's Armed Forces will find themselves facing nonnation-state conflicts and forces overseas. The point is that the same conflicts are coming here."

This leads to their startling conclusion: "The next real war we fight is likely to be on American soil."

As a coda to this, retired Col. Michael Wyly, another influential Marine thinker, and coincidentally James Webb's company commander in Vietnam, added a few months later in another *Gazette* article that "We must be willing to realize that our real enemy is as likely to appear within our own borders as without." He then swipes at the two fundamental principles of U.S. military professionalism: unwavering subordination to civilian control and nonparticipation in politics. "If our laws and self-image of our role as military professionals do not allow for this"—the recognition that the real enemy may be within—"we need to change them." He goes on to raise the possibility of the Marines refusing to enforce certain laws. Specifically, if Congress were to restrict gun ownership, then Marines need to understand that "enforcing such a restriction could quickly make us the enemy of constitutional freedom." (To its credit, the *Gazette* carried in the same issue a commonsense response to the Lind article from Maj. Mark Bean: "America is made of tougher stuff than the authors would have us believe." General Krulak, for his part, said in an interview that while he thinks the role of the U.S. military "may change a bit," he thinks that Lind and his coauthors "take it too far.")

The "culture war" trend of thinking seems at odds with the ethos of American military professionalism. Instead, it is closer to the stance taken recently by an Italian military officer, Comdr. Paolo Bembo, in a commentary in the magazine of the professional Navy, *Proceedings:* "The military is one of the few professions truly aware of the dangers surrounding the country."

When the military is politically active, when it believes it is uniquely aware of certain dangers, when it discusses responding to domestic threats to cherished values, then it edges toward becoming an independent actor in domestic politics. "A classic example of this situation happened in Chile," warns Major Newton at the conclusion of his report on "The Politicization of the Officer Corps." "The Chilean military was a very professional organization. The majority of the officer corps came from the middle class. When the society elected a communist president, the military broke from society. The officer corps believed this change threatened the basic principles upon which the society rested."

For all that, a U.S. military coup seems extremely unlikely. Professor Huntington seemed closer to the mark when, in a 1994 commentary in *The National Interest,* he attributed the civil-military turbulence of the Clinton administration to the process of seeking out a new post-Cold War equilibrium in the civil-military relationship.

But not all equilibria are equal. As Professor Huntington noted in the first paragraphs of *The Soldier and the State,* "Nations which fail to develop a balanced pattern of civil-military relations squander their resources and run uncalculated risks." The United States may be in danger of doing just that by drifting into a situation in which the military is neither well understood nor well used, yet—unlike in previous eras of military estrangement—is large, politically active, and employed frequently on a large scale in executing American foreign policy. If Professor Desch's analysis is correct, the military may even be, on top of all that, semiautonomous.

In addition, it isn't clear that the U.S. military, for all its political-military expertise, is best placed to decide how it should be used, either at home or abroad. For all the Clinton administration's ignorance of military affairs, for example, its estimate of the casualties that would be incurred in invading Haiti appears to have been far more accurate that those done by the Pentagon. Similarly, in the Bosnian deployment, the military's grim warnings about the U.S. military suffering widespread casualties as it became entangled in a guerrilla war haven't been realized. This is a testament in part to the professionalism of today's American soldier. But it also should cause future Pentagon estimates of the human costs of possible operations to be viewed with great skepticism.

Mutual distrust between the nation's political elites and military leaders ultimately could undercut American foreign policy, making it more difficult to use force. To repair the relationship, several steps could be taken.

First, consideration should be given to somehow reinstating a draft. Along the lines of the current German system, this could be combined with National Service under which youths could perform, say, eighteen months of military service, or two years of alternative work.

But resumption of conscription appears unlikely for the foreseeable future, so several other steps should be considered to engage the military with civilian society. Worried by the gap, military historian and analyst Prof. Eliot Cohen made several recommendations to the Army in a nervy 1995 speech at the Army War College. He advocated expanding ROTC programs, especially at elite institutions. In the same vein, the service requirement attached to attending the three military academies might be shortened in order to encourage more former military officers to pursue careers in civilian society—which, among other things, eventually should lead to more people in Congress with military experience. More civilians could attend the military's war colleges, but whenever possible, military officers pursuing higher degrees should be sent to civilian universities, even if this means closing some military schools. The skills of reservists could be used far more imaginatively by the military, especially in an era when civilian technologies are outpacing military developments. Professor Cohen even suggested bringing people into the military later in their lives, even at ranks as high as lieutenant colonel. And to help recruiters draw from the other end of the socioeconomic scale, Admiral Arthur suggests that the military establish special preparatory programs that would enable more of today's inner-city youths to enlist.

But the most important change that should be made involves the military only secondarily. This concerns the separation of professional Americans, or the upper middle class, from the broad concerns of society. Ignorance of the military is really just one manifestation of that larger problem. In this context, America's military problem is not unlike that facing parts of the former Soviet Union. Reviewing the depredations of private militias in thirty-one new states and "ministates" in the old East Bloc and the former Yugoslavia, Russian expert Charles Fairbanks recommended that to assert public control over those forces, "It is particularly important to involve the new middle class . . . in military service." America would do well to take that advice.

PARRIS ISLAND, OCTOBER 1996

E very year, about 320 platoons like 3086 pass through Parris Island. Recruits and drill instructors come and go, and by early in the next decade, a few members of 3086, those who want to make a career in the enlisted ranks of the Marines, will probably return to the island as DIs themselves. By October 1996, Platoon 3086 and two-thirds of its DI team have been scattered around the country, and around the world. But Kilo Company of the Third Battalion soldiers on at Parris Island. As the heat and humidity begin to give way to South Carolina's benign autumn, Staff Sergeant Zwayer prepares to pick up his last platoon before he leaves the island for a new assignment. His "heavy hat" on this final cycle is Sgt. Crawford Quick. (When 3086 was going through Parris Island, Sergeant Quick was a fresh-faced third hat newly graduated from DI school, working under Sergeant Humphrey and Staff Sergeant Frasier in Platoon 3085.) Quick, a drawling native of Rockingham, North Carolina, who keeps his head closely shaved, is pleased to draw Staff Sergeant Zwayer as his senior. "I always wanted to work with him," he says. "He has a rapport, and he carries himself well." The third hat is Sgt.

Charles Buck, a twenty-four-year-old former warehouse clerk who was a corporal just three weeks ago.

Staff Sergeant Zwayer is no longer the awkward junior DI who struggled with 3086. Now he has an ease of command, a confident bearing—he can drive the bus. "I like it," he grins. "I just like being a drill instructor. I like teamwork. And I like seeing recruits go from nothing to being Marines you would be proud to serve with."

The three drill instructors gather in an empty squad bay in Building 420, two floors below 3086's old haunt. Lt. Col. Patrick Strain, who has succeeded Lieutenant Colonel Becker as commander of the 3rd Battalion, begins the new cycle by meeting with all of Kilo Company's drill instructors and supervising senior sergeants. The DIs don't sit on the floor like recruits, but the meeting is still Marine Corps spartan—they perch instead on green wooden footlockers they have carried to the quarterdeck. "You must be the consummate professional in every aspect of your life, in everything that you do," lectures Lieutenant Colonel Strain, waving a black pen to emphasize his points. "In the appearance of your uniform. In the way that you speak. In the way you listen to people, look them in the eye, don't try to interrupt. In the way that you maintain your squad bay and your discipline."

Then come other officers bearing their own messages. Lieutenant Jefferson, the Navy chaplain, advertises himself as "the ethics artillery"—to be called in when the light infantry of the drill instructor just isn't bringing sufficient firepower to bear on the target. Lt. Robert Bartlett, the beefy commander of this series of platoons, advises them simply to give 110 percent effort.

Finally the officers move on and the senior sergeants take over. The drill instructors sit up a bit: They'll listen respectfully to officers, but they'll get down to the nitty-gritty of recruit training with their supervising NCOs. Gunnery Sgt. Roy Brown, a bald black man who bears a striking resemblance to the actor Lou Gossett Jr., and who will oversee the drill instructors for this series of three platoons, sits on an empty orange milk crate. "I'm not a screamer, and I'm not going to do doggone topsy-turvy flips," he tells the nine DIs facing him. "But if I have to stand on your chest, I will—with both feets."

The gunny moves on to particulars. "Now, this is October," he reminds the DIs. "Holiday season is coming. You're going to get all these recruits getting depressed."

At that, Staff Sergeant Zwayer, who had been reclining across a footlocker, with an elbow propped on a bunk bed at the edge of the quarterdeck, sits up. He has a message for the gunny about his plans to protect his own DIs. "Now, if a senior wants to give his hats a day off for the holiday," he says, "I don't want anybody coming in and saying, 'Why isn't Sergeant Quick here at 1400?' " Staff Sergeant Zwayer is drawing a boundary: Don't second guess my command of my platoon.

The gunny nods. He trusts Staff Sergeant Zwayer. "Good judgment wins over everything."

As the series DIs meet, the recruits who will become their platoons are moving toward Parris Island from all over the east coast. One group comes from the dying coalfields of southern West Virginia, another from the suburbs of Detroit. A third bunch gathers in the rockbound hills of northern New Hampshire, more fertile ground for recruiters than it is for farmers. They move from processing stations to airports, then fly to Charleston. At 2:30 A.M. on the morning of October 16th, their bus rolls onto Parris Island and pulls up to the receiving station. Young men, every single one wearing sneakers, most wearing T-shirts or sweatshirts bearing the names of professional sports teams, get off the bus and scramble to the yellow footprints. "Hurry up," shouts Sgt. Kenneth Donnelly, the thirty-one-year-old receiving sergeant on duty tonight. "Let's go. Let's go! *Let's go!*" He instructs them in the basics of standing at attention. He introduces them to Article 86 (unauthorized absence), Article 89 (disrespect), and Article 92: "Disobedience. You will do what you are told, when you are told—very quickly."

"You are now part of a team," he pronounces, standing in the humid night.

A few minutes later he informs them that they are Platoon 3002. One recruit is slow to pass up a form. "Take your time, son," Sergeant Donnelly says, introducing them to Parris Island sarcasm. "I'll stinkin' wait on you." When asked on one form to indicate nationality, several recruits think it means race: "black American," writes one, while another jots, "cocassion."

Two days later, Staff Sergeant Zwayer meets with his new DI team in his new squad bay, the third deck of Building 419, a mirror image of 3086's squad bay, which is visible a few yards away out the south side of the barracks. The drill instructors have reached into their own pockets to buy paint to spruce up the barracks. Then they festooned the latrine with "knowledge" signs. Above a urinal one asks, "What does the Marine Corps motto 'Semper Fidelis' mean? ALWAYS FAITHFUL." Above a sink another instructs: "Maximum effective rates of fire for the M16-A2: 45 RPM SEMI/ 90 RPM BURST."

Sergeant Quick hears the sound of marching feet. The drill instructors run to the window and look down on their new platoon being taken by a receiving sergeant to the battalion mess hall. The new recruits are horribly out of step, with right feet and left feet moving almost randomly. Even while marching their posture is stooped. Sweat streams down their faces in the humid October afternoon, still summery in South Carolina. They appear to be civilians dressed in fatigues, which is almost exactly what they are. "They look scared, so that's good," cracks Sergeant Quick.

A cold front blows in that night. The next day dawns dry, crisp, and sunny, the first real day of fall in the South. The bright morning of Saturday, October 19th invites a high energy response. Platoon 3002 will get one: This is the day of their "Pick-up." The new platoon marches into Building 419. They stand "on line" in the barracks—thirty-two on port side, thirty-three on starboard. They are white, black, Hispanic. Some are paunchy. All have their heads shaven, and all look bewildered.

Staff Sergeant Zwayer faces them. He takes a breath, and then he begins.

> *My name is Staff Sergeant Zwayer, and I am your senior drill instructor. We will make every effort to train you, even after some of you have given up on yourself. Every recruit here, whether he is fat or skinny, tall or short, fast or slow, has the ability to become a United States Marine. . . .*

THE MARINES' HYMN

From the halls of Montezuma
To the shores of Tripoli
We will fight our country's battles
In the air, on land and sea
First to fight for right and freedom
And to keep our honor clean
We are proud to claim the title
Of United States Marines

Our flag's unfurled to every breeze
From dawn to setting sun
We have fought in every clime and place
Where we could take a gun
In the snow of far off northern lands
And in sunny tropic scenes
You will find us always on the job
The United States Marines

Here's health to you and to our Corps
Which we are proud to serve
In many a strife we've fought for life
And never lost our nerve
If the Army and the Navy
Ever look on heaven's scenes
They will find the streets are guarded
By United States Marines

ACKNOWLEDGMENTS

I want to thank my wife, Mary Catherine Ricks, for her love, counsel, and encouragement, and for the title of this book. Also, my thanks to my children, Chris Ricks and Molly Ricks, for being themselves, and for tolerating the absences required by my work.

I am grateful to the editors and management of the *Wall Street Journal* for backing the original story that led to this book, and then for giving me the time to pursue it: Paul Steiger, John Brecher, Ken Wells, Alan Murray, Jill Abramson, and Robert Keatley. Thanks also to the people at the *Journal* who taught me to report and write: Eric Morgenthaler, Jim Montgomery, Nancy Beishline, Albert Hunt, Henry Oden, James B. Stewart, Dan Kelly, William Blundell, Thomas Petzinger Jr., and Ron Suskind. Thanks to David Wessel for good advice. Thanks also to Carla Robbins, Bob Greenburger, and my other colleagues at the *Journal*'s Washington bureau, the best place to work in American journalism today. I especially want to thank Alan Murray and Ron Suskind for two specific acts—Ron for sitting down over lunch and shaping the idea for a story about Marine boot camp, and Alan for pushing me beyond that original conception. Without them there would be no book.

Thanks to Scott Moyers, my editor at Scribner, for making the telephone calls that put me on the road to book writing, and then for doing a terrific job of editing this book. Thanks as well to Michael Carlisle, my literary agent, for introducing me to the world of publishing. Thanks to their assistants, Arnold Kim and Jennifer Chen, for their help in that world. Thanks to my old friend Jonathan Kaufman for talking to me like an old friend about how to make the transition from newspaper writing to book writing. Thanks as well to Marjorie Williams for pointing me in the right direction.

I also deeply appreciate the help given me by Professors Eliot Cohen and Andrew Bacevich, and also Alysia Banks, Lois Weiss, and the rest of the staff of the School of Advanced International Studies at Johns Hopkins University. They came to my rescue when I came back from Bosnia in December 1995 without a place in which to write this book. Thanks to Samuel Wells, Charles Blitzer, and the Woodrow Wilson International Center for Scholars for giving me a place in which to complete this book, and thanks to Kathryn Sweet for her energetic research assistance there. Thanks also to Harvard University's Samuel Huntington, Michael Desch, and Laura Miller for their thoughts about this book, and to their Project on U.S. Post-Cold War Civil-Military Relations at Harvard's John M. Olin Institute for Strategic Studies for support for the section of the book about the growing gap between the U.S. military and society. My deep thanks as well to Northwestern University's Charles Moskos and the Inter-University Seminar on Armed Forces and Society for tutoring me in military sociology—and for making it so much fun.

My deep thanks also to Peter Braestrup, a combat Marine in one U.S. war in Asia and an insightful reporter in another, for giving me a start in journalism—and for planting the first seeds of this book in 1979. Thanks to Robert Timberg, another Marine turned journalist, for writing *The Nightingale's Song.* Readers of my chapter 4 will note that I am indebted to him for his account of James Webb's early career. I also have used as a point of departure Kenneth Keniston's *The Uncommitted: Alienated Youth in American Society,* which presents a useful contrast to the Marines' ethos of "honor, courage, and commitment." It was with some pleasure that, seeking to understand my subject, I first picked up Keniston's classic text, only to see my father listed twice in the acknowledgments to that book. My thanks also to my parents, Prof. David Ricks and Annie Russell Ricks. And my thanks to my son's teachers at Eastern Middle School and its Humanities and Communication Magnet Program, and to my daughter's teachers at Woodlin Elementary School, Silver Spring, Maryland, for being such good teachers while I wrote this book about military teachers and their students.

My thanks also to the many other people—Marines, former Marines, and civilians—who patiently answered questions and sought to correct my views, successfully or not. I especially appreciate the patience shown me by James Webb, Gen. Al Gray, Tommy Lyons, and James Fallows.

Thanks also to Maj. Carol McBride, Maj. Rick Long, Capt. John Church, and Lt. James Rich of the Parris Island public affairs office, and to the officers and NCOs of the 3rd Recruit Training Battalion, then commanded by Lt. Col. Michael Becker. At Marine Corps headquarters, Lt. Col. Patrice Messer and Capt. Michael Neumann were always helpful and gracious in dealing with my requests. Thanks also to their colleagues and commanders in the Marine Corps public affairs operation.

Thanks also to the drill instructors of Parris Island for their candor, courtesy, and cooperation. Most especially, thanks to Staff Sgt. Ronny Rowland, Sgt. Darren Carey, and Sgt. Leo Zwayer, who let me into their workplace and lives.

Finally, and most of all, thanks to Platoon 3086 for cooperating—even more than they had to.

INDEX

Index

Bosnia, 24, 177, 178, 182, 183, 184, 185, 194, 266, 268, 275, 278, 279, 283, 287, 289, 290, 292, 296
Boston, *see* South Boston
"Bottom-Up Review," Clinton administration, 180
Bourassa, Paul, 33, 153, 240, 252-53
Braestrup, Peter, 219-20
BRASS-F, 121
Breaking the Phalanx: A New Design for Landpower in the Twenty-first Century (Macgregor), 185
Bright and Shining Lie (Sheehan), 146
Bronze Star, 134
Brooks, Johnny, 175
Brown, Roy, 300-301
Brown, Timothy, 269
Buchanan, Pat, 283, 294
Buck, Charles, 299-300
Buijs, Paul Adriaan, 75-76, 77, 127-28, 154, 165, 166, 167, 168-70, 205, 211, 248
    pacifism of, 76, 114, 156, 209
    transformation of, 169-70, 209-10
Builder, Carl, 188-90
Burk, James, 288
Bush, George, 144, 183, 285
Butler, John Sibley, 177
Butler, Smedley, 266

Cable, Larry, 145
Caldwell, Charles "Audie," 221-22
Camacho, David, 11, 88-89, 93, 109-10, 113, 114, 157, 206, 207, 214, 217, 249
Campas, Donald, 126, 161, 230, 259
Campbell, Recruit, 47-49, 175
Camp Lejeune, N.C., 60, 95, 99, 130, 136, 145, 204, 233, 239-44, 246-47, 250-51, 259
Camp Pendleton, Calif., 251-52, 265
Carbonari, Anthony, 120
Carey, Darren, 11, 52, 53, 54, 171, 189, 242, 243, 256-59, 291-92
    Force Recon and, 58-59, 78, 106, 148-49, 256
    in "forming" phase, 60-64, 65-66, 68, 72
    on graduation day, 208-9, 211, 213, 217, 218

as heavy hat, 56, 72, 88, 94, 107, 156, 208-9, 256
outspokenness of, 59-60
special warfare schools attended by, 59, 258, 267-68
in training cycle, 73-74, 78, 80-82, 84, 85-86, 88, 91-92, 93-94, 96, 106-7, 109-10, 111, 115, 120, 122, 131
as viewed by recruits, 61, 153, 232, 235-36, 239-40, 241, 243, 249, 251
vocabulary of, 162-63
in Warrior Week, 152, 153, 154-55, 156, 157, 159-62, 164, 165-66
Caselli, Art, 222
Cavellas, Herb, 32
Center for Naval Analyses (CNA), 203
Chaplin, Robert, 268
Chessani, Jeffrey, 11, 54, 60, 96, 157, 158, 206-7, 211
Chilean military, 295
Chosin Reservoir, 191-92, 194, 195, 214, 231
Christian, Lonnie, 162
Christopherson, Todd, 176
Church, John, 140
Clark, Larry, 222
Clark, Vernon, 266-67
Clint McQuade, USMC: The New Beginning (Duncan), 284-85
Clinton, Bill, 66, 136, 139, 150, 266, 269, 275, 283, 289, 295, 296
Cogdill, Mary, 44
Cohen, Eliot, 296-97
Cold War, 23, 179-80, 274-75, 278, 281, 291
Cole, John Henry, 225
Collins, Joel, 82
Command and Staff Action, 193
Command and Staff College, 282
Congress, U.S., 18, 277, 281, 289, 290
    Armed Services Committees of, 24, 180-81, 290-91
Conlin, Christopher, 194
Cook, Douglas, 174
Cooke, Christopher, 96
Cooper, Joseph, 270
Cordova, Armando, 18, 21, 193, 265
Country Such As This, A (Webb), 223, 283
Crandall, Kevin, 155

Index

Index

Index

Index

Index

Index